Prai

"VoIP   risks and
descr

—*Chr*

"At a   rt of their
comn   eak. This
book   rounding
secur   vet wear
their   feat!"

—*Rob*

"The   hreats and
vulne   et of security t

—*Joh*

"Rece   2007) and
YLE   15, 2007)
have   before it is
too la

—*Pro*
Pri   **PG) Head**
of

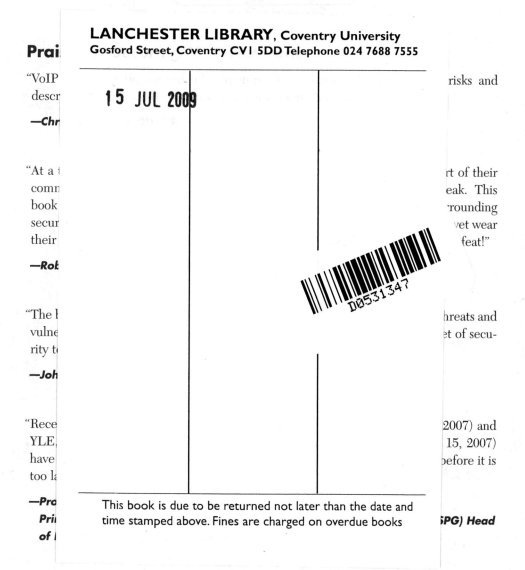

SECURING VoIP NETWORKS

SECURING VoIP NETWORKS

THREATS, VULNERABILITIES, AND COUNTERMEASURES

Peter Thermos and Ari Takanen

✦Addison-Wesley

Upper Saddle River, NJ • Boston • Indianapolis • San Francisco
New York • Toronto • Montreal • London • Munich • Paris • Madrid
Cape Town • Sydney • Tokyo • Singapore • Mexico City

Many of the designations used by manufacturers and sellers to distinguish their products are claimed as trademarks. Where those designations appear in this book, and the publisher was aware of a trademark claim, the designations have been printed with initial capital letters or in all capitals.

The authors and publisher have taken care in the preparation of this book, but make no expressed or implied warranty of any kind and assume no responsibility for errors or omissions. No liability is assumed for incidental or consequential damages in connection with or arising out of the use of the information or programs contained herein.

The publisher offers excellent discounts on this book when ordered in quantity for bulk purchases or special sales, which may include electronic versions and/or custom covers and content particular to your business, training goals, marketing focus, and branding interests. For more information, please contact:

U.S. Corporate and Government Sales
(800) 382-3419
corpsales@pearsontechgroup.com

For sales outside the United States please contact:

International Sales
international@pearsoned.com

This Book Is Safari Enabled

The Safari® Enabled icon on the cover of your favorite technology book means the book is available through Safari Bookshelf. When you buy this book, you get free access to the online edition for 45 days.

Safari Bookshelf is an electronic reference library that lets you easily search thousands of technical books, find code samples, download chapters, and access technical information whenever and wherever you need it.

To gain 45-day Safari Enabled access to this book:

- Go to www.awprofessional.com/safarienabled

- Complete the brief registration form

- Enter the coupon code PTMR-P4WM-ASPR-DBM1-7Z1N

If you have difficulty registering on Safari Bookshelf or accessing the online edition, please email customer-service@safaribooksonline.com.

Visit us on the Web: www.awprofessional.com

Library of Congress Cataloging-in-Publication Data:

Thermos, Peter.
    Securing VoIP networks : threats, vulnerabilities, countermeasures / Peter Thermos and Ari Takanen.
        p. cm.
    ISBN 0-321-43734-9 (pbk. : alk. paper) 1. Internet telephony—Security measures. I. Takanen, Ari. II. Title.
    TK5105.8865.H54 2007
    004.695—dc22

                            2007017689

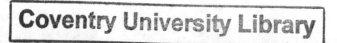

Pearson Education, Inc.
Rights and Contracts Department
75 Arlington Street, Suite 300
Boston, MA 02116
Fax: (617) 848-7047

ISBN-13: 978- 0-321-43734-1
ISBN-10: 0-321-43734-9
Text printed in the United States on recycled paper at Courier in Stoughton, Massachusetts

First printing August, 2007

Editor-in-Chief: Karen Gettman
Acquisitions Editor: Chuck Toporek
Development Editor: Songlin Qiu
Managing Editor: Gina Kanouse
Project Editor: George E. Nedeff
Copy Editor: Keith Cline
Indexer: Lisa Stumpf
Proofreader: Megan Wade
Publishing Coordinator: Jamie Adams
Cover Designer: Chuti Prasertsith
Composition: Bronkella Publishing

To our families: Peter dedicates this book to Elaine, Anastasios, and Dionysia, and Ari wants to dedicate this book especially to Anu and our newborn girl.

Also we both would like to dedicate this book to all the experts and specialists who remain anonymous but are willing to share their knowledge and wisdom and enable the rest of us to learn and improve.

CONTENTS

CONTENTS

FOREWORD

I have been teaching computer engineering in courses like Software Engineering and Operating Systems for more than 20 years. In all my teaching I have stressed making students understand the principles of the focal area of a course and not just having them memorize one technique or another. The increasing complexity of networks and our whole information society challenges this understanding even more. Different parts of the information structure can communicate with each other and understand each other via communication protocols. This opens up new threats in communication networks. Vulnerability in any of the communication protocols may make the whole system weak. It is of utmost importance that our developers and experts today and tomorrow have a good understanding of security aspects and can apply them.

Tomorrow, all communications will happen over IP. In the past, telecom operators handled most communications, and the main business for them was voice communication. In reality, almost all last-mile communications today still happen over the conventional telecom infrastructure. The backbone of the Internet has been going through a fast transition to faster and faster fiber optics and digital data transfer. The era of analog communications has been over for some time already. But, there are other changes in the communications landscape. I will describe some of them based on experiences we have had as one of the most advanced high-tech countries. This is so because here in Oulu, Finland, we have been surrounded by high-tech inventions, and several enterprises use the city as a test bed for their inventions and their business models.

In the past, the first GSM network was launched in Oulu. GSM technology took over the communications landscape quickly, and today in Finland we have people in their thirties who have never in their life owned a fixed-line telephone. Today there are more cellular phones in Finland than there are people. Less than 50% of households have a fixed-line phone, and the number of fixed-line connections is still dropping faster every year.

At the same time, the transition from fixed-line voice communications to fixed-line data communications has happened very rapidly globally. Most households now subscribe to broadband service, and they use services such as e-mail and the web in their everyday life. Necessary cabling to the households existed due to the transition from fixed-line to mobile, and the cabling was reused by the broadband providers.

Today the transition is from providing services to providing bandwidth. Recently, the next step in breaking traditional business models was taken in Oulu. One of the first free WiFi networks was also launched here. With the introduction of WiFi-enabled cellular phones, consumers in Finland are testing various free VoIP services, and that might be the end of all voice-based business models. The transition from voice to data, and from fixed to mobile, results in personal, always connected wireless communication devices.

Today, people speak of Voice over IP, but a better name for the Next Generation Networks is Everything over IP (EoIP). And all of that communication will be wireless. But what does that have to do with the topic of this book? It means the world has to finally wake up to the security of the communications networks.

To build security, you have to understand the application you use. For many, Internet security equals web security. This false impression is created by security companies, the media, and the software industry. For many, an application is the same thing as a web application. Application security equals web application security. But today, the web is not the biggest threat to your business. True, some businesses are built on web services, but other applications such as e-mail and voice can be much more critical for enterprises and for consumers. Web security can have a high profile, as a compromised server is seen by hundreds of thousands of people. A compromised voice connection or e-mail client might escape public attention but could result in the loss of the most critical assets of a company, or cause irreversible damage to an individual.

To be secure, you have to understand that wireless networks are always open. While in traditional telephone networks all the switches were kept behind locked doors and all the cabling was protected, in wireless technology there are no cables and everyone has access to wireless access points. One compromised infrastructure component, and the entire network is compromised. One virus-contaminated access device, and everyone in the network will be contaminated.

To be secure, you have to understand that client security is as important as, or even more important, than server security. Servers can be protected, upgraded, and updated and potential damages can be restored. These are standard processes for all IT administrators. Now, take laptops as an example of a mobile device of the future. Most, if not all, critical data is stored on the laptop. All the keys and passwords are there. Communication behavior is stored there. The laptop also can eavesdrop on all behavior, including listening to the surroundings of the user of the laptop. A mobile device of the future is all that and more.

This book by Peter and Ari is built around voice as the application to be secured, but the principles apply to any communications. Studying this book should be obligatory to all students in computer engineering and computer science, not only due to its content and deep understanding of VoIP security, but also to allow them to learn how to apply the best practices in other fields, no matter what their future field of study will be. The key to learning is not only studying things and memorizing the various topics, but learning how to apply the best practices of other fields in your own. Combining the best practices of traditional telecommunications, e-mail, and the web into new next-generation technologies is essential to be able to build reliable and usable communication technologies. Voice over IP is potentially the killer application, destroying conventional communication networks and creating a new IP-based communication infrastructure. I truly hope it will not be built by business people only, but also by people who understand the security aspects of the new technologies.

Prof. Juha Röning
Principal Investigator of Oulu University Secure Programming Group
(OUSPG)
Head of Department of Electrical Engineering
University of Oulu

May 30, 2007

PREFACE

Communication between people has changed with the invention of the telephone. The ability to communicate across continents in real-time has also helped our society in several dimensions including entertainment, trade, finance, and defense. But this new capability did not come without an investment. Building an international telephony infrastructure has required the cooperation of both commercial and government organizations to evolve into what it is today. It has also led to the formation of international standard bodies that both direct and support the industry towards an interoperable communication networks.

IP networks are the next step from the traditional telecommunications. For a while, IP family of protocols was only used in the Internet, and the main applications were file transfers and e-mail. With the World Wide Web, the Internet changed into a global and always open information distribution channel. And finally with the advent of VoIP, the Internet is becoming a real-time communication media that integrates with all the earlier multimedia capabilities.

Traditional telecommunication networks are critical to the survival of our society. The PSTN is a closed network and its operational intricacies are known to a few select individuals who have devoted much of their lives to building it. Although operations in PSTN are not entirely a secret, they were and still remain proprietary for several reasons such as competitive advantage and national defense. The PSTN was and remains a closed infrastructure that concentrated its intelligence in its core network elements and left the edge devices very simplistic. The equipment and resources to operate a TDM network require a substantial financial investment. This lack of direct access to core network elements from subscribers and the high price of connectivity alleviated the risk for attacks. Ergo, subscribers demonstrate greater trust for communications through the PSTN compared to the Internet. This is a misconceived trust once you start analyzing the PSTN components and protocols and realize the lack of protection mechanisms.

In the earlier days of the Internet, security was appalling. The Internet was an open network where anyone could attack anyone anonymously and many of the attack tools were, and still are, available. As such, security research became a standard practice in government, commercial, and academic worlds with globally known research groups in organizations such as DARPA, DISA, CERIAS, MIT CIS, Bellcore, Bell Labs, and many others. Things became a bit more complicated with the transition of critical services such as telephony on the Internet along with other multimedia applications such as video and gaming. And due to the performance, availability, and privacy requirements of these applications, their security requires new approaches and methods compared to traditional IP security. Nevertheless the traditional security objectives apply such as confidentiality, integrity, and availability of services.

Before gaining the interest of the academia, the topic of Internet security has been a secret science, or not even a science. The security field was a competition between hackers and system administrators, in a constant race of "patch and penetrate." Very few people knew what they actually were fixing in the systems when they applied new security updates or patches. And very few hackers understood what the attack tools actually did when they penetrated the services they wanted access to. People spoke of threats, attacks, and security measures that needed to be applied to protect from these attacks. The actual core reasons that enabled the existence of the attacks were not understood. For most of the users of communication systems, these weaknesses were hidden in complex, hard-to-understand protocols and components used in the implementations.

VoIP has been discussed at length in many textbooks and thus we avoid long discussions of its origins and details on introductory concepts. Instead the book focuses on the details associated with the security of multimedia communications including VoIP. Our purpose is to extend your knowledge of vulnerabilities, attacks, and protection mechanisms of VoIP and generally Internet multimedia applications. We deviate from listing a series of security tools and products and instead provide detailed discussions on actual attacks and vulnerabilities in the network design, implementation, and configuration and protection mechanisms for signaling and media streams, architectural recommendations, and organizational strategy—thus enabling you to understand and implement the best countermeasures that are applicable to your environment.

The book is structured so that we start by briefly explaining VoIP networks, and then go through the threats, attacks, and vulnerabilities to enable you to understand how VoIP attacks are made possible and their impact. The book discusses in great detail various attacks (published and unpublished) for eavesdropping, unauthorized access, impersonation, and service disruption. These attacks are used as proof of concept, but at the same time they also expose the reader to real-life weaknesses and serve as a mechanism to promote comprehension. In addition, this book discusses VoIP vulnerabilities, their structure, and their categorization as they have been investigated in enterprise and carrier environments.

Following VoIP vulnerabilities and attacks, the book discusses in great detail a number of protection mechanisms. In order to protect against current and emerging threats, there a number of areas that need to be considered when deploying VoIP. The book provides extensive coverage on the intricacies, strengths, and limitations of the protection mechanisms including SIPS, H.235, SRTP, MIKEY, ZTP, and others. Furthermore, the book focuses on identifying a VoIP security framework as a starting point for enterprise networks and provides several recommendations. Security architectures in enterprise and carrier environments are also discussed.

This first edition of the book aims in establishing the landscape of the current state of VoIP security and provides an insight to administrators, architects, security professionals, management personnel, and students who are interested in understanding VoIP security in detail.

ACKNOWLEDGMENTS

First, we both would like to acknowledge IETF and everyone participating in the work of IETF for their great work for VoIP and all communication standards. A portion of the proceeds is donated to IETF to support their efforts in standardizing the Internet. Keep up the good work!

Additional Acknowledgments from Peter Thermos

I have been fortunate to be acquainted with many people in the professional and academic community who generously shared their knowledge and experience throughout my career. These people have inspired me to research new topics and in turn share some of my experience and knowledge in the area of VoIP security with this book. I would like to thank them and I hope that I can inspire others including students and professionals to explore this field.

I would like to thank Henning Schulzrinne for his continuous support and academic guidance, John Kimmins for his professional wisdom and advisement, and Emmanuel Lazidis for the numerous and prolific discussions on information security. Also I would like to thank several people in two U.S. agencies that supported early research in the area of next-generation networks and security including Bill Semancik, Linda Shields, Gary Hayward, Tom Chapuran (Telcordia), David Gorman at LTS (Laboratory for Telecommunications Sciences), and Tim Grance and Richard Kuhn at NIST along with Dave Waring, Tom Bowen, Steve Ungar and John Lutin at Telcordia.

In addition, I would like to thank our reviewers John Haluska, Paul Rohmeyer, and Christian Wieser for their valuable comments and feedback. Also I would like to thank the many supporters of the VoPSecurity.org Forum and Dan York and Jonathan Zar for their community contribution of the BlueBox, The VoIP Security podcast. Furthermore, I would like to thank you, our reader, for your generosity and support. We welcome your comments and feedback!

Lastly but most importantly I would like to thank my beautiful wife Elaine and children Anastasios and Dionysia for their understanding and support during the writing of this book. The reader will appreciate the fact that the manuscript reads mostly in English and not Greek, which is largely due to the continuous support of my wife's instruction (an English teacher) in writing proper English!

Additional Acknowledgments from Ari Takanen:

There have been several people that have paved the way towards the writing of this book. Great thanks to Marko Laakso and Prof. Juha Röning from University of Oulu for showing me how everything is broken in communication technologies. Everything. And showing that there is no silver bullet to fix that. My years as a researcher in the PROTOS project in the OUSPG enabled me to learn everything there was to learn about communications security. Out of all those communication technologies we were studying, one family of protocols stood out like a shining supernova: VoIP. Thank you to all Oulu University Secure Programming Group members for all the bits and pieces around VoIP security. I know we did not cover all of them in the book, but let's leave something for the future researchers also! And a special thanks to Christian Wieser who did not get bored of VoIP after learning it, like many others did, but kept on focusing on VoIP security among all those hundreds of other interesting communication technologies being studied in the research team. Thank you Christian for all the help in putting this book together!

Enormous thanks to all my colleagues at Codenomicon, for taking the OUSPG work even further through commercializing the research results, and for making it possible for me to write this book although it took time from my CTO tasks. Thank you to everyone who has used either the Codenomicon robustness testing tools or the PROTOS test-suites, and especially to everyone who came back to us and told us of their experiences with our tools and performing VoIP security testing with them. Although you might not want to say it out loud, you certainly know how broken everything is.

Special thanks to Jeff Pulver and Carl Ford out of Pulver.com for your significant work in making VoIP what it is today, and for inviting me to speak in more than ten different conferences that you have arranged.

Through meetings with all key people in VoIP (a list too long to fit on one page), these conferences were probably the best learning experience for me in the VoIP area. I am terribly sorry for the time it took for me to understand that pointing out the problems was not the correct way of preaching but rather pointing out the solutions. I hope we contributed to the latter in this book!

I would like to thank everyone involved at Addison-Wesley and Pearson Education, and all the other people who patiently helped with all the editing and reviewing, and impatiently reminded me about all the missed deadlines during the process.

Finally, thanks Peter for inviting me into this project, although it was slow and painful at times, it certainly was more fun than anything else, and I will definitely do it again!

About the Authors

Peter Thermos is CTO at Palindrome Technologies, which acts as a trusted advisor for commercial and government organizations and provides consultation in security policy, architecture, and risk management. Previously Peter acted as Telcordia's lead technical expert on key information security and assurance tasks, including risk assessments, standards and requirements development, network security architecture, and organizational security strategy. He speaks frequently at events and forums including the IEEE, MIS, Internet Security Conference, SANS, ISSWorld, IEC, the 21st Century Communications World Forum, VON, and others. Peter is also known for his contributions to the security community through discovery of product vulnerabilities, the release of SiVuS (The First VoIP Vulnerability Scanner), and the vopsecurity.org forum. Peter holds a masters' degree in computer science from Columbia University where he is currently furthering his graduate studies.

Ari Takanen is founder and CTO of Codenomicon. Since 1998, Ari has focused on information security issues in next-generation networks and security critical environments. He began at Oulu University Secure Programming Group (OUSPG) as a contributing member to PROTOS research that studied information security and reliability errors in WAP, SNMP, LDAP, and VoIP implementations. Ari and his company, Codenomicon Ltd., provide and commercialize automated tools using a systematic approach to test a multitude of interfaces on mission-critical software, VoIP platforms, Internet-routing infrastructure, and 3G devices. Codenomicon and the University of Oulu aim to ensure new technologies are accepted by the general public by providing means of measuring and ensuring quality in networked software. Ari has been speaking at numerous security and testing conferences on four continents and has been invited to speak at leading universities and international corporations.

## CHAPTER 1

INTRODUCTION

The convergence of land-line, wireless, and Internet communications has stimulated the development of new applications and services which have revolutionized communications. The interconnection between PSTN (Public Switch Telephone Network) and IP (Internet Protocol) networks is referred to as the Next Generation Network (NGN). And the interconnection of Internet and wireless is referred to as IP Multimedia Subsystem (IMS). Both architectures play an important role in our evolution from traditional telecommunications to multimedia communications. You might also have heard of the term *triple play,* which refers to a service provider's ability to offer voice, video, and data to subscribers as a bundled service. Similarly, the term *quad play* refers to providing voice, video, data, and mobile communications.

Whatever marketing term one decides to use, the underlying protocols that define the NGN or IMS architecture remain the same. Voice over IP (VoIP) is implemented using a subset of the same protocols, and thus it is considered a real-time multimedia application that "runs" on NGN and IMS. Additional real-time multimedia applications include video and gaming.

Although the title of the book is *Securing VoIP Networks,* many of the concepts on attacks, vulnerabilities, and protection mechanisms are applicable to any multimedia application that is implemented using IP and the associated signaling and media protocols.

Because telecommunications is part of the national critical infrastructure, the security weaknesses of new technologies and protocols that support telecommunications are of great concern. In addition, the security and reliability of VoIP communications are an important requirement for commercial organizations in many sectors, including financial, pharmaceutical, insurance, and energy. Therefore, organizations that provide or use VoIP communications need to maintain the proper controls to support security and reliability.

VoIP communications can be a complex topic to understand at first, but ignorance can be your biggest threat—confusion is even worse. Therefore, to implement VoIP security effectively, you need to define and properly articulate security objectives and requirements that pertain to your environment. For example, some organizations require that calls between customers and clients remain confidential, other organizations may monitor calls for quality assurance, and some organizations can't afford to have any communications compromised. For those who are considering deploying VoIP, the task of defining security objectives and requirements has to take place during the design phase prior to the deployment of the VoIP network. For those who already have deployed VoIP, they should identify their security objectives and requirements and evaluate their current posture to identify any inconsistencies that may exist. This book will help you understand the threats and attacks associated with VoIP and, most importantly, the protection mechanisms that you can use to defend against those threats and attacks.

Deploying security in VoIP networks can be a challenging task, and it requires interacting with subject matter experts from several areas, including network security, engineering, operations, management, and product vendors. The level of interaction is proportional to the size of the organization and the size of the VoIP implementation. A Fortune-100 company with thousands of employees requires more coordination and planning compared to a small enterprise network that supports 250 employees. As with any IP application, it is important to know what you want to achieve with the deployment of VoIP and enforce appropriate security controls accordingly. Many organizations erroneously perceive security as an add-on device or technology that can be added when needed. Security is a process, not a product. As such, it is important to understand its role and how it needs to be applied through the network life cycle, from the inception and design phase to the retirement phase. This is also applicable to a VoIP network, service, or product. Defining security requirements early in the process will eliminate the perceived "added" cost of security if it is added at later phases. In addition, it will help in building a proper foundation to support mechanisms to mitigate current and emerging threats.

Some consider the primary drivers for implementing security to be regulations[1] and FUD (Fear, Uncertainty, and Doubt), which can cause a reckless response and hinder the ability to develop an understanding of the strengths and limitations of the deployed technology and thus enforce reactive security rather than effective security. Understanding "what" we need to secure and "why" helps us develop applicable security requirements and controls without hindering functionality for the sake of security and vice versa. The security of a network is as strong as its weakest link. Therefore, identifying and analyzing the weakest link in the security of a network, service, or product is critical. The topics discussed in this book will help build a good understanding of the attacks and vulnerabilities associated with VoIP, but most importantly it discusses in detail the protection mechanisms that can be used to alleviate and manage the associated risks.

Although this book covers basic concepts of VoIP protocols and technologies, it purposefully avoids detailed discussions on introductory concepts since they are covered extensively in other books. Chapter 1 starts with a brief introduction on telephony, and Chapter 2, "VoIP Architectures and Protocols," provides a high-level discussion of the basic components and protocols that support VoIP to help you quickly assimilate the associated concepts. These discussions will provide a foundation in understanding the chapters that follow. Each subsequent chapter focuses on a specific area of VoIP security. Chapter 3, "Threats and Attacks," discusses threats associated with VoIP and provides examples of attacks related to eavesdropping, unauthorized access, denial of service, and fraud. Specific attacks can be performed in a number of ways, so we demonstrate some variations to help you understand the importance of protection mechanisms and their relation to the attacks. Chapter 4, "VoIP Vulnerabilities," focuses on vulnerabilities and provides a detailed discussion and categorization of vulnerabilities associated with signaling and media protocols. Chapter 5, "Signaling Protection Mechanisms"; Chapter 6, "Media Protection Mechanisms"; and Chapter 7, "Key Management Mechanisms," focus on analyzing protection mechanisms associated with VoIP protocols along with their strengths and weaknesses. Chapter 8, "VoIP and Network Security Controls," discusses some of the components that are currently used to support security in VoIP networks and also

---

1. *The Global Information Security Survey 2005 by Ernst & Young notes that since 2005, compliance with regulations is the key driver of security investment, considered even more important than the threat of viruses and worms.*

presents related architectural considerations. Chapter 9, "A Security Framework for Enterprise VoIP Networks," presents a security framework, aligned with the ISO 17799/27001 standard,[2] for enterprise VoIP networks. Finally, Chapter 10, "Provider Architectures and Security," and Chapter 11, "Enterprise Architectures and Security," discuss service provider and enterprise network architectures and security considerations.

Although this book purposefully does not discuss all the intricacies of the functionality and operation of the associated VoIP protocols and network elements, it provides enough information to help you understand the issues related to VoIP security. We also provide links to additional material for those who want to study the operation of VoIP protocols and components in more detail.

VoIP and Telecommunications

To understand the security issues related to VoIP, you need to understand some of the fundamental principles associated with circuit-switched networks. An example of a circuit-switched network is the Public Switched Telephone Network (PSTN). The PSTN is composed of interconnected circuit-switched networks that are built, owned, and operated by private or governmental organizations. The end devices are typically easy-to-use dumb terminals that are connected to a smart and complex network, the AIN (Advance Intelligent Network). AIN was introduced in 1991 by Bellcore (Bell Communications Research) as a replacement to the existing network to provide more flexible and sophisticated telecommunication services (for example, call forwarding, call waiting, 800-toll free) for residential, business, cellular, and satellite customers. Other intelligent end devices are ISDN phones and PBX stations (Private Branch Exchange). One fundamental property of circuit-switched networks is the physical separation of signaling messages and circuit data (voice), whereas in VoIP signaling media traffic is transmitted using the same physical medium. Another fundamental property is access to the network. In circuit-switched networks, access is limited to government or commercial organizations that have financial and operational resources to connect and maintain their infrastructure. To launch an attack against a circuit-switched network, the

---

2. *www.iso.org/iso/en/prods-services/popstds/informationsecurity.html*

attacker has to have access to a core network element such as a Signal Transfer Point (STP).[3] The cost of owning an STP or Service Switching Point (SSP) and interconnecting to a circuit-switched network runs into hundreds of thousands of dollars, whereas access to a VoIP network comes at a fraction of the cost or even unrestricted. For example, in an enterprise environment, access to the VoIP network is established by connecting the user's device (for example, a laptop or VoIP phone) in to an Ethernet connection. In PSTN, terminals are dumb and cheap and are always physically connected, making location of the device easy. An exception to this is mobile telephone networks, where roaming has been enabled with agreements between service providers. Still, in mobile telephony the device is authenticated using a SIM card and other tamper-proof hardware.[4] But the user can not be authenticated to the network unless an authentication mechanism is implemented in which the phone passes the user credentials to the network for authentication and authorization (for example, biometric authentication or voice recognition). This is difficult to implement in a service provider environment since subscribers will have to provide identifiable attributes to the provider upon subscription. Thus, currently users may enforce pin authentication to prevent access to their phones and call initiation. Also, the location of each cellular phone can be traced by law enforcement agencies whereas in VoIP the actual phone (hard phone or soft phone) may be located anywhere on the Internet.

A common business model for traditional fixed-line telephony networks or PSTN is time-based interconnection charging. Subscribers are charged by usage—more calls, higher bill. Although, lately, both fixed-line and mobile telecommunication providers have established monthly plans with unlimited calls for a fixed fee. However, these plans are applicable only to local communications or to calls within a coalition of service providers, as long-distance and international calling still carries a high charge per minute. With the introduction of VoIP this charge for long-distance calls diminishes. The international service may be provided at

---

3. *STP is one of the fundamental components of the PSTN, which routes signaling messages to other STPs to establish, manage, or disconnect a call. Other components include the SCP (service control point) and SSP (service switching point).*

4. *Note that although in mobile networks the client devices are authenticated, the network is not necessarily authenticated.*

lower cost by a VoIP service provider or an incumbent carrier that provides VoIP. In traditional telecommunications there is a clear separation between service providers and carriers, although some companies can act as both. Carriers provide the core network connectivity between service providers (the cabling and call termination/hand-off to PSTN) and service providers build the last interconnection to the PSTN ensuring that the consumers and enterprise customers have the required telephony services available.

Telecommunication networks are part of the critical national infrastructure and need to maintain requirements for high availability, security, and quality of service. These requirements were emphasized by New York's State Office of Communications after reviewing the effects of 9/11.

Telecommunications network reliability, increasingly viewed through a prism of national security and public safety considerations, is a political and economic mandate.[5]

This need is also recognized in other countries around the world. For example, the Australian Communications Authority (ACA) is carefully monitoring the performance and reliability of the telecommunications networks of any universal service provider that operates in Australia.[6] The Australian Network Reliability Framework (NRF) provides a good example of how government agencies can set and enforce regulations or recommendations that promote equal service and better quality of service nationwide. In the U.S. the National Security Telecommunications Advisory Committee (NSTAC) "provides industry-based advice and expertise to the President on issues and problems related to implementing national security and emergency preparedness (NS/EP) communications policy[7]." Besides reliability, the various national regulations typically have other requirements for some of the services and functionalities, including

---

5. *Network Reliability After 9/11. A Staff White Paper on Local Telephone Exchange Network Reliability. November 2, 2002. New York State Department of Public Service, Office of Communications.*

6. *The related documents mainly indicate Telstra as the main service provider. For more detail, see Connecting Australia, Report of the Telecommunications Service Inquiry, September 2000. Network Reliability Framework (NRF) Review 2004 (Revised June 2005) is available at www.dcita.gov.au, and Telstra Web pages at www.telstra.com.au/ publish the related reports.*

7. *http://www.ncs.gov/nstac/nstac.html*

limitations on who can provide Internet and telecommunications services.[8] In extreme cases, a named operator has exclusive rights for either national or international telephony, or both.[9] Special regulations exist for the legal intercept of communications and for emergency services, including the location of the emergency call. In addition, with regard to postal service, telephony has requirements for privacy, but regulations for privacy of telephone conversations vary internationally.

A Brief Look at the PSTN

The PSTN comprises thousands of interconnected network elements over dedicated circuit-switched facilities that use the SS7[10] for signaling. Various protocols, including ISDN and X.25, are used to interface with the terminals and databases. Although recently the X.25 has become less prevalent and mainly used to maintain backward compatibility with "legacy" systems. A simplified network architecture of a PSTN is shown in Figure 1.1. The PSTN network relies on a model of trusted neighbors. The PSTN has been maintained as a closed network, where access is limited to carriers and service providers. Access to route traffic within the PSTN requires a great financial investment and resources including equipment and personnel. Therefore, access to the PSTN core network has traditionally been protected by price, because costs can exceed hundreds of thousands of dollars per month. These two characteristics of the PSTN (closed network and very high cost of access) have established the false perception that the PSTN is a secure network. In fact, many people believe that it is more secure than the Internet. This claim is quickly discredited when you start to analyze the security controls, or lack of, that are available in the PSTN.

---

8. *For the United States, see the Communications Act of 1934 and its amendments, such as the Telephone Consumer Protection Act (TCPA) of 1991, the Telephone Disclosure and Dispute Resolution Act (TDDRA) of 1992, and the Telecommunications Act of 1996. See also regulations set by the specific state law, especially related to setting up telecommunications businesses, and to powers related to building wireless and wired networks over or through private or public property. For more detail, see the Federal Communications Commission website at www.fcc.gov.*

9. *In Panama, the incumbent telephone service carrier has an exclusive concession for the exploitation of local, national, and international voice-transmission services, regardless of whether the voice transmission takes place via the Internet, satellite link, or leased lines.*

10. *Common Channel Signaling System No.7, SS7 or C7.*

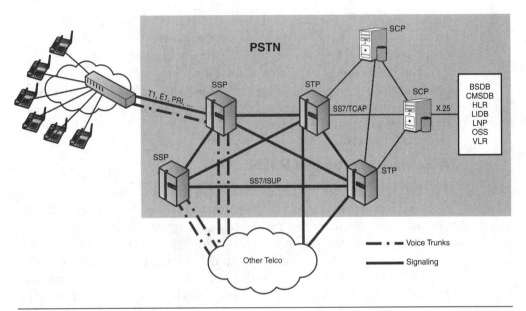

FIGURE 1.1 Traditional PSTN network.

The "last mile," the final leg of connectivity to the actual telephone handset, the legacy POTS, or Plain Old Telephony Service, uses dedicated-pair cable connections for signaling and voice and for circuit-switched connections in the network topology. A typical POTS line is connected via a single pair, with loop closures, Dual Tone Multi Frequency (DTMF) tones, ringing voltage, and various other tones and voltage transitions used to signal incoming and outgoing calls. ISDN lines utilize a digital interface instead, which can use either two or four wires. Physical security is always an issue because anyone with access to the wiring has full control of the end device and can impersonate that end device, as shown in Figure 1.2.

FIGURE 1.2 On the left, a switching board for about 3,000 subscribers; on the right, a red phone known as a "butt set" directly connected to listen in to an existing call.

VoIP and IP Communications

IP communications are implemented using the IPv4 or IPv6 protocols to support applications such as email, Web, or telephony.[11] All traffic traverses the same cable (or "pipe"). Since capacity in IP based networks is less expensive, compared to PSTN, the IP network is viewed as a simple packet forwarding infrastructure in which application servers and terminals maintain the intelligence. End devices can be complex and expensive but the infrastructure is cheap compared to traditional telephony networks.

One fundamental area of research in VoIP communications is quality of service, where some aspects are related to security (for example, denial of service). Because of the nature of packet switching, the traffic can at times consist of bursts of packets, and is thus subject to latency, delay, and jitter. IP packets can be sent through different routes and can be received in a different order from which they were sent. The packets can be collected and reassembled at any location, and then transmitted again in different packet sizes from what was initially used.

---

11. *Besides Ethernet, the transport can also be Frame Relay or ATM. The focus of this book is on the application layer, not the underlying protocols.*

Communication protocols operate in different layers. In IP communications, both connectionless (User Datagram Protocol [UDP]) and connection-oriented (Transport Control Protocol [TCP]) transport layer protocols are available. Packet loss is possible, and therefore protocols such as TCP are used to ensure reliability in communications. When an unreliable transport protocol is used, the application layer protocol must ensure reliable delivery of protocol messages. An example application connectivity with SIP is shown in Figure 1.3.

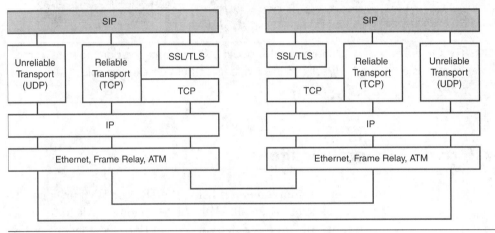

FIGURE 1.3 Application connectivity through the IP protocol stack.

It should be noted that frame relay and ATM are declining in use due to the deployment of MPLS (Multi Protocol Label Switching). The business model in IP networks is typically based on selling bandwidth,[12] for a fixed monthly fee. The charging is not based on usage time, used services, or volume of actual traffic. A special case is a peering model, especially in the core network. In a peering model, there is typically a minimal or no charging for interconnection between networks. This interconnection model has enabled the birth of the Internet. And the Internet has resulted in one global network with no international barriers and no extra cost for

---

12. *Many IP connectivity service providers have a data limit, after which they start invoicing for the amount of data transferred. Most such service providers, at least in Europe, have moved to a completely flat rate.*

international communications. Any IP-enabled device can theoretically be connected to any IP-enabled network, making it possible for end devices to roam for free as long as IP connectivity is provided. Although currently there are cases where wireless connectivity to the Internet is provided for a small fee, there are organizations that provide wireless Internet access for free (for example, hotels and coffee houses). Separation between carrier and service provider is more difficult because a broadband service provider does not necessarily provide any services. All that is needed is plain IP connectivity to the public or private network. With Internet connectivity, consumers can subscribe to any value-added services globally. [13] Many Internet connectivity providers try to package services with their offering, but consumers have the freedom of choice as to which services they use. Typically, there is no service provider at all, but enterprises can implement their own services, and consumers can interconnect directly through peer-to-peer networks.

A common misunderstanding is that IP is synonymous with the Internet; however, this is not the case. Not all IP networks are Internet connected. Private and dedicated physical connections are common, especially in critical infrastructure and business-critical enterprise networks, and these networks typically have no connection or a very limited connection to the Internet. Internet communications consist of IP networks connected to the public Internet in one way or other, allowing them to share each other's resources according to specific routing rules. Even there, not every end device has a public Internet address. Private and closed networks can be connected to the Internet using private addressing schemes. Therefore, an Internet-connected device is commonly understood to mean any device with access to the public Internet, whether or not it has a unique and public Internet address, and whether or not it is behind security perimeters such as proxies, firewalls, or private networks. IP is a transport protocol, not the network. Figure 1.4. shows examples of IP devices used to provide IP connectivity, such as switches and routers.

---

13. *Google, eBay, Yahoo!, AIM, Amazon, Hotmail, Skype, and iTunes are good examples of globally reaching Internet services.*

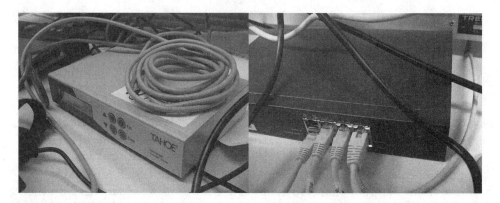

FIGURE 1.4 IP devices.

In addition, the Internet access is part of the Critical National Infrastructure (CNI), and therefore has requirements for maintaining high availability, security, and quality of service. This is expected that similar to telephony services, national regulations will apply in the future to Internet services and service providers.

VoIP Deployments

VoIP does not come in one flavor, and unfortunately there are several perceptions of what is VoIP. For example, IP telephony *and* VoIP do not mean that Internet connectivity is involved. Internet telephony, on the other hand, means that the IP connectivity is established through the Internet, with or without encryption services such as Virtual Private Networks (VPNs) or IPSec to protect the communications.

The first way to implement enterprise VoIP is probably through private dedicated lines or VPN connections between different sites, as opposed to using the public Internet to route the calls. Enterprises do this because (at least partially) of the risks involved with the "hostile" Internet. In these types on deployments, the VoIP infrastructure is built and maintained by the enterprise or bought as a hosted service, and there is necessarily no connection to the Internet or PSTN.

Internet-based VoIP deployments consist of smart software-based clients that register into an Internet-based service, or registry. For a service provider, this requires minimal investment in infrastructure resources as compared with traditional telephony and instead exploits the "free" Internet connectivity. Subscribers use the available broadband connectivity to connect to the server provided by the service provider. The first widely used deployment was Microsoft Messenger, which used the Hotmail "registry" to locate and identify people. Another popular implementation is Skype, where a proprietary protocol and software client are used to provide the service over the Internet, with the central registry being managed by Skype. Examples of commercial, but still Internet-based, services built on top of open standards include Vonage, Broadvoice, SunRocket, and Packet8.

VoIP can also be provided as a closed commercial service by a traditional or new telecom operator, as part of their PSTN offering or as its replacement.[14] A closed VoIP offering consists of the broadband connection as a hidden or additional service to the telephony services. The end devices are typically standardized devices that subscribe to the service provider's infrastructure only. Figure 1.5 shows a sample VoIP device. To the consumers, this appears as legacy telephony devices that support more features that are provided by the VoIP infrastructure. Whether the Internet is used as the infrastructure by telecommunication carriers or service providers is irrelevant, except from a security and quality of service perspective.

Telecom operators might see VoIP as a threat to existing revenue streams because the most widely deployed services are not based on the same business models used in legacy telephony. VoIP services can be based on fixed monthly fees with no additional cost related to the call minutes, or the VoIP service can be completely free. Billing and other service provider functionalities for VoIP have come as a solution, enabling the VoIP service provider to still use existing business models. The IP Multimedia Subsystem (IMS) infrastructure has been designed from this perspective. The elements that exist in IMS enable the service providers to transition from legacy telephony into VoIP without changing their existing business models. Infrastructures such as the 3G and others that are designed by the incumbent telecoms have used the IMS approach. IMS is not a technology itself, but a network architecture that is built upon protocols and components that are discussed in this book. Although some of the naming conventions of components in IMS, VoIP, and NGN may differ, the fundamental function is the same.

---

14. *See, for example, the 21CN from British Telecom, or Telio in Norway.*

FIGURE 1.5 VoIP phone.

Wireless VoIP terminals and roaming enable nomadic use of VoIP. Whether the soft client is on a mobile phone or a laptop computer, Internet telephony will enable users to use the same VoIP service wherever they are as long as Internet connectivity is provided. Poor security controls in areas such as confidentiality, authentication, and authorization of users and devices and the openness of the infrastructure expose the infrastructure, the service, and the subscribers to various attacks. Wireless terminals can also be restricted to a closed enterprisewide wireless network, where the roaming is restricted by access to the VoIP infrastructure. This network design will still enable free enterprisewide calls (for example, in warehouses or other places where mobility is required), but openness of the telephony service is not needed.

A special case of IP telephony is the Sigtran protocol, which essentially is SS7 over IP, tunneling traditional PSTN signaling over an IP network.

VoIP deployments come in many flavors, and it is difficult to compare the penetration of VoIP in the telephony market. Additional complexity comes from mobile phone networks adapting VoIP technologies in the 3G infrastructure and as a built-in functionality to the handsets. Some metrics for VoIP deployments are the sales statistics of VoIP phones and download statistics for VoIP-enabled soft clients. Another metric is the number of subscribers to commercial or free VoIP services. An important consideration is separating the number of subscribers and the number of "minutes" VoIP subscribers have used for VoIP calls. According to ISP-Planet statistics,[15] the top five VoIP service providers in 2006 were Vonage, Skype, Time Warner Digital Phone, Comcast Digital Phone, and CableVision. In total, these five provide service to about eight million VoIP subscribers.

Challenges in VoIP Security

To understand security in VoIP, you must first analyze the business threats that you are trying to protect against. The analysis should identify the impact of the potential risks that may be realized if the network is not secured properly.

One example of a business threat is damage to the organization's profile in case a security breach is publicized. The media is extremely interested in security-related incidents. A failure to properly secure a service or the release of an insecure product will definitely attract public and media attention. This attention might result in reduced revenue and the potentially permanent loss of customers.

Security incidents also cause direct costs related to analysis of the incidents and recovery of the systems. Even without an incident, a bad-quality product or service results in increased costs in maintenance and other product life cycle costs through regular and urgent patches, updates, and upgrades.

An additional and extremely important emerging factor today is regulatory concerns, which is extremely problematic for nomadic users, because a service or a product may be under several international regulations. As such, the costs and risks related to regulatory compliance need to be considered.

Vendors and their software products have until now enjoyed the protection of End-User License Agreements (EULAs). However, these agreements do not always protect the service providers with enterprises or consumers as customers. Legal liabilities related to damages, lost revenue, or even loss of human life have to be factored into the risk analysis. Negligence in building services without security and robustness can prove to be expensive.

---

15. *VoIP Ranking by Subscriber: Q3 2006, ISP-Planet, www.isp-planet.com/research/rankings/2006/ voip_q32006.html.*

Although IP telephony differs from traditional legacy telephony, it maintains common features, and business requirements. Only the underlying communication protocols and physical attributes differ. From a security perspective, the threat-analysis practices relevant to a traditional telephony network are still applicable to IP telephony, but they need to be adjusted to support VoIP. The IP protocol family has inherent vulnerabilities related to the core IP services, such as Domain Name Server (DNS), and problems that relate to the message sequences used in, for example, the TCP handshake. These vulnerabilities affect all services built on top of IP networks and can be used to perform various attacks, including, but not limited to, service disruption, unauthorized access, eavesdropping, masquerading, and fraud. Because access to the Internet is not restricted (as it is in PSTN), it is easier for attackers to generate attacks and exploit weaknesses. Because the Internet is global and anonymous, it is usually more difficult to track down and catch the perpetrators after a security incident compared to a closed network such as the PSTN.

VoIP networks provide an extended range of telephony services, including the services provided by the traditional PSTN, but the services are implemented using a different transport medium. Nevertheless, the same reliability and security requirements need to be maintained as for traditional telephony services. The same regulations are being developed for IP telephony similar to those that apply to traditional telephony, including legal intercept,[16] emergency services,[17] and privacy[18]. But, there is an additional factor of complexity related to Internet telephony. For example, from a privacy perspective, the regulations are easy to circumvent in IP communications by forking or routing traffic to places where data can legally be monitored. Service providers must ensure privacy, and one way they can do so is by encrypting all telephony traffic. In addition, national and international regulations related to lawful intercept, censorship, and encrypted data communications must also be considered when offering Internet services.

---

16. *See, for example, CALEA requirements for legal intercept in the United States. AskCALEA explains: "The objective of CALEA implementation is to preserve law enforcement's ability to conduct lawfully-authorized electronic surveillance while preserving public safety, the public's right to privacy, and the telecommunications industry's competitiveness." http://www.askcalea.net/*

17. *See, for example, the E911 requirements for emergency services and locations in the United States.*

18. *Separation and definition of public data communications services and public telephony services is difficult from a regulation perspective. See, for example, the European definitions for ECS and PATS and the related regulations. The same applies for the Telecoms Act in the United States. Note also that there is no global regulations body, and enforcing any regulations for exterritorial services is challenging. It is also difficult to limit consumers' access to services that do not follow national regulations.*

Unfortunately, security is often an afterthought when deploying products or applications. The primary focus when building communication networks is whether the business features are in place but disregarding potential security risks. After the first security incident happens, network architects might finally realize the importance of the actual security requirements. Proactive thinking and a well-conducted risk assessment will assist in planning for and building a secure IP telephony network. If this is not done, vendors, manufacturers, and service providers in IP telephony will be caught in the patch-and-penetrate race, where system administrators run to fix problems with patches and workarounds before hackers compromise the system.

Although it is difficult to change users' poor habits, and many users might already be accustomed to insecure practices, you can integrate seamlessly several security mechanisms in order to protect the users by carefully designing technologies with properly defined security requirements.

To identify security requirements for VoIP the following should be considered (but not limited to):

- How critical is IP telephony to the organization?
- What critical information may be carried by the system, network, or service?
- What are the recovery mechanisms when the system fails?
- What supporting technologies does the service depend on?
- What systems and networks are the services integrated into, and are those exposed to threats?
- Is there a service provider dependence, and is the service provider liable for any damages?
- What are the responsibilities inside the organization?
- What is the cost of downtime and data loss?
- What are the past security incidents internally (or known in other deployments)?
- What are the regulatory compliance requirements?
- What are the short-term and long-term planned initiatives and changes?

Risk Analysis for VoIP

As with any critical network including legacy telephony or an Internet-connected data network, a VoIP infrastructure requires careful risk analysis. The starting point to various risk-analysis tasks is gaining an understanding of the system through collecting and analyzing system requirements. All key functionalities in VoIP service need to be listed and a risk value should be associated. System complexity increases the opportunity of error and the introduction of weaknesses into the design of the network, system, or service. Traditionally, the number of flaws in a system is directly proportional to the number of lines of code of the final product. Not necessarily all functionalities add significant value, and therefore not all functionalities need to be implemented. If there are unnecessary features in the system, you can reduce the complexity of the system by minimizing the set of features, otherwise referred to as the KISS principle (keep it simple, stupid).[19]

For the required value-add features, you can define three types of information security requirements: confidentiality, integrity, and availability. To make these easy to remember, they are commonly called the CIA (Confidentiality Integrity Availability) set of security objectives.[20] Again, remember the KISS principle. Too many security mechanisms make the system more complex and more difficult to maintain, implement, and use.

In any VoIP implementation the areas that should be protected include the signaling and media protocols that support the service, the service infrastructure (for example, SIP proxy, PSTN gateway, phones) and the supporting infrastructure (for example, routers and switches, DNS servers, NTP servers, etc.). In addition, areas such as APIs for provisioning and management, network peering, and administration interfaces need to be evaluated and secured appropriately.

The first set of requirements relates to data confidentiality. As a starting point for risk analysis, you need to develop confidentiality requirements for every feature and function of a network element. This is an important step because you need to understand whether confidential data is traversing or being stored in the corresponding network element.

---

19. *KISS (keep it simple, stupid). A maxim often invoked when discussing design to fend off creeping featurism and control development complexity. Possibly related to the marketroid maxim on sales presentations: Keep It Short and Simple. Source: The Jargon File. www.catb.org.*

20. *CIA is a mnemonic for confidentiality, integrity, and availability.*

Confidential data can also reside in the client software. Examples of confidential data include encryption keys, identity, presence, and location data. Analyzing and understanding how data traverses the network can identify critical weaknesses in the design.

The second set of requirements relates to data integrity. Besides integrity of the data exchanged between VoIP network elements, the data that is stored in end devices may need to support data integrity. Security mechanisms for integrity include checksums, signing, and filtering.

Availability requirements for all services and components are the third essential objective. In VoIP implementations availability is required for any component that supports the VoIP service including security (for example, authentication and authorization) controls, packet routing, domain name services, and network time service. A denial-of-service (DoS) attack (load-based or syntax-based) can aim in shutting down a service or resource and thus disrupting operations. Protection mechanisms for availability include perimeter defenses, secure programming principles, redundancy, and load balancing.

VoIP implementations often focus on a fourth requirement: Quality of Service (QoS). A bad network design or physical implementation of the cabling can ruin the user experience for VoIP. Although some aspects of QoS overlap with security, it is addressed in this book in relation with security (because the lack of QoS mostly results from bad network connectivity, the physical quality of the connections, or bad compression algorithms in both signaling and media). Security-related aspects of QoS, such as reducing voice quality with DoS and other attacks, are covered in Chapters 3 and 4.

A simplified risk equation consists of analyzing the probability of an incident based on the existence of a vulnerability associated with the technology, the ease of exploiting these vulnerabilities, and the extend of exposure (risk) through these vulnerabilities. *Threat* here means the existence of an opportunity and the attacker's incentive. If one of these parameters is eliminated, the risk is minimized or alleviated. Vulnerabilities, attacks, and threats should be given numeric values that represent probabilities; however, this numeric assignment is sometimes challenging because it is difficult to measure them objectively. The actual risk relates directly to the probability of an incident. You can use a simple formula that multiplies the probability metrics for vulnerabilities, attacks, and threats, resulting in the probability of an incident, for example:

Incident probability = Vulnerability × Attack × Threat

For all features, you should be able to measure the risk probability (or more specifically the incident probability), as just shown. You also need to measure the value of a security incident—that is, what does it cost if the threat is realized and security is compromised (incident cost). This is typically the easiest metric because the value of the service or feature can be taken directly from the business metrics, such as loss from downtime or loss of revenue. You can then calculate Annual Loss Expectancy (ALE) from these two components as a factor of time, as follows:

ALE = Incident probability × Incident cost × Time

Mitigation techniques reduce vulnerabilities, attacks, or threats and therefore directly affect the ALE value. If one of these is halved, the total probability is halved. Therefore, the mitigation factor can be added to the equation, giving the mitigated ALE (mALE):

mALE = Mitigation factor × ALE

Savings related to the mitigation equals the change in ALE:

Savings = ALE – mALE

Finally, knowing the cost related to the mitigation gives you the Return On Security Investment (ROSI):[21]

ROSI = Savings – Mitigation cost

Although these equations give a simplistic view to various aspects of quantification of risk, the resulting metric for ROSI is an important value for making informed decisions about various security investments. These equations are typically are used by large organizations when they consider making considerable investments in technologies such as firewalls and antivirus software, but they apply equally well to a product-development environment. When looking at code-auditing tools or robustness-testing tools, you should analyze the benefits and costs and make informed decisions about what is best for the product life cycle. Security is always about

---

21. *For more information about ROSI calculations, see the article by Scott Berinato at www.csoonline.com/read/120902/calculate.html.*

risk analysis—that is, understanding the probabilities, values, and costs related to mitigating those risks.

VoIP as Part of IT and the Security Organization

VoIP security can be challenging depending on the size of the organization because it crosses both the IP and telephony side of the IT infrastructure. Organizational changes might be required, such as designating a Chief Security Officer (CSO) or a Chief Information Security Officer (CISO) and creating a separate organization for the information security aspects of the IT infrastructure. As with any changes to the organizational structure, careful planning should take place. One way to set up an information security organization is as follows:[22]

1. Identify executive leadership.
2. Select a point person.
3. Establish the security organization.
4. Assemble the implementation teams.
5. Assign, schedule, execute, and discuss deliverables.
6. Measure the outcomes with metrics.

Without the support of the executive leadership, security will be perceived as an obstacle rather than a strength or a differentiator. Whether the responsible person for security issues is the CTO,[23] CIO,[24] CSO, or a dedicated CISO, they should report directly to an executive management person such as the CEO.[25] On the operational side, the organization should reach across both the telephony and IT infrastructure for maximum communication capabilities. It is also important that a corporatewide

---

22. *Loosely based on a 13-point plan suggested by Stan Gatewood, CISO of the University of Georgia, according to an online article, available at www.csoonline.com/read/030106/ security_group.html.*

23. *A CTO, chief technology officer, is a person typically responsible for the manufacturing and implementation of networks and services. He typically leads the research and the engineering teams.*

24. *A CIO, chief information officer, is a person leading the IT infrastructure and relationships to external service providers that the infrastructure depends on.*

25. *A CEO, chief executive officer, is the highest operational person, typically appointed by the board of directors. A CEO is typically called a managing director in Europe.*

policy be in place, and that it be enforced. Improving the resulting security practices is crucial, especially on the engineering side where such practices might be lacking at the moment. Lack of uniform corporate-wide policies introduces inconsistencies in standards and operations between groups within the organization which leads to poor service or product quality and resistance to change. Vulnerability analysis and penetration testing can be a useful mechanism to identify weaknesses on a consistent basis in an organization's operations, management, and technology implementation. Furthermore, the CSO's team together with the IT organization is typically the champion for user awareness and education which is critical for the organization's overall security strategy.

Operational tasks in a VoIP enterprise environment such as user provisioning and account management are typically handled by the IT staff, but the processes should be approved and maintained by the security group. In addition, there are many areas, such as network controls and data classification requirements, where close cooperation is required between the IT personnel and security personnel. Thus although the CSO's organization assumes the audit role, the personnel in the IT organization act as the practitioners of the CSO's security directives. Building networks is still the responsibility of the CIO's organization, but the design and architecture is also evaluated by the security team. Therefore, IT initiatives typically require the approval of the CSO. Figure 1.6 show a sample organization.

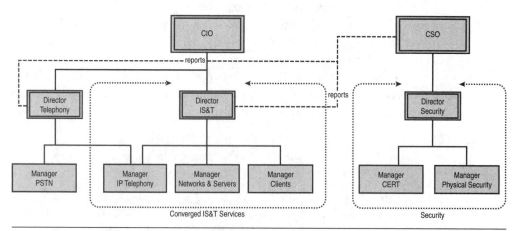

FIGURE 1.6 Converged IS&T and security organizations.

Security Certifications

Certification processes have been introduced (and certainly even more will emerge in the future) in order to provide a uniform mechanism in evaluating the security of a product, network, or service. For a certification process, typically a standard needs to exist. For VoIP, currently no security-related standards can be used for certification purposes. However, to understand future needs, let's first review various types of security standards and certifications in widespread use today. The main standards and certificates fall into three segments: professional, product, and infrastructure.

Professional certificates include training and tests so that professional engineers can receive accreditation for their work in critical networks, such as IP telephony. These are provided by vendors/manufacturers[26] and engineering organizations.[27] In security, the most widely accepted certifications include CISSP[28] and SANS-GIAG[29]. One typical certification method requires passing a written examination provided by various international organizations or vendor training organizations and then maintaining that certification through reexaminations.

Certifications are also applied to products. The purpose of product certification is to validate that the product passes third-party evaluation. The focus can be on the quality of the product or on the security mechanisms used in the product. Commercial testing laboratories typically conduct product certifications against their own acceptance criteria[30]. In

---

26. For example, in early 2002, Cisco introduced their Cisco IP Telephony Support Specialist, Cisco IP Telephony Design Specialist, and Cisco IP Telephony Operations Specialist accreditations.

27. The Telecommunications Industry Association (TIA) endorses the vendor-neutral Certified in Convergent Network Technologies (CCNT) and Certified Convergence Technologies Professional (CTP) certifications.

28. The International Information Systems Security Certification Consortium (ISC) is the internationally recognized gold standard for educating and certifying information security professionals throughout their careers (www.isc2.org).

29. GIAC stands for Global Information Assurance Certification. GIAC was founded in 1999 to validate the real-world skills of IT security professionals. GIAC's purpose is to provide assurance that a certified individual has practical knowledge and skills in key areas of computer security (www.giac.org).

30. For example, ICSA Labs tests security products such as firewalls, but the test criteria are their proprietary process.

some cases (for example, for doing business with government agencies), the assessment has to be performed against publicly recognized standards such as FIPS[31] and Common Criteria[32]. The problem with many product certification programs is that they validate the security mechanisms present in the products and typically include no vulnerability assessment of the products. This is because security assessment is typically an ad hoc review that is very difficult to specify. The torture-test specifications for SIP and Sigcomp published by the IETF are examples of defining test criteria for robustness of VoIP implementations. However, although they are valuable for educating engineers to prepare for security attacks, they do not provide adequate test coverage to validate security of the products themselves.

The third category includes best practice standards that focus on validating the infrastructure used and organizational practices. These certifications are very similar to generic quality certification (such as the ISO9000 series of standards). Examples of security-related certifications include ISO/IEC 17799, ITSEC, and GASSP. These standards promote good security practices within organizations, and typically they are a requirement for providing services for networks that support the Critical National Infrastructure (CNI), including power distribution, healthcare, and the military. Different organizations have different conformance requirements based on national/international standards.

When a service is finally deployed, different certifications are available to show to consumers that the service or network has been implemented using a set of security controls based on best industry practices. Although this type of service certification does not appear to be available for VoIP, corollaries can be drawn from Web services. Web site certifications include certifications such as the BBB Online Privacy Seal[33] and AICPA/CICA WebTrust Program;[34] in similar fashion, the security mechanisms in place can be advertised for VoIP services. It should be noted that certifications

---

31. *FIPS 140 was issued by NIST (National Institute of Standards and Technology) to be used as a validation criteria for cryptographic modules. It is not a guarantee of security, but focuses on the good validation practices of the software and its documentation.*

32. *Common Criteria (CC) and the Common Evaluation Methodology (CEM) are accepted as an international standard (ISO/IEC 15408). For more information, see www.commoncriteriaportal.org and www.iso.org.*

33. *BBBOnLine's mission is to promote trust and confidence on the Internet through the BBBOnLine Reliability and Privacy Seal programs (www.bbbonline.org).*

34. *The American Institute of Certified Public Accountants is the national, professional organization for all Certified Public Accountants (www.aicpa.org).*

should not be perceived as a state of perfection but rather a mechanism to demonstrate consistency of operational practice, knowledge, or support of certain functionality.

Besides the various certifications previously mentioned, international security organizations and product manufacturers have published checklists and technical guidelines that define how a network must be configured securely. For any device that you depend on for reliable operations, you should verify whether the manufacturer has written a guideline for secure deployment.

Summary

Many compare the development and evolution of VoIP protocols such as SIP to HTTP (which enabled Web services and the launch of the Internet to the general public). However, just as with Web and email, security will play an important role in the evolution of VoIP and other multimedia applications including video and gaming. Traditionally, people have thought of the PSTN as the infrastructure for all communications and of IP as one of the many payloads that can carried by this infrastructure. Now, however, IP is considered the underlying transport of all multimedia communications. VoIP is one of the applications that uses the protocols that are covered in this book which inherit weaknesses that can be exploited in order to carry out various attacks. And thus the same weaknesses are applicable to any multimedia application along with protection mechanisms that are discussed in this book.

This chapter covered the background of VoIP, looking at the basics of legacy telephony and IP communications. Since 1980 to the present, we have seen the transition from legacy POTS systems to digital telephony using ISDN, and from fixed-line communications to wireless NMT, GSM, and CDMA telephony. The development of both quality and speed of packet networks has resulted in the introduction of voice as one of the services that Internet connectivity can offer to consumers. Because increasing numbers of people have high-bandwidth Internet connectivity to their home, incumbent telephone service providers suddenly face a new business threat: free calls over the Internet. This "threat" has initiated enormous infrastructure changes and has spawned challenges related to regulatory requirements and implementation of VoIP services.

VoIP has a long history, and the various architectures have gone through several different phases and iterations. IP connectivity has been used to tunnel enterprise voice traffic between different sites, and for communications in Internet games and entertainment systems such as Internet chat. Because of the unregulated service offerings and international connectivity of both the Internet and related services, software developers and device manufacturers have basically set the pace of VoIP development. Free, proprietary VoIP offerings (such as Skype) and commercial enterprise VoIP deployments by equipment manufacturers (such as Cisco) have both impacted the diversity of VoIP. It was finally the adoption of industry standards such as SIP that opened up the VoIP market for interoperability and wider deployments. However, open communication networks have also created the need for security and reliability. And, the Internet was never intended to be secure; it was intended to be open.

The possibility of anyone being able to contact anyone else over the Internet has also created security requirements for Internet applications. Over time, standardization organizations have extended the technologies with security mechanisms and capabilities, and these same technologies have now been adopted for voice communications. Legacy telephony had no requirement for security because it was a closed network; there were no open interfaces into which attackers could inject worms or viruses (and there was no malicious signaling or media). With free Internet calls, however, the same problems that plague the Web and email will also influence voice communications. This chapter introduced the starting points for preparing your organization for security requirements: risk analysis, organization structures, and certification models.

The most important point to understand about risk analysis is that for every security improvement, there is a cost associated (and in some cases a return on investment). Risk analysis is always the starting point for security. You need to understand the value of the assets you are trying to protect and the cost of protecting those. It is the only way to make informed decisions when selecting network components and security mechanisms. For example, a closed network may not need external security controls because no external threat exists, but it may require internal security controls. The cost of downtime of the VoIP service is measured according to the reliance of the organization's operations on the service and the robustness of the network—because, after all, a business-critical network must not crash. Security has to be measurable.

Organizations also evolve and as technologies converge it's natural for organizational teams to also converge. The legacy telephony team becomes part of the IT infrastructure team. Security roles have to exist in any organization (regardless of size) with security-critical assets. Any change in the organizational structure is always difficult because of general resistance to change (both at the organizational level and the individual level).

Finally, certifications are the proof of maturity, not only for the technology and organization, but also for the marketplace. Subscribers expect from the VoIP industry reasonable quality of service and security. Certification is considered as a mechanism to demonstrate uniform controls according to industry best practice. Although VoIP does not introduce any new security requirements or objectives to the security of a network owner or service provider, some of the associated weaknesses and threats are new to some and thus need to be understood properly. VoIP consists of concepts and technologies between traditional telecom and data networks. Therefore, the security practices used in both of these domains are still applicable to the newly converged network. A successful VoIP deployment can only result from informed decisions when choosing the processes and technologies properly. But that said, no one will guarantee the security of any network.

## CHAPTER 2

VoIP ARCHITECTURES AND PROTOCOLS

The transition from legacy Public Switched Telephone Network (PSTN) into communications using IP-based networks has sparked the development of real-time multimedia applications with many sophisticated features at a lower cost. VoIP is one of the applications that provides global interconnectivity at a low cost. And in cases where calls are established between peers in an IP network the cost is negligible or non-existent. This chapter focuses on the most commonly used architectures of VoIP communications and discusses the protocols and components that are used to support VoIP and generally any multimedia application. Chapter 10, "Provider Architectures and Security" and Chapter 11, "Enterprise Architectures and Security" expand on the discussion of enterprise and carrier architectures, along with security considerations.

VoIP architectures can be studied from several different perspectives. When studying the various architectures of VoIP, we need to understand the underlying elements that comprise the network and their respective functions that support the VoIP service. The underlying IP infrastructure ensures interconnectivity and proper routing of the call traffic between end users. The network architecture for VoIP is neither simple nor homogeneous. Although there are similarities between VoIP networks at the moment, no single industry-standard architecture for VoIP exists. Enterprise VoIP architectures differ from carrier grade architectures which also differ from government architectures. Each of these architectures is driven by the organizational requirements in place which are defined based on many distinct drivers such as monetary gain (in case of a service provider), cost-reduction, quality of service, and others. Although security is not a primary requirement for switching from TDM (Time Division Multiplexing) to IP-based communications, it has become an apparent requirement. Traditionally, the PSTN has been perceived as a trusted network. Note the word "trusted" is purposefully chosen instead of the word "secure." In general, people make an assumption that their communications through the PSTN are secure, which is not the case. But, throughout the years we have established a misconceived trust that we expect it to be present when we use VoIP. As such, VoIP security has become a hot topic.

Both network and service access have to be considered when planning the security of a VoIP network whether it is offered over broadband or wireless networks. The protocols and services that are used to support Internet connectivity, such as NTP, DNS, SMTP, and so forth, can also be implemented in a closed network. In addition, they support a variety of VoIP architectures, the selection of which usually depends on who is providing the service and which type of business model is used. At the enterprise level, the IT department of the company can provide the entire IP and VoIP architecture, with interconnections to commercial VoIP carriers or to the PSTN. In a VoIP service provider architecture subscribers may access the service through their respective ISP (Internet service provider). In which case access to the IP backbone (Internet) is provided by the ISP and access to the service is provided by the VoIP service provider through the ISP. At the carrier level, the voice traffic can be routed over the Internet or a private IP backbone (MPLS) depending on the type of service. Thus IP connectivity can be provided through legacy networks such as PSTN, cable TV, satellite, or cellular. It is expected that the components and protocols used in the deployment of enterprise and carrier VoIP architectures will be standardized. An example of such a standard is the Internet Protocol Multimedia Subsystem (IMS) architecture, which is used to support multimedia applications in both fixed telecommunications and in mobile networks.

To enable interconnection between products from different manufacturers, the industry has agreed on a set of industry standard protocols defined by organizations such as IETF, IEEE, 3GPP, and ITU-T. Different protocols are needed depending on the used service and network architecture. Internet access depends on protocols that provide IP addresses, name resolution, and the routing of the packets. VoIP is implemented using different signaling and media protocols. Both signaling and media connections can be protected as necessary. Signaling protocols are used to establish, maintain, and tear down connections between end points. In addition signaling protocols are used to support billing and negotiate call parameters such media ports, encryption keys, and codecs. For interoperability between devices, signaling protocols are also used to negotiate the media codecs that are used to convert the analog audio signal into digital packets.[1] Media protocols are used to transfer the actual content between the end points over the network. In addition they are used to carry events such as dialtones to support menu navigation for IVR (Interactive Voice Response) systems. Because of the real-time requirements, the media protocols almost always use unreliable transport (UDP). The most commonly used protocol for media streams is RTP (Real Time Protocol). Some of the well-known signaling protocols that are used in VoIP include SIP, RTP, MGCP, H.323, and Sigtran.

Protection of signaling and media protocols is necessary due to the various attacks that can be performed as discussed in Chapter 3 "Threats and Attacks." For example, eavesdropping can be prevented by using traffic encryption. The encryption can be performed at various levels starting from the link layer (for example, link encryptors) up to the application layer using SRTP (Secure RTP). Alternatives include the use of secure VPN (virtual private network) tunnels. Other mechanisms for protecting signaling and media traffic are network segmentation using VLANs (virtual LANs) which are discussed in Chapter 9, "A Security Framework for Enterprise VoIP Networks," along with several other architectural considerations in Chapter 10, "Provider Architectures and Security," and 11, "Enterprise Architectures and Security."

Subscribers are typically connected to the Internet using various methods including ADSL (Asymmetric Digital Subscriber Line), DOCSIS (Data Over Cable Service Interface Specification) via cable modem, wireless, or even through a cellular network that provides GPRS (General Packet Radio Service) or similar data service. For enterprise networks the network connectivity may be through a Gigabit Ethernet or ATM and in some cases a T-1 line. Although in some cases end users may be restricted to a dial-up connection for Internet connectivity, in many countries broadband access is becoming the standard mechanism for subscriber Internet access. Thus the landscape for bandwidth requirements has paved the road to support real-time applications such as VoIP. As such, telecoms and cable operators invest in deploying fiber or cable connectivity to end users. A fully converged "triple-play" service requires quite a lot of bandwidth to be able to transport all multimedia services over one single IP connection.[2]

---

1. *Codec is the encoding and the decoding standard for digital media. Different codecs have varying properties for compression rate, voice quality, and data bandwidth requirements.*

2. *Triple-play generally refers to bundling broadband connections and the various IP services together with video (IPTV) and voice (VoIP).*

The following paragraphs discuss the fundamental components and protocols associated with VoIP. In addition, enterprise and carrier-grade VoIP architectures are discussed further in Chapters 10 and 11 from a security stand point of view.

Architectures

The organizational objectives should dictate the requirements for the used VoIP architecture. For example, an enterprise architecture is different from a carrier-grade architecture which is different from a service provider architecture. In enterprise networks we typically observe two types of VoIP architectures. One is the hybrid-IP architecture in which the traditional PBX supports IP connectivity, and the other is the all-IP architecture in which the PBX has been replaced by components such as a SIP proxy or an H.323 gatekeeper or a call manager.

In addition these architectures are further decomposed based on the physical and logical components that comprise them. A physical composition of the architecture describes the network elements and provides specific description of the actual network implementation (for example, routers, switches, SBCs). Whereas the logical composition of the architecture provides a generic view of the functionality that is supported by the components (for example, call agent, gatekeeper, SIP gateway). For example the call agent function may be supported by four physical hosts that are dispersed throughout a geographical region for continuity purposes. The VoIP network architectures have many similarities to both legacy telephony networks and traditional IP networks. After all, the features, network design, functional components, and deployment principles are drawn from traditional networks such as PSTN telephony, peer-to-peer communications, and enterprise IP networks. All ideas in VoIP peer-to-peer are drawn from legacy systems. We will next provide an overview of some of the most commonly used architectures for VoIP.

VoIP in Peer-to-Peer IP Telephony

The simplest architecture for VoIP consists of a direct connection between VoIP phones, a peer-to-peer connection. Due to popular and free implementations this is also the most common VoIP setup. Peer-to-peer (P2P) communication networks do not rely on the existence of centralized servers. A P2P network transfers the work of the servers to the end points themselves, and therefore each new node in the P2P network adds resources such as storage and processing power to the entire network. P2P networks can prove difficult to monitor because they can easily be encrypted from end to end, to protect from eavesdropping using existing monitoring technologies from IP communications. In P2P networks, the communicating parties can also achieve anonymity by implementing or using anonymizing services.[3] In such an anonymizer network, the routers forward different packets in the communication streams semi-randomly, making it very difficult to catch all the packets related to a stream, potentially at the same time encrypting the payload.[3] The origin and the destination identifiers can be anonymized by the communicating parties themselves. P2P networks can be implemented with industry-standard protocols such as P2P SIP[4] or with proprietary protocols such as Skype.[5]

All soft phones that are not bound to centralized servers can be set up in a simple P2P setup. The simplest form of P2P VoIP is a direct connection between two voice-enabled end points, which may be personal computers (PCs), relying on the private or existing IP addressing scheme, as shown in Figure 2.1. Numerous VoIP soft clients are available for all industry-standard operating systems. If two people have soft clients installed, and know the public IP address of each other, they can create a direct VoIP connection. One of the main problems with P2P VoIP comes from the limitations of the IP addressing scheme[6] associated with DHCP (Dynamic Host Control Protocol) and in some cases NAT (Network Address Translation). If the other party in the communications does not have a public IP address, but relies on some internal dynamic addressing scheme provided by the service provider, the communication to that direction requires prior knowledge of the destination's current IP address thus making it difficult to initiate a connection. Without a centralized server with a known IP address, the communications between two devices in private networks will be impossible because neither party has a public IP address that can be contacted to initiate the call. Another obstacle is

3. David Goldschlag, Michael Reed, and Paul Syverson have developed the onion routing technique; see http://en.wikipedia.org/wiki/Onion_routing for more information, A free patent-free implementation of onion routing is available in Tor networks: http://tor.eff.org/.

4. P2P is a standardization effort in progress by the IETF. For more information about P2P SIP, see www.p2psip.org.

5. Note that Skype is a trademark of Skype Technologies S.A. For more information about Skype, see www.skype.com.

6. Note that the address space limitation exists in IPv4; IPv6 is supposed to fix this problem by extending the address space.

created by mobility. A device will change its service provider and IP address every time it moves from one network to another. It is important to remember that in most use scenarios, the IP addresses cannot reliably be used to identify people or devices. A VoIP address does not identify a device but a user that can be using any device.

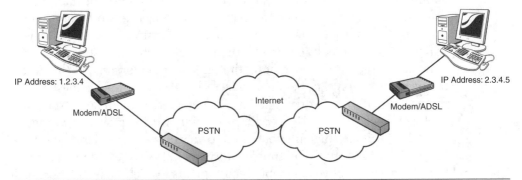

IP Address: 1.2.3.4

Modem/ADSL

Internet

PSTN

PSTN

Modem/ADSL

IP Address: 2.3.4.5

Figure 2.1 P2P communications between two workstations.

The user database and the location database can also be implemented using P2P technologies. One example of a P2P VoIP is Skype, from the developers of the Kazaa file-trading network. Skype uses a proprietary Global Index (GI) approach to finding people in the network. The GI technology used by Skype takes advantage of a multiple-tiered architecture where super nodes take the responsibility of distributing the presence of the subscribers. Any Skype client with a public Internet address and adequate resources such as bandwidth can become a super node. Skype uses intelligent routing to enable efficient routing of encrypted end-to-end communications through the Internet.[7] Skype is not completely peer to peer; it appears to be using a centralized login server for user authentication.[8] Figure 2.2 shows how a Skype client can find other parties in a Skype network and connect with them. Skype is not a completely closed network; Skype-out and Skype-in services interconnect with traditional PSTN.

7. *Skype's approach to P2P VoIP is explained at www.skype.com/products/explained.html, and third-party articles have been collected at www1.cs.columbia.edu/~salman/skype/.*

8. *Salman A. Baset and Henning Schulzrinne. An Analysis of the Skype Peer-to-Peer Internet Telephony Protocol. Columbia University Technical Report CUCS-039-04.*

Those calls must travel through the VoIP-to-PSTN gateways located in different countries. Incumbent telephony companies typically provide the PSTN termination.

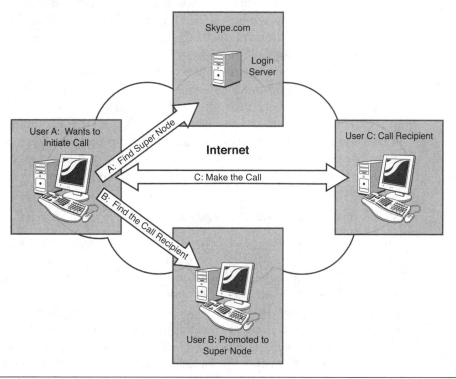

Figure 2.2 Overview of various connections taking place in a Skype network.

Creating an industry standard for P2P is much more challenging and time consuming than creating a proprietary and closed communication protocol. The requirements set by heterogeneous networks and challenges for privacy and confidentiality are much easier to resolve with closed communication standards, although third-party review of the used techniques becomes more difficult. The shrinking size of the available IPv4 address space has been addressed by the implementation of Network Address Translation (NAT), but that poses problems to P2P communications. P2P communications traverse NAT devices using various methods, which usually involve contacting "rendezvous servers" [9] with fixed IP address or other P2P clients that have a public IP address. These devices will then keep track of the IP addresses of the corresponding P2P clients. Although P2P SIP standardization is still work-in-progress[10], it appears that the peer-to-peer network (P2P Overlay) will be a separate layer, and the SIP protocol will remain unchanged. When the standardization work is completed, the final specification for P2P VoIP may raise security concerns since P2P networks completely open up the connections between the two hosts, avoiding all perimeter defenses in between. The open connectivity between any two hosts through the P2P Overlay could end up giving attackers an advantage to propagate attacks through the overlay network. Protection against P2P threats requires the implementation of strong user and node authentication in addition to enforcing authorization on functionality available by the service or application (such as directory listing).

VoIP in Enterprise Networks

VoIP is adopted in enterprise networks principally because of the benefits derived from reducing the complexity of the network infrastructure, and because of the advantages that accrue from the improved productivity applications available with VoIP.[11] With VoIP, the enterprise also reduces costs by implementing most or all of the subscriber services at the company site. The control of the telephony subscribers is in the hands of the telephony people inside the company. Cost savings can be sizable when inter-company calls inside one logical entity never go through the telephony service provider, and the savings can be enormous when communications of two remote sites can be routed over the internal telephony system.

Whereas in consumer networks end users can choose to use any applications they want, additional legal challenges exist in enterprise networks and limit the opportunities available. The enterprise is typically liable for the communications both internally and toward third parties outside their network. An enterprise will take enormous risk if it allows anyone to

---

9. *Bryan Ford, Pyda Srisuresh, Dan Kegel. Peer-to-Peer Communication Across Network Address Translators. Available at www.brynosaurus.com/pub/net/p2pnat/.*

10. *When we were writing this book, the P2P SIP was still in draft status. For the current status, see http://tools.ietf.org/wg/p2psip/.*

11. *IDC white paper by William Stofega. Enterprise VoIP: Adding Value While Reducing Cost. 2005.*

connect with anyone outside the organization without any authentication of the communicating parties and without any validation of the actual traffic. In similar fashion, only authorized parties can connect into the enterprise network from outside. The lack of control is why P2P traffic is seen as the "ultimate evil" for enterprise data networks.[12] Client/server architecture is much easier to monitor and control. An enterprise VoIP network can be built from several different perspectives. The most common implementation strategy is a step-by-step transition from fixed-line enterprise telephony based on Private Branch Exchange (PBX) to using an IP-PBX to control both legacy telephony and IP-based telephony and to interconnect the IP network and the PSTN. On the other hand, companies with no legacy fixed-line networks or companies that will make the transition without PSTN access can step directly into pure IP telephony without thinking about the architectural restrictions from legacy PSTN.

Generally, an enterprise VoIP network involves a PBX. The transition from a legacy PBX-centric approach to IP-PBX typically happens through a hybrid model, in which an IP interface card is added to the PBX and connected directly to the same enterprise IP network used for data connections inside the office. The first application for this IP interface is typically aimed at reducing the costs related to intercompany calls by routing the calls between two company sites, by connecting each IP-PBX over the enterprise data network. This setup is extremely easy to implement securely by using dedicated lines between the sites, or a secure VPN connection if the voice traffic is routed through the public Internet. Things change when the IP-PBX allows any IP device to subscribe to the VoIP service. Suddenly, any IP-based phone, or any PC in the office, can make a call through the PBX. This is a natural evolution because most of the telephony services can be transferred to the IP network, and the converged network will allow a wider range of telephony services to all subscribers. The final steps in this transition to VoIP result in an IP-PBX with only one PSTN connection directed out from the enterprise, and finally no interconnection to PSTN at all, but direct broadband access to a VoIP carrier.

2. VoIP Architectures and Protocols

---

12. *Skype appears to be an exception to this distrust of P2P networks. System administrators appear to trust the company behind Skype to provide adequate confidentiality for the service. Perhaps one thing that influences this trust is that Skype is a closed architecture that is thought to transfer voice and messages, and nothing else, and therefore the risk is quite limited. The features of Skype should be compared to your corporate policy. Users of Skype can, for example, use file sharing over third-party networks, and that might be against your security policy.*

When VoIP is built from the scratch, it can be built just like any other IP communications service. Similar to all other IP communications, VoIP in an enterprise environment consists of perimeter defenses, gateways, servers, and (finally) the clients. Servers authenticate the clients, and gateways provide access to other communication networks. Perimeter defenses such as firewalls ensure that only approved communications take place between authenticated communication devices. Because all VoIP components are basically software, each "service" can be installed to the same servers where other IP services reside. In addition, the IP-to-PSTN gateway can simply be an interface card on a server. A pure VoIP deployment could potentially be implemented on existing hardware.

VoIP in Carrier Networks

A carrier network typically provides very high bandwidth interconnections between networks located in other states and countries. A carrier can provide interconnections to both local and international telephony service companies and Internet service companies. Carriers can also provide interconnections directly to large global enterprise customers. The carrier can provide either circuit-switched or packet-switched connections. Typically, a carrier network consists of a 100% fiber network with Synchronous Optical NETwork (SONET) ring architectures, which guarantees reliability. Common bandwidths for the links are 51Mbps (OC-1), 155Mbps (OC-3), 622Mbps (OC-12), 2.5Gbps (OC-48), 10Gbps (OC-192), and 40Gbps (OC-768). This can be a dedicated circuit all the way to the customer or can run packet-switched protocols such as ATM, Frame Relay, SMDS, IP/MPLS, and X.25 inside virtual circuits. A multilayer/multiservice switch can support several different protocols over a single link or circuit. A carrier is in the business of providing (and guaranteeing) bandwidth and the optimal route to the final destination.

A VoIP carrier will tunnel telephony services over their network. The interconnection to a local service provider can be a dedicated fiber circuit or a network interface optimized for a specific application such as VoIP or PSTN. When the connection is for voice, the carrier does its best to ensure that the call takes the best possible route to the final destination. Whereas traditional circuit-switched PSTN voice traffic was easier to estimate (due to dedicated links), carriers are now dealing with customers that want to send more bursty IP traffic over their network. VoIP is one of these IP payloads, but with a specific requirement for quality of service (QoS). This separation of voice from other IP traffic is the challenge for the carriers and their customers.

VoIP in Service Provider Architectures

Service providers for VoIP come in three different flavors. The first category consists of converged telecommunications service providers, who bundle the fixed-line access with an additional service for VoIP. The second category is Internet service provider (ISP) companies, who can provide VoIP services to their customers, providing a full service, including identification of their customers and sometimes even the terminals (for example, VoIP phones). There are several business models for ISPs. An ISP can provide the VoIP access as an add-on service to broadband access, similarly to how they provide email service. The VoIP service can also include access to the PSTN telephony through a gateway. The third category includes Internet-based service providers. They host the VoIP service remotely. They do not need to be concerned about the infrastructure required for the consumer connectivity because their customers receive the plain broadband connection from their local ISP. Internet-based VoIP service providers typically provide a global VoIP registry that anyone can join. Some Internet-based VoIP providers also partner with local ISPs, who will sell their service to the consumers.

Softswitch Architecture

A softswitch refers to a logical entity that supports signaling in NGN/VOIP VoIP architecture. A softswitch is a VoIP-enabled network component (for example, a router integrating many of the functional elements used in typical VoIP architectures). The softswitch architecture is also the basis of the IMS architecture. The softswitch architecture introduced logical entities to the VoIP architecture and made it possible to move and separate services from the PBX-centric approach into different industrial-grade servers on the network. Distributing the functionality made it possible to simplify the switches and to make them more cost-effective. In 1998, an industry organization called the International Softswitch Consortium was founded to facilitate the adaptation of VoIP to replace the large central office (CO) telephony switches in the enterprise environment. This organization was later called the International Packet Communications Consortium (IPCC) and now is called the IMS Forum.[13] Similarities between softswitch architecture and IMS are quite apparent because the same logical entities such as signaling gateways, media gateway controllers, media gateways, and application servers are used in both approaches.

2. VoIP ARCHITECTURES AND PROTOCOLS

The idea behind the softswitch architecture is the separation of the physical switching of telephony from the logical operations. For promoting interoperability between different vendors through similar functionalities, the softswitch architecture is divided into four functional planes: transport, call control and signaling, service and application, and management. The transport plane is responsible for the interconnection of call setup, signaling, and media, and includes both IP and non-IP transports. The media gateway controller operates the call control and signaling plane and is responsible for setup and teardown of media connections. Application servers and various add-on features are implemented in the service and application plane. The management plane provides subscriber and service provisioning and can be implemented with management protocols such as Simple Network Management Protocol (SNMP). In practice, however, one single network element, also called softswitch, can implement all these functionalities.

Internet Protocol Multimedia Subsystem

The Internet Protocol Multimedia Subsystem (IMS) extends the softswitch approach into building a standard architecture for realtime multimedia applications. Just as with the convergence of voice and data communications, we have seen the convergence of mobile and fixed telecommunications networks. A challenge with traditional Internet connection is that it has been designed for fixed access. With mobile devices, however, we need access to services wherever the device happens to be. IMS is a key architecture for transitioning to mobile Internet access. Mobile devices are always-on and always-connected devices that contain a rich set of features and applications, including large displays, cameras, instant messaging, and email. With VoIP moving to mobile devices, the mobile operators required a way to control the voice traffic. Although mobile operators were the first to embrace IMS, fixed-line operators are now adopting it, too. This is not only because of the adoption of wireless connection technologies such as WiFi and WiMAX, but also because IMS supports and extends the business models of legacy mobile and fixed-line operators. The most critical asset to the service providers is the network, and they need to maintain control of that network. IMS is the natural choice because it is designed to enable mobility, roaming, billing, and monitoring of services. IMS is the architecture for operators who want to provide reliable and secure IP connectivity to their mobile users, anywhere. The architecture has been specified by 3GPP, in Releases 5, 6, and 7.[14] The protocols used in IMS are specified by IETF, with potentially minor modifications by 3GPP. Important protocols for IMS include SIP, RTP, Diameter, IPv6, and IPSec.

With the introduction of IMS, basically all mobile services, including voice, will be used on top of IP. IMS can enforce strong authentication of the user and device, similar to that used in GSM mobile phones.[15] When authenticated successfully, the device has full access, with all the capabilities that can be offered. The home operator can choose to remain in control of the services.[16] This could, for example, mean that the user of the device can only use VoIP services authorized by the operator, and also therefore billed by the operator. This control will also guarantee access and QoS to services such as push-to-talk, presence/location, voice, and video. The same security mechanisms covered in this book are used in IMS, if the service provider chooses to use them.

VoIP Network Components

Similar network components can be recognized in all VoIP architectures regardless of the network topology. Understanding the building blocks and their usage will help you to understand, select, and deploy the chosen VoIP technology. We next cover the various network components available in VoIP.

Terminals

A VoIP phone, or terminal, is used to initiate and receive calls. A soft phone is a software-based VoIP implementation that runs on desktop PCs or on any other industry-standard platforms, including PDAs and mobile phones. They use the sound capabilities of the used host system. The VoIP software can also run on an appliance ("hard phone") and therefore can appear to be very similar to traditional phones. Because some VoIP implementations use text-based user identities, a hard phone with only a numeric keypad can be very cumbersome to use without a numbering

14. For details about IMS history, see www.3gpp.org.

15. Note again that similar to the GSM networks, IMS does not necessarily mean that the network is authenticated.

16. 2G mobile networks used "visited service control" mode, which means that the operator where the device was roaming had control of the services. In IMS, "home service control" is used, ensuring the same set of services wherever the device is located.

plan. Depending on the architecture, the VoIP terminal can also be a called user agent (UA) or terminating user agent. Note that not all terminals are human controlled, but they can be software-based providing a VoIP service. For example, a VoIP terminal can also consist of software that automatically receives (voice mail) or makes (auto-dialer) calls.

Call Manager

VoIP end points need to know how to identify and reach each other. A call manager is responsible for authenticating users. Call manager can also act as an address(ing) server, responsible for translating telephone numbers into the VoIP addressing space, or the other way around. A call manager is typically the first entity a new VoIP terminal has to interact with. When the call manager is aware of the subscriber, however, where the user has registered or subscribed to the service, the call manager can step aside and let the other infrastructure take care of the actual call handling. Other names for a call manager function or device include gatekeeper or registrar. In IMS, a Home Subscriber Server (HSS) or Home Location Register (HLR) can handle the call manager functions. In P2P networks, the call manager function is either a fixed host on the Internet or distributed among different nodes.

Signaling Server/Gateway

In VoIP, signaling and media take different paths. A signaling gateway is responsible for routing the signaling messages to the correct signaling server. In a P2P VoIP call, the destination server can actually be a terminal and act as a server (super node). In enterprise VoIP, the first gateway/server can be the IP-PBX. In carrier VoIP networks, the signaling gateway functionality is implemented in a softswitch. In conferencing systems, the signaling gateways are called multipoint controllers, and they are responsible for coordinating a call between several subscribers. A gateway can operate between similar networks, or it can act as a proxy between different architectures and protocols. A redirect server would be responsible for redirecting the call to the right destination. In IMS, signaling is routed through the CSCF (Call Session Control Function) components into an MGCF (Media Gateway Control Function) responsible for setting up the call. Super nodes handle the gateway function in P2P networks.

Media Server/Gateway

Whereas the signaling can take a longer route through various servers and gateways, the actual media takes its own typically shorter and faster path from one end point to the other. In some VoIP architectures, the media travels directly between the terminals according to the routing mechanisms of the IP network. In service provider architectures and in security-critical enterprise environments, the owner of the network prefers to have at least some control over what the acceptable media formats are, and what is the acceptable path for the media. A media gateway (MGW) is responsible for controlling the media flows, and it can also be responsible for media conversion from one protocol or codec to another. In conferencing systems, this can also be called a multipoint processor and can mix and separate several different media streams together to save bandwidth, instead of all terminals sending and receiving the media streams to/from all participants. In IMS, the CSCF has control over the media, but the logic is handled by the MGW and MGCF. In P2P networks and any VoIP architectures with end-to-end encryption, there typically is neither interest in nor even the possibility of controlling the media.

Session Border Elements

Session border elements are very difficult to define. Session border elements are responsible for policing the connections. The simplest session border element is a VoIP-aware firewall, an Application-Level Gateway (ALG). Some functions that can be present in a session border element include signaling and media gateway operations, firewall functions, NAT functionality, and even encryption or VPN support. In SIP/IMS, these elements are called Session Border Controllers (SBCs) or security gateways. These SBCs are not really part of any of the VoIP specifications, but have been added by the carriers to provide some security perimeters to VoIP. Another potential benefit from an SBC is the improved interoperability through "repairing" VoIP messages, which on the other hand can lead to an aggressive or intrusive SBC breaking the operation of VoIP by altering the packets in transit. P2P networks are typically designed, through the implementation firewall/NAT traversal and strong encryption, to be invisible to session border elements.

Signaling Protocols

In IP telephony, signaling and media are typically separated and are handled by different protocols. Traditionally in PSTN, signaling is used to identify the calling parties and to negotiate the voice trunks or channels used by the media streams. The same applies for most VoIP architectures today.

Interestingly, this separation of media and signaling was introduced to PSTN telephony because of security reasons. Before the introduction of SS7, in-band signaling allowed attackers to send signaling tones using the same path. SS7 was developed to support more sophisticated operations and one side effect was the eliminiation of call fraud because SS7 provides out-of-band signaling.[17] An out-of-band signaling protocol called SS7 was introduced to separate the signaling from the media to protect against these phreakers sending their malicious signaling messages when they had access to the telephony networks, potentially even through the terminal itself.[18] Quite often in VoIP networks, signaling and media use the same physical network even though the signaling and media are implemented by two different protocols. In PSTN, the path for signaling and media are distinct and the network maintains the intelligence that is responsible for the signaling; whereas, in VoIP a terminal maintains a lot of functionality through the signaling messages. A hacker (or phreaker) with access to the VoIP signaling can impersonate signaling messages to perform various attacks, which are discussed in Chapter 3, "Threats and Attacks," and Chapter 4, "VoIP Vulnerabilities."

We next look at industry-standard signaling protocols. Proprietary protocols are beyond the scope of this chapter, although there are many similarities in all multimedia protocols. Also, various proxies and gateways handle interoperation between different signaling protocols; so in a real-life deployment, you can see all of these happily mixed together. For example, a softswitch can support all the signaling protocols mentioned in the following sections and provide service to subscribers no matter which technology they depend on.

---

17. For more information, see Wikipedia for "Blue box" at en.wikipedia.org/wiki/Blue_box.

18. Phreaker and phreaking are terms used for telephony hackers and hacking.

SS7, Q.931, and Sigtran

The protocol used for network-to-network signaling in PSTN is called Signaling System #7, or SS7, which is comprised of a suite of related protocols. SS7 is defined by ITU-T.[19] The same SS7 protocol family, or network, is also sometimes be called Common Channel Signaling System 7 (CCS7) or CCITT number 7 (C7).[20]

Although media in PSTN is circuit switched, SS7 is a packet-switched protocol. It travels on top of Frame Relay networks between carriers that negotiate and allocate used circuits. SS7 consists of underlying layers starting from the physical (MTP[21] 1), link (MTP 2), and network (MTP 3) and the application protocols such as ISUP (ISDN User Part), TCAP (Transaction Capabilities Application Part), and SCCP (Signaling Connection Control Part). Signaling parts of the SS7 are implemented in MTP 3, ISUP, and TCAP. In the ISDN functionality, Q.931 is also used for signaling.[22] RFC 2719 explains the interworking requirements between SS7 networks and IP networks.[23]

Sigtran is a functional model for IP interconnection with SS7. As you can see from Figure 2.3, Sigtran is basically the IP variant of MTP Layer 1 through three protocols. Sigtran implements the same (or similar) SS7 user and application protocols as SS7. Sigtran may also implement the SCCP part, and when interconnecting with an ISDN network, it can also implement the Q.931 layer. Because of the high QoS requirements of the PSTN, Sigtran also has very high reliability requirements, and therefore requires good bandwidth and tolerates very few collisions on the network. Basically, Sigtran can be used to tunnel SS7 between two PSTN networks over IP connections, or even over the Internet.

2. VoIP ARCHITECTURES AND PROTOCOLS

---

19. *ITU-T Recommendations Q.700-775, Signaling System No. 7.*

20. *ITU-T was earlier called CCITT.*

21. *ITU-T Recommendations Q.701-6, Message Transfer Part of SS7.*

22. *ITU-T Recommendation Q.931, ISDN user-network interface layer 3 specification (5/98).*

23. *L. Ong et al. RFC 2719, Framework Architecture for Signaling Transport. 1999.*

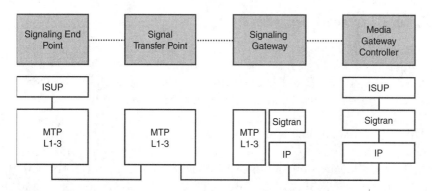

Figure 2.3 SS7 access to MGC (according to RFC 2719).

ISUP is an application protocol of the SS7 protocol family and is specified by ITU-T as part of the Q.7xx series of protocols. ISUP used in Europe is standardized by ETSI. ISUP is a binary protocol that defines the circuits that need to be connected to set up the call between two parties, and it identifies when the call is set up, when the phone is finally answered, and when the resources are released. ISUP can also be used in other signaling protocols such as Sigtran.

H.323

H.323 is a set of protocols recommended by ITU-T and is widely adopted in the enterprise environment because of its easy integration with PSTN. The battle for the most accepted VoIP technology appears to be between H.323 and SIP. H.323 is an umbrella of specifications and contains a number of signaling protocols with different purposes and a selection of media protocols. H.323 is a binary protocol,[24] which closely resembles the PSTN business logic. H.323 uses reliable transport (TCP) extensively in the signaling and therefore has a bad reputation for consuming more resources from the network services. H.323 uses the H.225 protocol for the initial signaling. H.225 is similar to, and partially implements, the functionality of Q.931 messages. After the initial signaling, H.245 is used to continue the negotiation of capabilities and media properties. QoS is set up

---

24. Note that binary protocols are often more compact in size as compared to text-based protocols.

using the Resource Reservation Protocol (RSVP). And finally, media is transferred using Real-time Transport Protocol (RTP).

RTSP

Real Time Streaming Protocol (RTSP) is specified by the IETF in RFC 2326. RTSP establishes and controls media streams such as video and audio. RTSP is a text-based protocol that resembles HTTP. RTSP is connectionless, although it can use TCP streams for sending the messages on one or several connections. Media streams use RTP, but other streams are also possible. The media server maintains the RTSP state. RTSP is a two-way protocol, which means that both the client and the server can send messages to each other.

SIP

The Session Initiation Protocol (SIP) today is considered the standard protocol for multimedia signaling, and the result is a very generic protocol. SIP is specified by the IETF in RFC 3261. From a structural perspective, SIP is a text-based protocol very similar to HTTP used in Web services. SIP can transfer different types of payload with different encodings. SIP is a stateful protocol that supports both UDP and TCP as transports. From the network perimeter perspective, the dynamic operation of SIP and most other signaling protocols is very similar to FTP, but without the benefit of "passive mode." This means that SIP negotiates dynamic UDP port pairs in both ends for the RTP media streams. Besides signaling, SIP is also used for instant messaging. Although originally intended as a simple lightweight protocol, the complexity of SIP has really exploded because of the many application areas and use cases. SIP specification is probably the longest specification ever released by the IETF and is extended further in numerous other specifications.

In contrast to many traditional IP protocols, VoIP implementations are required to implement both the server and client functionality. In SIP, any SIP-enabled entity can initiate and terminate a SIP session. This is built by the separation of SIP into two parts: User-Agent-Server (UAS) and User-Agent-Client (UAC). The UAC initiates a session by sending SIP signaling messages to the server-side implementation of UAS. UAC is always listening for incoming SIP connections. This setup is like implementing a Web server in every Web browser and has been a great challenge to security components such as firewalls. A SIP gateway or proxy is basically a back-to-back user agent that processes SIP messages, terminates the call on the other side, and it initiates the same (or similar) session on the other side. Most next-generation architectures, including softswitch architecture and IMS, have adapted SIP as the signaling protocol. SIP uses SDP as a payload for negotiating the media properties.

SDP

The Session Description Protocol (SDP) is defined by the IETF in RFC 2327.[25] The purpose of SDP is to communicate the media capabilities and desired properties between the communicating parties. SDP can be used in connection with many different signaling protocols and media gateway control protocols. The session description in SDP is represented in a text-based list of variables and their parameters.

MGCP and H.248/Megaco

The Media Gateway Control Protocol (MGCP) is defined by the IETF in RFC 2705, whereas H.248 is specified by the ITU-T. MGCP is a text-based protocol running on top of UDP, and H.248 is a binary protocol over TCP. Both fulfill the same purpose—that is, separating the media control signaling from the other signaling responsibilities. MGCP follows the softswitch and IMS architecture by breaking the signaling into the following functionalities: media gateway, media gateway controller, and signaling gateway. MGCP is a protocol that media gateway controller functionality uses to coordinate the operation of media gateways. Although MGCP uses UDP, it still handles the retransmission of lost packets on the application level. Packet loss of MGCP messages is therefore not very efficiently handled, setting high quality and bandwidth requirements for the connections. H.248 is used in IMS.

25. Handley, M. and V. Jacobson, *SDP Session Description Protocol, RFCC 2327, April 1998.*

Media Transport Protocols

The actual media, whether it is voice or video, is transferred using different media streaming protocols. Some media protocols contain features for exchanging media properties and quality metrics, but most of the signaling is left for the various signaling protocols covered earlier.

RTP and RTCP

Almost all VoIP implementations use Real-time Transport Protocol (RTP) for media transport. RTP is an extremely simple protocol specified by IETF in RFC 3550 and RFC 3551. RTP runs on top of UDP and therefore has best-effort delivery but does not guarantee delivery of the packers. Real-time properties of the streams are more important than the reliability of the underlying transport. A packet lost in transit is lost for good because in real-time communications it would be too late to resend it. The actual media codec in the payload of the RTP messages defines the quality and fault tolerance of the stream, and different error-correction algorithms can fix the problems created by packet loss. The bandwidth requirement depends on the compression rate and quality of the codec used. Some applications and multimedia codecs can create extensive RTP streams with large packet sizes, whereas others can send huge numbers of small packets, or everything in between. The encrypted variant of RTP is called SRTP.

The Real-time Transport Control Protocol (RTCP) is used together with RTP, but it is not necessary for RTP streams to work. RTCP messages are sent on the same route as RTP, typically originate from the terminal, and therefore should not be trusted. If correctly used, RTCP proves useful for collecting data on the quality of the connection. The feedback that RTCP provides might not help you locate the problems but still provide useful information on the efficiency and quality of the connection. At least the following metrics are available through RTCP reports: latency, jitter, and packet loss. Media gateways are typically responsible for collecting and responding to the RTCP messages.

2. VoIP ARCHITECTURES AND PROTOCOLS

Other IP Protocols Used in VoIP

Most VoIP protocols are application layer protocols. A fully functional VoIP implementation depends on both the underlying transport protocols and on other protocols responsible for providing necessary supporting services. VoIP depends on many non-VoIP protocols, some of which are summarized here.

IPv4 and IPv6

IPv4 and IPv6 contain numerous IETF-specified protocols, all of which have many extensions by all standardization organizations. The latest additions include Mobile IPv4, Mobile IPv6, and IPSec. UDP is one of the IP protocols and provides unreliable transport; TCP is the sister protocol and ensures reliable transport for message streams.

SCTP

As part of developing Sigtran, the IETF specified the Stream Control Transmission Protocol (SCTP) in RFC 2960. SCTP provides similar services as TCP and runs directly on top of IP. SCTP can sometimes be tunneled over UDP.

TLS

TLS is an authentication and encryption protocol. It is a standard encryption method used to encrypt any TCP connections. It was originally developed by Netscape as SSL2 and SSL3 and was initially used to encrypt HTTP traffic. TLS was finally adapted by IETF with very small modifications compared to SSL3 and became an accepted Internet standard used across many different applications. Both SSL2 and SSL3 are still widely used in Web browsers.

DHCP, DNS, and ENUM

DHCP and DNS are specified by the IETF for dynamic IP address reservation and for IP address name resolution, respectively. ENUM is a DNS extension for Telephone Number Mapping (E.164), providing a naming convention and directory for VoIP. ENUM is being developed by the IETF in, for example, RFC 3761. ENUM should not be confused with the VoIP URI addressing scheme. DHCP/DNS is also used with IMS, but not for discovering the user identities. They are used only for discovering some of the network elements (such as P-CSCF) when a new device joins the network. IMS also uses ENUM to convert a telephone URI (such as "tel:+358-9-123-45678") into SIP URI (such as sip:ari.takanen@codenomi-con.com).

SigComp

Signaling Compression (SigComp) is specified by the IETF in RFC 3320 and RFC 3321. SigComp is used to compress text-based application protocols such as SIP and RTSP, and it can use TCP, UDP, or SCTP as transport. SigComp proves especially useful in mobile networks and is adapted in IMS by 3GPP. SigComp uses a Universal Decompressor Virtual Machine (UDVM) for the decompression and can be configured to support many different compression algorithms.

RSVP

RSVP is a standalone protocol, but it is also used in connection with the Multiprotocol Label Switching Protocol (MPLSP). Note that the Internet does not guarantee that all packets take the same route, and this can be challenging to real time, where the requirements for QoS are higher than for protocols used in non-real-time communications such as email or other messaging. Version 1 of RSVP is covered in RFC 2205. Originally, RSVP was used to indicate resource requirements to the devices on the path, and it was later extended to work more closely with MPLS core networks.

Summary

Our aim in this chapter was to provide an overview of the technologies used in VoIP. This provides a short introduction to help you understand the security-related topics covered in the rest of this book. Many of the architectures and protocols are discussed later in this book, including those used by various security mechanisms such as encryption and authentication. VoIP draws its design, architecture, and protocols both from traditional telephony and from legacy IP communications. Understanding the principles of VoIP architectures, network components, and the protocols used will help in analyzing the networks from a security perspective. This is not by any means a complete list of architectures and protocols. Several variants of these protocols exist, such as SIP SIMPLE for SIP instant messaging. In addition, a number of vendor-proprietary protocols are used in VoIP, such as SCCP or "Skinny" used by Cisco. Some of the protocols are open, but are mostly used by one implementation, such as the IAX used by Asterisk. In any case, when studying your own VoIP architecture, it is helpful to understand the various technologies in use. Comparing and selecting new technologies requires an understanding of the differences between these choices.

## CHAPTER 3

THREATS AND ATTACKS

The security of communication networks can be analyzed from several different perspectives. This and the following chapters take a closer look at VoIP security by analyzing the threats, vulnerabilities, and attacks. This chapter focuses on the threats and attacks specific to VoIP. Some of the presented attacks are studied in more detail in Chapter 4, "VoIP Vulnerabilities," in which we analyze the technical details of vulnerabilities that enable these attacks to succeed.

Definitions of Threats and Attacks

To understand the difference between the terms *threat*, *attack*, and *vulnerability*, we need to establish the proper definitions in the context of VoIP security. Often, people use the terms *threat* and *vulnerability* interchangeably to define the risk associated with a network resource, service, or user interaction. Before we continue discussing threats and vulnerabilities in VoIP networks, we must establish an agreeable definition for threat. Webster's dictionary defines threat as follows.

> *The expression of an intention to inflict evil or injury on another; the declaration of an evil, loss, or pain to come.*

The NSA has defined *threat* as follows:[1]

> *The means through which the ability or intent of a threat agent to adversely affect an automated system, facility, or operation can be manifest. A potential violation of security.*

---

1. *Webster's Revised Unabridged Dictionary (1913)*

The U.S. National Information Assurance Glossary defines threat as follows:[2]

> *Any circumstance or event with the potential to adversely impact an IS through unauthorized access, destruction, disclosure, modification of data, and/or DoS.*

Although several dictionaries and sources define threat, the NSA definition provides an adequate association of the relationship between threat and vulnerability as it pertains to communication networks, among other dimensions. Therefore, we use this definition throughout this book. Note that for a threat to be effective, an associated vulnerability must exist that ultimately can be exploited. If the vulnerability does not exist or it is not possible to be exploited, the threat is categorized as minimal. If that vulnerability can be exploited, given the available resources, the threat level increases accordingly.

There are two common ways to identify threats to a network or an asset (threat object). The first method is to look for the subjects (or agents) of threat—that is, who can threaten your infrastructure assets or operations? The second is to look for the menaces—that is, threat of what, or how can attackers threaten the network? The first approach looks for the attackers, whereas the second approach looks for the business threat events. A combination of these means, both attackers and the menace, and how they can affect infrastructure assets or operations are being analyzed. Example threats are a DoS on the gateway, a disk failure on a server, an earthquake at a server location, and eavesdropping on communications.

An attack is the actual attempt to impact infrastructure assets or operations, and it is carried out by a threat agent. Someone or something is actually physically launching an attack against an asset. The NSA defines attack as follows:

> *An attempt to bypass security controls on a computer. The attack may alter, release, or deny data. Whether an attack will succeed depends on the vulnerability of the computer system and the effectiveness of existing countermeasures. The act of trying to bypass security controls on a system. An attack may be active, resulting in the alteration of data, or passive, resulting in the release of data. Note: The fact that*

---

2. *U.S. National Information Assurance Glossary www.cnss.gov/Assets/pdf/cnssi_4009.pdf*

an attack is made does not necessarily mean that it will succeed. The degree of success depends on the vulnerability of the system or activity and the effectiveness of existing countermeasures.

Both threats and attacks can be categorized as active or passive, depending on whether the realization (the attack) of the threat requires changing the system or network. Eavesdropping and traffic analysis of communications can be passive or active, whereas a denial-of-service (DoS) threat is almost always active. Attacks are also called exploits or exploit scripts by hackers and the media.

RFC 3067 defines a vulnerability as follows:[3]

A flaw or weakness in a system's design, implementation, or operation and management that could be exploited to violate the system's security policy.

To be able to define a condition as a vulnerability, we first need to identify the corresponding service provided by the resource. Any feature in the system can introduce a vulnerability or become a vulnerability. Many times, we have heard the statement "it's not a vulnerability, it's a feature" to comically refer to an obvious condition that may be exploited. In telecommunications and computer networks, a vulnerability is a flaw that allows a threat agent to carry out a successful attack. The vulnerability may exist in the configuration specification, software, architecture, or operations process of the network, enabling attacks to succeed (thus realizing threats against the business system). In almost every instance, the vulnerability can be corrected and thus eliminate the attack against it.

Eliminating a vulnerability involves installing a patch (update, correction, or workaround) or reconfiguring the system so that the attack/exploit is not effective anymore. One method of vulnerability protection without correcting the actual flaw is to add a perimeter defense such as a firewall or intrusion prevention system to mitigate the attack. Eliminating vulnerabilities (and attacks) does not mean that the threat is eliminated because new vulnerabilities and attacks are expected to emerge.

One of the critical requirements in traditional PSTN systems is to maintain high availability, otherwise known as five nines (99.999 percent uptime), which is measured by collecting an extensive amount of data

---

3. *RFC3067. J. Arvidsson, A. Cormack, Y. Demchenko, J. Meijer. 2001. TERENA'S Incident Object Description and Exchange Format Requirements.*

regarding the voice traffic over a period of time. The measurements are performed in a simulated and controlled environment in which there is a set of known variables and typically maintain a uniform distribution.[4] In packet-based networks such as the Internet, there are variations in the types of traffic, protocols, and performance requirements used to support applications and services. Packet-based networks can support both data and real-time multimedia applications such as VoIP or Video over IP. Furthermore, packets may traverse disparate networks that support different performance requirements, and therefore the quality of service (QoS) is questionable. In addition, in open networks, data and message sequences can be nonconformant to any protocol specifications because of traffic corruption or intentional hostile activity to disrupt the services.

Threats in VoIP

In August 2006, S. Niccolini submitted a draft to the IETF outlining a taxonomy for VoIP threats.[5] Earlier, the VOIPSA[6] had created an enormous classification for VoIP threats and attacks, but that was "too complete" for practical VoIP security analysis. Although one can argue that any element including the supporting components or protocols in a VoIP deployment can introduce vulnerabilities, it is difficult to foresee every possible future attack and protect every VoIP deployment. Therefore, focusing the analysis on the VoIP application layer is a logical continuation from the existing foundation of best practices and procedures to secure a network. On the other hand, the threats listed in the IETF "VoIP Security Threats" draft are threats that should be considered in the protocol design. The first version of the IETF draft listed the following threat categories:[7]

- Interception and modification threats
- Interruption-of-service threats
- Abuse-of-service threats
- Social threats

---

4. *For example, only voice needs to be supported in PSTN, whereas in packet-based networks there is voice, video, and data.*

5. *An IETF draft is a document submitted for review. After it has been reviewed thoroughly by the IETF members, it will later receive an RFC status.*

6. *Voice over IP Security Alliance (VOIPSA). www.voipsa.org/*

7. *S. Niccolini. 2006. VoIP Security Threats. http://tools.ietf.org/id/draft-niccolini-speermint-voipthreats-00.txt*

There are many different categorizations and taxonomies, and different classifications have different purposes. The VOIPSA takes a very detailed look at threats, to give as much information as possible, which might be overwhelming for some organizations. Nevertheless, it is an important contribution that helps us understand the associated threats. The IETF threat classification categorizes threats based on how the protocol specifications can be improved to minimize the impact of an attack and therefore does not consider issues associated with the supporting infrastructure, such as operating system platforms and network configuration.

In this book, we build on and extend the threat taxonomies to distinguish certain attacks that overlap and include attacks that are not specific to the protocol design. Threats associated with VoIP are narrowed into the following categories:

- **Service disruption and annoyance**—The attempt to disrupt the VoIP service, including management, provisioning, access, and operations. Attacks in this category can affect any network element that supports the VoIP service, including routers, DNS servers, SIP proxies, session border controllers, and so on. Such attacks can be initiated either remotely, without having direct access to the target network elements and manipulating the VoIP protocols, or locally, by issuing disruptive instructions or commends. An attacker can target an edge device (for example, a VoIP phone), a core network component, or a collection of components such as SIP proxies that may impact a community of users. This category also includes annoyance attacks such as SPIT (spam through Internet telephony).
- **Eavesdropping and traffic analysis**—The attempt to collect sensitive information to prepare for an attack or gain intelligence. In VoIP (or, generally, Internet multimedia applications), this means that the attacker has the ability to monitor unprotected signaling or media streams that are exchanged between users. This category includes traffic analysis and can be passive or active (that is, collect, store, and analyze or real-time decoding/translation of media packets). The attack aims to extract verbal or textual (for example, credit card number or pin) content from a conversation or analyze communications between parties to establish communication patterns, which can later be used to support other attacks.

- **Masquerading and impersonation**—The ability to impersonate a user, device, or service to gain access to a network, service, network element, or information. This is a distinct category because masquerading attacks can be used to commit fraud, unauthorized access to information, and even service disruption. A special case of a masquerading threat is impersonation, where the attacker can pretend or take over someone's identity in the service. In this category, targets include users, devices, and network elements and can be realized by manipulating the signaling or media streams remotely or through unauthorized access to VoIP components (for example, signaling gateways, the SIP registrar, or DNS servers). For example, if a telecommunications provider is using only caller ID information to authenticate subscribers to their voice mailboxes, it is possible for an attacker to spoof caller ID information to gain access to a user's voice mailbox. Masquerading attacks in VoIP networks can also be realized by manipulating the underlying protocols that provide support for VoIP (such as ARP, IP, and DNS).

- **Unauthorized access**—The ability to access a service, functionality, or network element without proper authorization. Attacks in this category can be used to support other attacks—including service disruption, eavesdropping, masquerading, and fraud—because the attacker has control of a device, resource, or access to a network. The difference between masquerading and unauthorized access is that the attacker does not need to impersonate another user or network element, but rather can gain direct access using a vulnerability such as a buffer overflow, default configuration, and poor signaling or network access controls. For example, an attacker that has administrative access on a SIP proxy can disrupt VoIP signaling by erasing the operating system's file system, and thus cripple the host and service. Another example is where an attacker has access to a media gateway and installs malicious software to collect media packets and ultimately perform passive eavesdropping on subscriber communications. Unauthorized access can be correlated with threats such as eavesdropping, masquerading, and fraud.

- **Fraud**—The ability to abuse VoIP services for personal or monetary gain. This category of attacks is one of the most critical for telecommunication carriers and providers, along with service continuity and availability. Fraud can be realized by manipulating the signaling messages or the configuration of VoIP components, including the billing systems. Some fraud scenarios feasible in current VoIP implementations can be performed by manipulating the signaling flows of a call. It is expected that more sophisticated fraud techniques will surface as VoIP becomes mainstream.

These categories provide a succinct structure in which current and new attacks can be categorized. For example, an attack against the authentication mechanism used by a signaling protocol can be categorized under unauthorized access if the attack allows access to information but does not have financial impact on the organization, or it can be categorized as fraud if it has a financial impact (or overlap in both if necessary).

Service Disruption

Disruption of service can target different planes of a VoIP implementation, including the management, control, or user plane. Several areas in VoIP can be targeted during a DoS attack. Figure 3.1 depicts the areas in a VoIP infrastructure that can be targeted during a DoS attack.

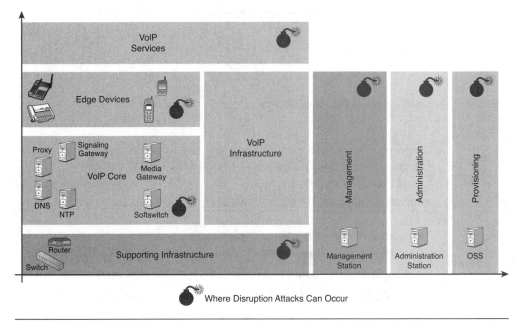

FIGURE 3.1 Disruption attack areas.

DoS attacks can be performed against any of the components that support the VoIP infrastructure and associated services. The attacks can target components in the supporting infrastructure; core VoIP components (including edge devices, signaling, and media gateways); and components used for management, administration, and provisioning of VoIP services.

Figure 3.2 depicts a logical representation of the layers that can be targeted by an attacker during a disruption attack and the affected areas.

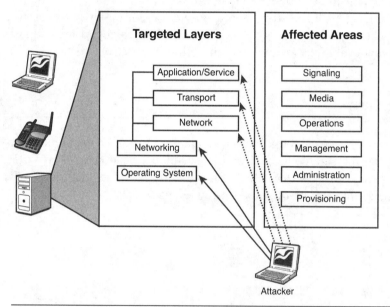

FIGURE 3.2 Targeted layers during a disruption attack.

DoS attacks can be directed toward any network element to disrupt the system's functionality or the networking capabilities of the corresponding component. The components that can be targeted during a service disruption attack include the following:

- Network components:
  Edge/user devices

  Core network elements (such as a signaling gateway)

  Underlying supporting infrastructure (for example, routers)

- Service or application components
  Signaling
  Media
- Operations systems
  Management
  Billing
  Fraud
  Security
  Provisioning

Obviously, "defense in depth" is a fundamental requirement in VoIP because VoIP protocols must maintain a client/server model on the core network elements and on the edge devices (for example, user phone) and thus extend the applicability of DoS attacks. VoIP differs from other applications such as email and Web browsing because these do not need to support presence for real-time communications.

Attacks Related to Telephony Services

Telecommunications is part of the Critical National Infrastructure (CNI). Therefore, various national and international laws require the confidentiality, integrity, and availability of some of the telephony services. The service-disruption category will definitely be under constant change as new services are introduced to VoIP. In VoIP networks, the operation of any service can be disrupted, denied, or altered in such as way that the original service is not any more confidential, trusted, or available. Examples of services include voicemail, caller ID, international calling, telephone number, call waiting, call transfer, location, confidentiality of signaling or media streams, lawful intercept, and emergency services.

Example threats against VoIP services and features include the following:

- **Voicemail**—An example threat is unauthenticated people potentially accessing your confidential voicemail messages. This is a common flaw in all telephony if people do not set a good password on their voicemail. A typical attack is to guess the voice mailbox password using common passwords such as 0000, 1234, 2580, or the telephone extension number. If attackers can access a subscriber's voicemail, they can perform a number of attacks, including deleting messages, changing greetings, or enabling call forwarding to another phone number.[8]

- **Caller ID**—An example threat is someone impersonating a subscriber by spoofing her caller ID. Services such as automated answering systems for banks, insurance companies, or telecommunication providers are implemented to authenticate subscribers using caller ID information. Caller ID spoofing can be performed by manipulating the signaling messages as discussed later in this book, but also provided as a service from companies such as SpoofCard, cidspoof, and others. For example, an attacker may spoof caller ID information to activate a new credit card as part of a credit card fraud scheme because some credit card companies use caller ID to verify the card owner.

- **Follow-me service**—The ability to associate several phone numbers with one distinct number is a desirable feature for many. At the same time, if an attacker can exploit a vulnerability in the subscriber's profile management interface to associate a rogue telephone number, the attacker can hijack the subscriber's calls. This threat emphasizes the need to maintain proper security, not only at the network and service levels, but also at the application level.

- **Call forwarding**—The ability to forward incoming calls to another telephone number is another feature that can be targeted for abuse. If an attacker gains access to the subscriber's profile or VoIP component that provides call routing services (for example, SIP proxy), the attacker can alter the configuration to route calls to another number. Another scenario is where an employee abuses the feature by forwarding calls to an international location or pay-per-call services (for example, 900 numbers) through the company's telephone system. Instead of calling the international number directly, the user can configure his office phone to forward a call to that international telephone number, with the toll charges going to the company.

---

8. *For more details about PBX voice mailbox hacking, see Kingpin's (Joseph B. Grand) article. Kingpin (Grand J): Compromising Voice Messaging Systems, Published on @stake Web site, April 2000. www.grandideastudio.com/files/security/general/compromising_voice_messaging.pdf*

Organizations should restrict such activity by limiting international calling and outbound calls to pay-per-call services.

- **Location and presence services**—Location and presence service are used in VoIP to provide better quality of experience to the user. At the same time, privacy laws require the protection of user data associated with these services. An attacker who compromises a server that provides location and presence information can expose the subscribers to many attacks, including traffic analysis and access to personal information.

- **Confidentiality**—Confidentiality of subscriber communications is an expectation rather than a feature, although some might argue otherwise. Although many users claim that their daily casual conversations over the phone do not carry important information, sensitive information may be exchanged over VoIP—such as checking an account balance, applying for a loan, talking to an attorney, or discussing a business strategy. Attacks against confidentiality include DoS against the end points and bid-down attempts to weaken the strength of encryption or eliminate it all together.

- **Lawful intercept**—Telecommunication carriers and providers are mandated to support CALEA[9] (Communications Assistance for Law Enforcement Act) in the United States (and in other countries under similar laws) with regard to intercepting communications. The associated threat is that someone may gain unauthorized access to this feature to eavesdrop on communications for personal or monetary gain or espionage. A good example is the case in which this feature was used to spy on the Greek prime minister's phone, his cabinet members' phones, and 100 other telephone numbers, including some from the U.S. embassy in Athens.[10] Although the Greek authorities did not disclose the details of the investigation, the agency of Assurance of Information and Communication Privacy (ADAE) which investigated the matter released a list of the people that were targeted[11].

---

9. FCC. *Communications Assistance for Law Enforcement Act (CALEA)*. *www.fcc.gov/calea/*

10. *Spy software used in mobile eavesdropping*. *www.ekathimerini.com/4dcgi/_w_articles_politics_100014_03/02/2006_65958*

11. *John Brady Kiesling, former U.S. Foreign Service Officer. Vodafone Eavesdropping Scandal. www.bradykiesling.com/vodafone_scandal.htm*

- **Emergency services**—Support for emergency services through VoIP is also a regulatory requirement for VoIP providers. Attacks against network elements that support VoIP can impact prompt response and threaten human lives. Therefore, proper protection mechanisms need to be considered and implemented to detect and prevent against attacks that might impact emergency services. Negative impacts, for example, might inhibit the proper routing from VoIP service providers servicing residential subscribers to enterprise networks (for example, voice gateway) and PSAPs (Public Safety Answering Points) that use VoIP technologies.

Denial of Service

The primary effect of DoS attacks is rendering the attacked service or system useless. Organizations may simulate DoS attacks to measure the reliability of their system or service and to evaluate their intrusion detection and incident response capabilities. The primary categories of DoS attacks are load based and malicious packet based. Load-based attacks saturate a network, system, or service with thousands of packets to degrade network bandwidth and ultimately service quality. In VoIP (and, generally, Internet multimedia applications), a load-based attack consists of establishing thousands of sessions in parallel or rapid succession to degrade or disrupt the targeted service (for example, voice or video). Malicious packet-based attacks consist of generating a single malformed message that will force the receiving service to disrupt or terminate processing or even cause the target host to reboot.

The VoIP network elements that can be targeted during an Internet-based DoS attack are, for example, a VoIP user agent, a VoIP proxy, a router that supports VoIP, or a SBC. The attack can also be targeted to a specific edge device such as a cable modem, a set-top box (STB), or a telephony adaptor that supports multimedia services such as voice and video. In addition, DNS servers can be targeted to disrupt VoIP communications in cases where ENUM is used.[12] ENUM has been defined by the IETF as the standard to provide address-to-name resolution of telephone numbers. An attack against a DNS server that is part of a VoIP implementation that uses ENUM can be devastating.

---

12. Faltstrom, P. and M. Mealling, "The E.164 to Uniform Resource Identifiers (URI) Dynamic Delegation Discovery System (DDDS) Application (ENUM)," RFC 3761, April 2004.

Although the following list provides a good start to identify components that can be affected by DoS attacks, along with the associated impact, it is not an exhaustive list. It is expected that as new threats and vulnerabilities emerge, the list will expand. Any protocol interface can be attacked with a DoS attack. Examples from VoIP-enabled devices include the following:

- **Content/protocol layer**—SDP, encoded voice, encoded video
- **Application**—H.323, SIP, RTP, RTCP, Radius, Diameter, HTTP, SNMP
- **Application-level encryption**—TLS/SSL
- **Transport**—TCP, SCTP, UDP
- **Network-level encryption**—IPSec
- **Network**—IPv4, IPv6
- **Link**—PPP, AAL3/4, AAL5
- **Physical**—SONET, V.34, ATM, Ethernet

Table 3.1 outlines in more detail some of the layers that can be targeted by attacks that aim to disrupt the service/operation provided by the respective component that supports the VoIP service.

Table 3-1 Target Layers

Layer	Attack	Target Component(s)	Area of Impact
Network	ICMP Attacks include flooding, reflection, amplification, and service corruption (for example, by sending a malicious packet).	Underlying network routing components such as routers and switches Edge devices (for example, VoIP phones) Core VoIP components (for example, signaling and media servers) Supporting infrastructure components (for example, NFS, NTP, DNS, HTTP)	Network routing Management Administration Signaling Media

(continues)

Table 3-1 Target Layers *(continued)*

Layer	Attack	Target Component(s)	Area of Impact
	ARP Attacks include flooding, cache poisoning, and service corruption (for example, by sending a malicious packet).	Edge devices (for example, VoIP phones) Core VoIP components (for example, signaling and media servers) Supporting infrastructure components (for example, NFS, NTP, DNS, HTTP)	Network routing Management Administration Signaling Media
	IP flooding	Underlying network routing components such as routers and switches Core VoIP components (for example, signaling and media servers) Supporting infrastructure components (for example, NFS, NTP, DNS, HTTP)	Network routing Management Administration Signaling Media
	BGP Attacks include SYN flood, prefix flood, and route injection.	Routers	Network routing, especially between peering networks
	TCP Attacks include flooding, reflection, and service corruption (for example, by sending a malicious packet).	Underlying network routing components such as routers and switches Edge devices (for example, VoIP phones) Core VoIP components (for example, signaling and media servers) Supporting infrastructure components (for example, NFS, NTP, DNS, HTTP)	Management interfaces Administrative interfaces Signaling ports

Layer	Attack	Target Component(s)	Area of Impact
	UDP Attacks include flooding, reflection, and service corruption (for example, by sending a malicious packet).	Underlying network routing components such as routers and switches Edge devices (for example, VoIP phones) Core VoIP components (for example, signaling and media servers) Supporting infrastructure components (for example, NFS, NTP, DNS, HTTP)	Management interfaces Administrative interfaces Signaling ports Media ports
Application/ service	SIP/H.323/MGCP Attacks include message injection, flooding, and service corruption (for example, by sending a malicious packet).	Edge devices SIP proxies/registrars H.323 gatekeepers Signaling gateways SBCs Voicemail system	Caller ID Call waiting Call forwarding Follow-me Voice applications Video applications Conferencing applications Online gaming applications
	RTP Attacks include message injection, flooding, and service corruption (for example, by sending a malicious packet).	Edge devices Media gateways Voicemail system SBCs	Voice applications Video applications Conferencing applications Online gaming applications
	RTCP Attacks include message parameter tampering to invalidate performance reporting, flooding, and service corruption (for example, by sending a malicious packet).	Edge devices VoIP core components (for example, SIP proxies, signaling gateways, and media gateways)	Voice applications Video applications Conferencing applications Online gaming applications

(continues)

Table 3-1 Target Layers *(continued)*

Layer	Attack	Target Component(s)	Area of Impact
	DNS Attacks include flooding, cache poisoning, and service corruption (for example, by sending a malicious packet).	DNS server	Address/name resolution. Attacks against DNS servers can impact the discovery of VoIP components such as phones and domain SIP proxies.
	NTP Attacks include flooding and service corruption (for example, by sending a malicious packet).	NTP server	Skew system time, which can impact proper logging of system and network events and generation of billing records.
	STUN Attacks include flooding, reflection, and service corruption (for example, by sending a malicious packet).	Edge device STUN server	DoS attacks against a STUN server or an edge device will disable the ability of an edge device to properly perform network address discovery.
	HTTP Attacks include flooding and service corruption (for example, by sending a malicious packet).	Edge devices VoIP core components (for example, SIP proxies, signaling gateways, and media gateways) Any associated components that use HTTP for management and administration or support a service through HTTP	Management interface Device configuration User profile configuration

Layer	Attack	Target Component(s)	Area of Impact
	TFTP/FTP Attacks include flooding, file force overwrite, and service corruption (for example, by sending a malicious packet).	Edge devices VoIP core components (for example, SIP proxies, signaling gateways, and media gateways)	Retrieval of component configuration files. This includes components such as edge devices and core VoIP components such as the signaling gateway.
	DHCP Attacks include IP address exhaustion, flooding, and service corruption (for example, by sending a malicious packet).	Edge devices such as VoIP phones	This attack prevents devices from completing their configuration and ultimately their operation in the VoIP network.
	POP/SMTP Attacks include flooding and service corruption (for example, by sending a malicious packet).	Mail server Voicemail server Unified messaging server	Can impact applications such as unified messaging and voicemail.
	SSH Attacks include flooding and service corruption (for example, by sending a malicious packet).	All associated network elements, including, but not limited to, routers, switches, DNS, NTP signaling and media gateways, and sometimes even the VoIP phones.	SSH is used for remote administration of network elements. An attacker can launch a DoS attack against the SSH service and thus prevent administrators or support personnel from performing any administrative tasks.

When preparing for a DoS attack, attackers typically first analyze the target system. This will involve scanning the potential services that are open for attack. After the open services are listed, the attacker verifies that he can connect to the service by sending a valid message sequence to the target system. These valid message sequences can be used to analyze the available feature sets that could potentially be used for the DoS attack. If SIP communications is open, for example, the attacker will send a valid SIP sequence that will negotiate the call parameters to the service. Potential targets can then be selected from the various layers of the SIP negotiation:

- Attacks against the lowest layers of the communication can use IPv4, UDP, or TCP connections for the attack.
- The security protocols such as TLS or IPSec can be used for the attack.
- SIP sessions can be used for the attack.
- By negotiating the media parameters in SIP signaling, the attacker can open connections through the perimeter defenses and use the RTP streams for the attack, potentially with series of streams with the same identifiers launched against a single target device.

The target of DoS attacks can be anything in the message path, including the perimeter defenses, the SIP proxy, or the user agent (UA). The attack can be launched as a malformed message DoS or as a flooding-related DoS. In a malformed message DoS, a single packer can crash the target device, whereas in flooding attacks, the attacker launches a number of message streams against the target. The attack can originate from a single host or a number of hosts in parallel. The attack can also be launched from the PSTN network or can be targeted toward a PSTN network behind a VoIP proxy. The target of the attack can also be a single host, or the attack can target several targets simultaneously. The result can be a crash, or the DoS can also result from filling up resources (such as the available storage in a voicemail system). When the attack is targeting an intermediary device, the attacker does not necessarily need to know any real end devices behind the network infrastructure.

The victim of the attack can also be a third party because the source address of the originating messages can be faked to use the victim's Internet address. In reflection attacks or in amplification attacks, the destination of the messages responds to the attack messages but sends those messages to the final target of the attack. In flooding attacks, metrics such as data sizes and number of messages are valuable information to the attacker. For a successful amplification attack, the destination system should respond with larger packets than are sent by the attacker, thus amplifying the message stream needed to initiate the flood.

Malformed Packet Denial of Service

The DoS attack can also consist of individual malformed packets. The process of generating malformed packets randomly or semi-randomly is called *fuzzing*. In 2002, PROTOS researchers from the University of Oulu released a freely available test suite for SIP protocol that uses a small set of efficient tests instead of randomly generating millions of malicious packets. Figure 3.3 shows an example of how software from 2006 still fails when tested with these PROTOS tests.

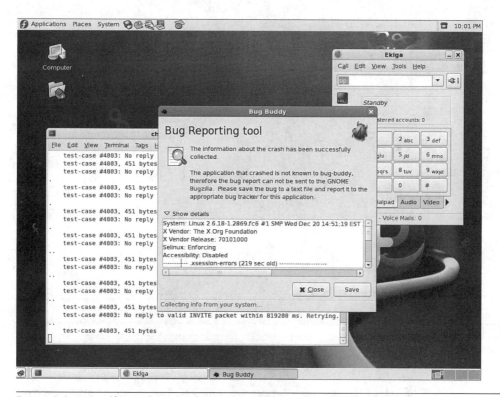

FIGURE 3.3 A malformed packet from PROTOS test suite crashes Ekiga SIP client.

SIP Flooding Attack

One of the well-known DoS attacks in VoIP is resource consumption through message flooding. The attacker generates thousands of messages to render the target network, device, or service inoperable. Figure 3.4 demonstrates a SIP flooding attack in which 10,000 INVITE messages are sent to a user's phone.

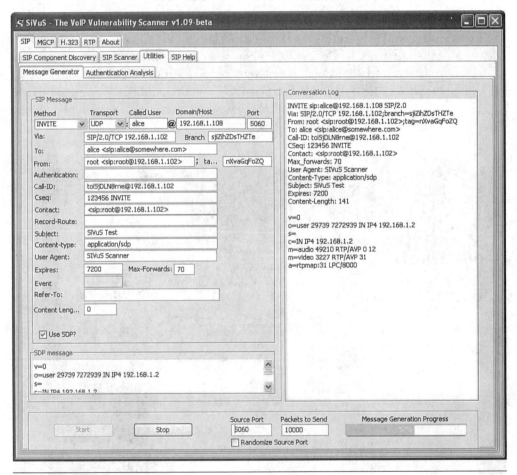

FIGURE 3.4 SIP flooding attack.

The attack causes the remote phone to ring continuously and thus prevent the user from making any phone calls. In addition, the SIP proxy has allocated resources to support all the INVITE requests it has received and has to forward to the destination. A similar technique can be used to carry out a SPIT attack. The performance of a system is an important factor for flooding attacks. To prepare for flooding attacks, test the VoIP system with performance testers or load generators.

A special case for flooding-based DoS is the distributed DoS (DDoS) attack. VoIP networks can be both the originator and the target of DDoS attacks. In DDoS attacks, a large number of hosts are compromised and controlled by an attacker to launch a targeted attack against a service. Typically, these attack programs are integrated with viruses and worms to infect unsuspicious victims to join the attack. A network of compromised hosts is often called a *botnet,* because the network consists of autonomous software robots, or bots. An example attack in VoIP could include all VoIP phones trying to call the same target at the same time.[13]

SIP Signaling Loop Attack

In the near future, we expect to see new DoS attacks that will target the signaling messages across a VoIP infrastructure to degrade or disrupt service. An example of an attack that can have a devastating impact in a VoIP network is the Max-Forwards problem that was discovered during a SIP interoperability event.[14] The attack requires the establishment of a pair of accounts on two distinct SIP proxies/registrars that do not perform loop detection. Figure 3.5 depicts the two steps of the attack.

In Step 1, the user registers in both domains, one.com and two.com, using the two user accounts, user1 and user2. Note that in each registration, the Contact header has two values, one pointing to one account and the other to the other account in the same domain. These are legitimate registration requests that are processed successfully by the corresponding SIP registrars/proxies. In Step 2, an INVITE request is received by one of the registrars/proxies (in this case, one.com), which in turn forks two INVITE request to domain two.com for users user1 and user2. When these INVITES are received by the SIP proxy/registrar in domain two.com, four requests are forked to the proxy/registrar in domain one.com. When these requests are received by domain one.com, eight requests are forked and so on until the Max-Forwards header is set to zero.

13. For more information about DDoS, see: J. Mirkovic and P. Reiher, A Taxonomy of DDoS Attacks and Defense Mechanisms, ACM SIGCOMM Computer Communications Review, Volume 34, Number 2, April 2004, pp. 39–54.

14. S. Lawrence, et al., Problems with Max-Forwards Processing (and Potential Solutions) IETF Draft. http://tools.ietf.org/html/draft-lawrence-maxforward-problems-00

RFC 3261 defines the default value of Max-Forwards to be 70, which means that there would be 2^{70} outstanding requests in the network! In addition, there will be another set of failure messages generated by the proxies (for example, 408, CANCEL). This attack can cripple a VoIP network's service within minutes. A number of solutions can be implemented to mitigate this attack. One approach is to disable forking or limit the number of the Max-Forwards value, which may be applicable to small, confined SIP networks but not to carrier networks where peering is also required. Another approach is to enable loop detection, which may impose some performance impact on the proxies.

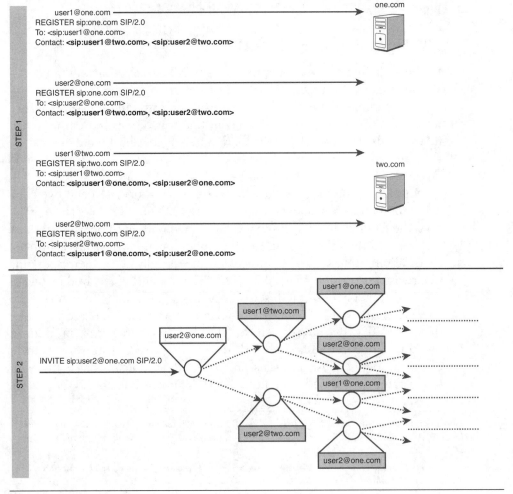

FIGURE 3.5 SIP loop-detection DoS attack.

Annoyance (That Is, SPIT)

An annoyance threat is a summary of different means by which people annoy each other by making calls that one cannot prevent receipt of. Blacklisting callers or muting the phone works in most cases where there are only a few callers who need to be blocked, or if everyone needs to be blocked for the duration of a meeting, for example.

Spam in the form of unsolicited calls exists in the PSTN. These are primarily based on telemarketers. However, these are limited because spamming over PSTN is expensive, particularly with respect to the bandwidth cost. Spam for/over Internet telephony (SPIT) is the transmission of unsolicited calls in VoIP networks and is a special case of a well-known problem in email services. When a service is free or low cost and you can remain anonymous, people are tempted to send commercial or political messages over that form of communications. A simple attack is to create a script that initiates calls to a wide number range or IP address range and sends a recorded speech. Spam (for email) has simple solutions because the entire message can be statically analyzed and compared against typical patterns and blacklists without significant delay in the message transfer. A spam message that matches the filters will not be forwarded. SPIT has a special problem with regard to prevention mechanisms because the content is not known when the call is "ringing." Blacklisting (restricting known spam originators) and whitelisting (allowing only good users and domains through) are potential solutions for VoIP. Some researchers have also proposed multilevel grayscaling techniques to detect SPIT.[15] Another solution is to modify answering machines so that a machine actually answers the call and decides whether to forward the call based on a simple question to restrict machines from calling. And example question could be "Please say what is the opposite of black?"

Calls set to high priority (calls that you want to receive even when you are in a meeting) are one category of an annoyance attack. If anyone can set the call as urgent, or the equivalent of the highest priority, you would lose control of who can call you when you want to remain unavailable. A possible attack is to change the call priority to high at the protocol level to create an urgent call that can bypass call filters.

One category of annoyance attack in VoIP security is related to poor handling of broadcast and multicast messages. These are known since the

15. D. Shin and C. Shim, "Voice SPAM Control with Gray Leveling," Proceeding of 2nd VoIP Security Workshop, Washington DC, June 1–2, 2005.

3. THREATS AND ATTACKS

first SIPIT (Session Initiation Protocol Interoperability Testing) events. One attack method is broadcasting the signaling (INVITE) messages. This will make everyone's phone in the same broadcast area ring simultaneously; and if the source (caller) number is faked, the result is that everyone will basically attack the originating source address with his or her responses. Besides SIP INVITE messages, many other VoIP protocol messages can be used in similar fashion.

Another similar broadcast-based annoyance attack in the media plane is sending corrupt invalid media (RTP) messages to a broadcast address, inserting them into the media streams of ongoing calls, creating noise or DoS to the legitimate calls. Sometimes sequence numbers, different codecs, and wrong source addresses/ports protect against this attack, but unfortunately, most implementations ignore these or use easily guessable values.

Unauthorized Access

Unauthorized access has been one of the traditional attacks associated with physical and logical security. Three common methods of gaining unauthorized access are as follows:

- Impersonation
- Man-in-the-middle attacks
- Total compromise

Impersonation attacks involve stealing or guessing the authorization keys, such as the username-password combination, and using that to impersonate the user.

In man-in-the-middle attacks, the real user does the authentication, but the attacker sees the message exchange and can even take over the active session after authentication.

In total compromise, the attacker has full control of the system and can execute any services, commands, and processes on behalf of the user. An example of total compromise is a worm attack in which the worm runs on the victim's computer, impersonating him when making new communication sessions.

In the context of VoIP communications, unauthorized access can occur in the following areas:

- VoIP service. An attacker may use vulnerabilities in service signaling to gain unauthorized access to the VoIP network.
- VoIP infrastructure. An attacker can exploit vulnerabilities to gain access to VoIP network elements.
- VoIP network elements such as signaling and media gateways, soft switches, proxies, registrars, SBCs, DNS, NTP servers, and others.
- VoIP end devices.
- Supporting infrastructure.
- Transport network elements such as routers and switches.
- Management and administration systems. An attacker can access management or administrative interfaces and perform tasks by bypassing access controls or taking advantage of the lack of controls.
- Provisioning/operation support systems.

Figure 3.6 provides a logical representation of the components and areas that can be impacted by unauthorized access. Note that this is not an exhaustive list of the components used in all the areas but rather a representative sample.

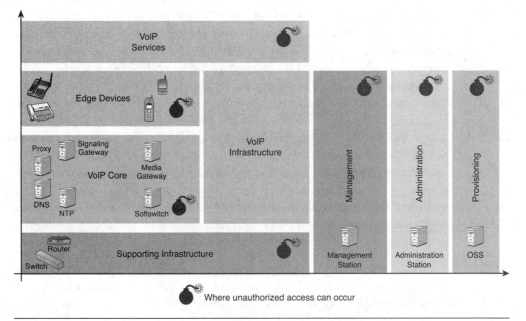

FIGURE 3.6 Areas where unauthorized access may occur in VoIP networks.

A malicious user can exploit a vulnerability (or a combination of vulnerabilities) to gain unauthorized access to services, data, or controls (privileged or unprivileged) of a system or network and carry out various attacks. Poor security controls increase the likelihood and impact of this threat.

The number of components and protocols required to provide support for VoIP create a complex environment in which several opportunities arise for gaining unauthorized access. Attempts for unauthorized access can occur against any of the software components that manage, administer, or support the VoIP infrastructure and include the exploitation of the following:

- Default configuration settings (for example, fail to remove unnecessary user accounts, manuals, libraries, compilers)
- Default account passwords
- Unrestricted access to management interfaces
- Unrestricted access to services (for example, TFTP, FTP, Telnet, RPC)
- Lack of adequate authorization controls (for example, file and directory permissions, program execution)

Although unauthorized access is typically associated with operating system resources, it can also be exercised at the application layer (signaling and media). An attacker may attempt to gain access to a VoIP network by exploiting weak signaling message controls. For example, an attacker may attempt to place a call through a VoIP network by exploiting the weak authentication used for signaling messages. In a VoIP fraud case in 2006, the perpetrators were able to generate more than $1 million by routing VoIP traffic through various service providers by gaining unauthorized access to the VoIP infrastructure and modifying the routing tables to accept fraudulent traffic.[16]

The ability to gain unauthorized access to network elements or network services and applications can be used to leverage other attacks, including service disruption, annoyance, eavesdropping, and fraud. To prevent unauthorized access, the following controls should be considered when designing and deploying VoIP networks.

---

16. *Miami Man Arrested in Network Hacker Fraud that Victimized New Jersey Voice-Over-Internet Provider.* U.S. Department of Justice. http://newark.fbi.gov/dojpressrel/2006/nk060706.htm

- **Application controls**

  User and device service registration

  Signaling message authentication and integrity

  Media message authentication and integrity

  Enforce logging and auditing of components that generate, process, modify, and terminate VoIP calls

- **Network controls**

  Enforce device network admission controls, including MAC address verification and 802.1x port authentication

  Segment the network. Implement VLANs to isolate VoIP components

  Enforce VLAN ACLs. Enforce ACLs to prevent authorized traffic traversing VoIP VLANs

  Implement stateful inspection for signaling and media streams using VoIP firewalls or SBCs

- **Management**

  Enforce proper network access controls on management interfaces to restrict connectivity from remote authorized origins

  Enforce proper authorization and role-based access controls on management functions

  Enforce logging and auditing of user accounts and processes that perform management or administrative functions on VoIP network elements

- **Billing**

  Enforce controls to maintain integrity of billing records

  Enforce controls to maintain confidentiality of billing records

  Enforce authentication and authorization controls to prevent unauthorized access to billing records

  Enforce logging and auditing of user accounts and processes that modify CDRs (customer detail records)

- **Provisioning**

  Enforce proper network access controls to restrict remote connectivity to the provisioning systems from unauthorized sources

Enforce authentication and authorization controls to prevent unauthorized access to provisioning system functionality from unauthorized parties

Enforce logging and auditing of user accounts and processes that initiate, modify, or delete service orders

This introductory list of controls provides the basis for strengthening the security posture of a VoIP network in the critical areas in which unauthorized access can occur. Later chapters discuss in further detail network security controls for VoIP networks, along with protection mechanisms that can be deployed to prevent unauthorized access to network elements, services, applications, and associated data.

It is important to understand that unauthorized access can occur at the application layer (VoIP service) by manipulating or spoofing signaling and media messages, at the transport and network layers, by manipulating packets or at the operating system level, by exploiting a software vulnerability or default configuration. The following sections provide examples of such attacks. These examples help emphasize the need for defense in depth when designing and deploying VoIP.

SIP Authentication Dictionary Attack

One of the methods to gain unauthorized access to a VoIP service is by guessing subscriber credentials through a brute-force password attack. In VoIP implementations that use SIP, the REGISTER request can be used to guess passwords.

An example of a brute-force attack in SIP is shown in Figure 3.7. The attack sends multiple REGISTER requests using a combination of user IDs and passwords from a dictionary file. In this example, the SIVuS tool is used, but the concept can be implemented using other tools, too. When the attacker identifies the password of an account, she can register as the corresponding user and hijack the user's registration (see Figure 3.8).

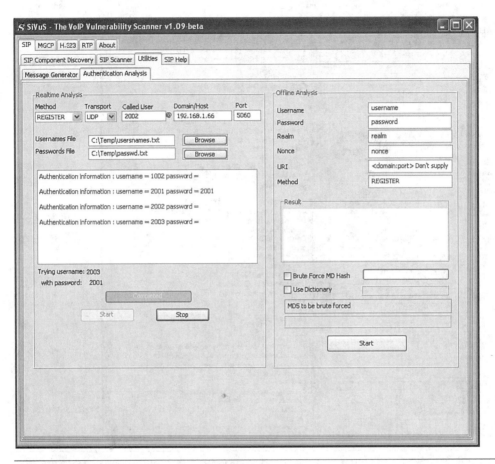

FIGURE 3.7 SIP authentication dictionary attack.

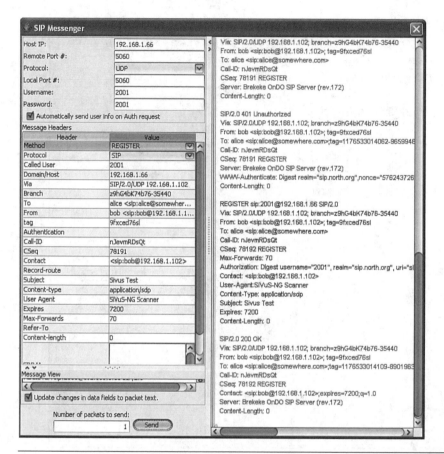

FIGURE 3.8 SIVuS-NG 2.0 SIP messenger used to register with a brute-forced username.

Note that traditional security best practices recommend enabling account lockout or timeout to prevent authentication by brute-force attacks. This might not be feasible in VoIP because subscribers will not be able to make phone calls. And because the phone tends to be a natural extension of our personal ecosystem of appliances, it is challenging to identify the most appropriate solution to prevent this attack. One approach may be to slow down the authentication process between the user and the SIP registrar. For example, if the first login request fails, the SIP registrar should wait for two minutes before it responds to a consecutive request. If the second request fails, it should wait for four minutes. On additional failures, the SIP registrar should wait 16 minutes and so on.

Exploiting a Software Vulnerability

Another way to gain unauthorized access to a VoIP network is by exploiting software vulnerabilities that may exist on a network element such as a call manager. For example, an attacker may exploit a buffer overflow vulnerability and gain administrative access. Figure 3.9 shows an example in which a Cisco call manager was compromised through a buffer overflow that existed on another service that was running on the same component.

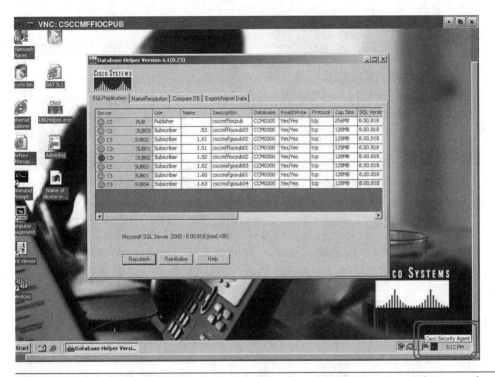

FIGURE 3.9 Exploiting a software vulnerability in other services running on the target host. (Courtesy of Cisco Systems, Inc. Unauthorized use not permitted.)

This example underlines the importance of defense in depth and enforcing good security practices on the operating system and associated services such as eliminating unnecessary services, keeping up-to-date software patches, and changing default configuration settings.

Eavesdropping

Privacy and confidentiality are key aspects of security, and in some environments are the primary security objectives when implementing VoIP networks. Privacy in some network implementations may be dictated by legislation; telecommunications have traditionally had strict requirements for privacy. Encryption is one of the fundamental components in providing confidentiality and privacy in multimedia communications, including VoIP, along with key negotiation.

For our purposes, we consider eavesdropping to include the following:

- Traffic analysis (link, network, and transport layers)
- Signaling eavesdropping
- Media eavesdropping

Traffic analysis (on link, network, and transport layers) is always possible even when there is no encryption.[17] Traffic analysis of VoIP communications can reveal information about the user's call patterns, behavior, and habits, which helps in profiling a target.

In addition, if a master key is used for encryption, this master key can be used by the traffic analyzer to open the stored recording and see the contents of the encrypted communication. Looking at a VoIP packet with a network analyzer, we can see the entire layered protocol stack with all the technical data related to the communication. Any confidential data is available to anyone on the data path.

Eavesdropping on communications can be performed in several ways. An attacker may take advantage of vulnerabilities that exist in protocols or software implementations of VoIP components, to intercept communications between parties. Based on historical evidence from attacks on IP-based networks, it is possible to intercept communications (signaling and media) between users who reside in the PSTN and IP-based networks, respectively. In such scenarios, an attacker with access to an IP network (that is, corporate network) has the ability to monitor and capture signaling and media messages between two unsuspecting parties. Such an attack is easier to perform in IP-based networks because of the ease of access. Some may argue that switch-based IP networks prevent eavesdropping on

---

17. The encrypted traffic can also be analyzed, but data available to the eavesdropper is significantly less critical.

18. In the past, when many networks were built with hubs, all traffic was visible to all ports in the network hub.

the IP layer by not broadcasting all frames to everyone in a network segment[18]. This is true if an attack such as ARP poisoning is not successful or a network element has not been compromised by an attacker who may have installed a network sniffer. As discussed later in this book, various methods can be used to perform eavesdropping.

Eavesdropping Using Ethereal/Wireshark

Wireshark (earlier versions are known as Ethereal) is a well-known free network traffic analyzer and has many powerful features, including analysis of packet streams for SIP, H.323, and RTP. When network traffic is captured, the program provides the ability to filter and select VoIP calls.

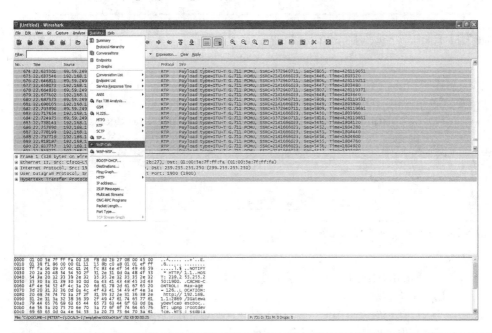

FIGURE 3.10 Capturing network traffic using the Wireshark network sniffer.

The Statistics drop-down menu provides the VoIP calls selection to filter traffic associated with VoIP. When selected, the software analyzes the captured traffic and displays the available VoIP calls.

3. THREATS AND ATTACKS

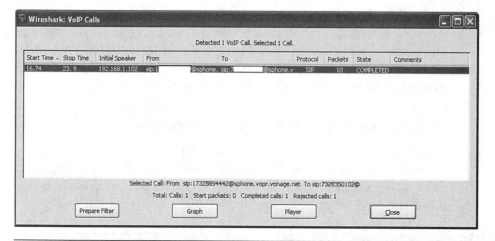

FIGURE 3.11 Filtering network traffic for VoIP calls.

When the streams are assembled, the user can select which one to decode by highlighting it in the list. When selected, the user can press the Player button to proceed with packet re-assembly and decoding.

FIGURE 3.12 Selecting an RTP stream for decoding.

Finally, the user can play the audio of the RTP streams, as shown on Figure 3.13.

The user can select to play the streams individually or combined (for example, half duplex or full duplex).

Eavesdropping Using Cain & Abel

Another tool that you can use to capture VoIP traffic is Cain & Abel.[19] The tool uses ARP poisoning to launch a man-in-the-middle attack and relay SIP and RTP traffic to the unsuspecting end points (see Figure 3.14).

---

19. *Cain & Abel. www.oxid.it/cain.html*

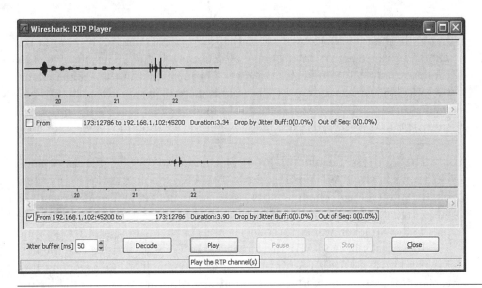

FIGURE 3.13 Playing the audio of an RTP stream.

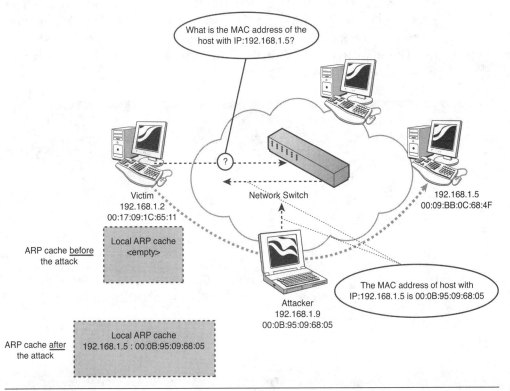

FIGURE 3.14 ARP poisoning attack.

ARP poisoning, also known as ARP spoofing, is used to divert network traffic through an attacker's host so that the attacker can act as man in the middle or cause a DoS by dropping all Ethernet frames. This attack can be exercised only between hosts on a LAN. During a man-in-the-middle attack, the attacker can eavesdrop on communications between two or more end points (hosts) and harvest sensitive information such as account credentials (user IDs and passwords) and media streams (for example, voice and video traffic).

The Address Resolution Protocol is used to resolve the association between a host's MAC and IP address. The ARP spoofing attack is operating on the principle of changing the association between the MAC and IP address that has been cached by a host's ARP table (ARP cache). For example, if the attacker wants to collect traffic between host 192.168.1.2 and 192.168.1.5, it will send ARP broadcasts to the LAN advertising that the new MAC address for 192.168.1.5 is 00:0B:95:09:68:05. The unsuspecting host caches this association and uses it to forward Ethernet frames in the future. Similar spoofed packets will be generated on behalf of the attacked victim (192.168.1.2) to force traffic destined for the victim to be routed through the attacker's host (192.168.1.9). So, the attacker will spoof ARP packets for both hosts to poison their cache tables and collect traffic from both directions.

The steps to perform VoIP call eavesdropping using Cain & Abel are depicted in the following figures.

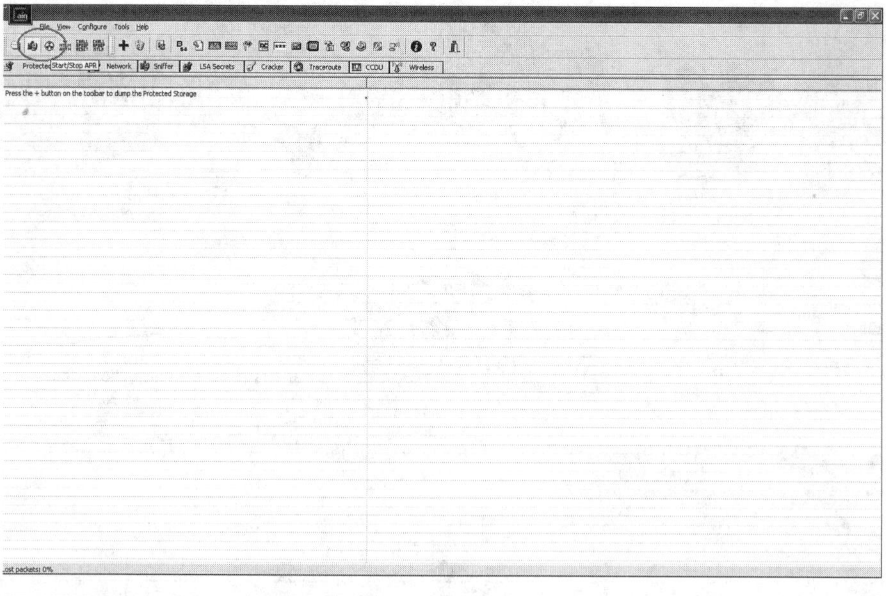

FIGURE 3.15 Press the buttons Start/Stop Sniffer and Start/Stop ARP.

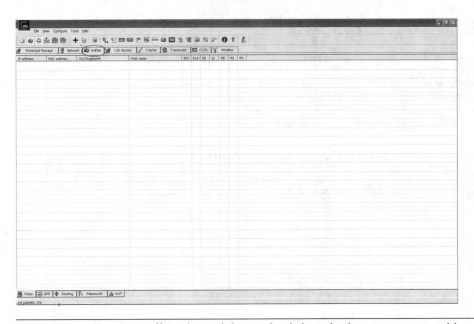

FIGURE 3.16 Select the Sniffer tab, and then right-click and select Scan MAC Addresses from the menu.

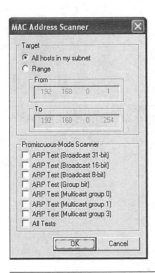

FIGURE 3.17 Select OK from the Target menu.

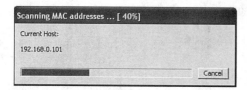

FIGURE 3.18 The program will initiate a scan to identify hosts on the local network.

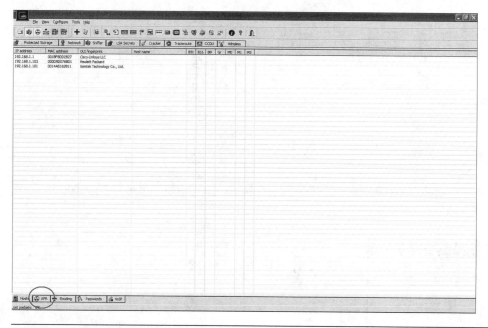

FIGURE 3.19 When the scan is complete, and a list of IP addresses is shown, select the ARP tab to switch to the "Poison" selection.

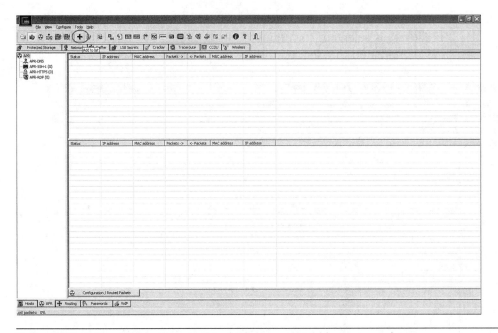

FIGURE 3.20 Select Add to List to add which hosts should be poisoned.

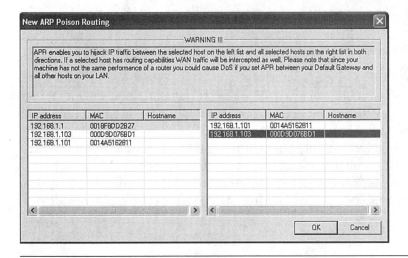

FIGURE 3.21 Select the target IP addresses that will be targeted.

Initially, the left pane is populated with IP addresses only. When the IP address is selected (for example, VoIP phone, gateway), the right pane is also populated to select the other end of the conversation.

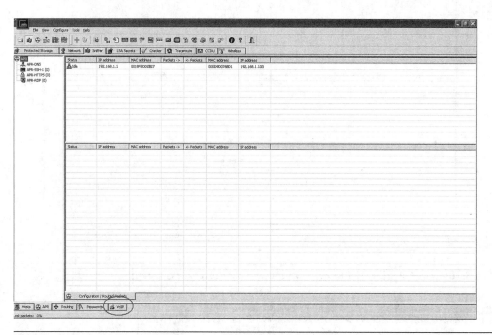

FIGURE 3.22 When the selection is made, the tool initiates the ARP poisoning attack.

When the tool detects a VoIP call (SIP), it starts capturing its traffic. You can view the call by selecting the VoIP tab at the bottom of the tool's interface.

At this point, you can highlight the call that you want to listen to and right-click to drop down a short menu that provides you with the selection to play the audio. The default audio player (for example, RealPlayer or Windows Media Player) of your host will be invoked to play the audio file.

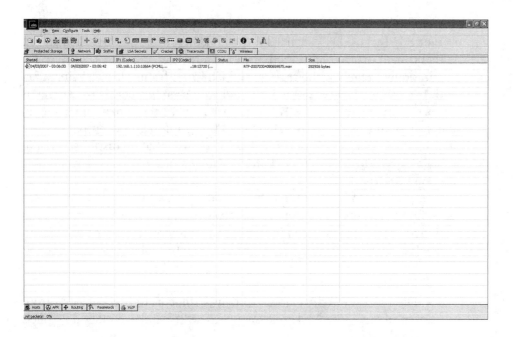

FIGURE 3.23 The tool lists all captured calls.

Eavesdropping Using VLAN Hopping

The previous section discussed eavesdropping through man-in-the-middle attacks using ARP poisoning. Typically, this attack is carried out against hosts that reside on the same LAN. This section discusses how to perform ARP poisoning using VLAN hopping and ultimately eavesdrop on communications between users in disparate LANs in a multiswitched network. This is not applicable to a single-switch network where a trunk link can be exploited to relay packets.

Traditionally, the ARP poisoning attack was thought to be effective only against hosts that reside in the same LAN. Currently, there are two publicly known VLAN hopping attacks: switch spoofing and double-tagging. The attacks are effective when a network switch has an incorrectly configured trunk port.

During switch spoofing, the attacker configures his system to advertise ISL or 802.1q and DTP signaling, thus making it masquerade as a switch with a trunk port that has membership to all targeted VLANs.

In double-tagging, the transmitted Ethernet frames are carrying a tag with two 802.1q headers. When the network switch receives the frame, it strips the first tag off and forwards the frame with the remaining tag to all the switch and trunk ports. Therefore, the frame can be propagated by intermediate switches based on the VLAN ID that is displayed in the remaining 802.1q header. The double-tagging attack works even when port trunking is turned off.

To protect VoIP communications from attacks that exploit this weakness, implementers can enforced the protection mechanisms for signaling and media streams discussed in this book. Additional recommendations to protect against VLAN-hopping attacks include the following:

- Disable all unused switch ports.
- Disable DTP[20] (Dynamic Trunking Protocol) to prevent ports from "trunking." For backbone switch-to-switch links, configure explicit trunking.
- Assign dedicated VLAN IDs to all trunk ports.

A publicly available tool that can be used to demonstrate VLAN hopping is Yesirnia.[21] This tool can perform attacks on several protocols that are used by switches for network management, including DTP (Dynamic Trunking Protocol), STP (Spanning Tree Protocol), VTP (VLAN Trunking Protocol), ISL (Inter-switch Link Protocol), 802.1x, 802.1q, HSRP (Hot Standby Router Protocol), DHCP (Dynamic Host Configuration Protocol), and CDP (Cisco Discovery Protocol).

Real-Time Eavesdropping by Manipulating MGCP

In many enterprise and carrier VoIP implementations, the MGCP protocol is typically used between a call agent (or call manager in Cisco terminology) to create, modify, and terminate calls—although in some implementations it is used between the edge devices and the signaling or media gateway (for example, ATAs). Figure 3.24 depicts the use of the protocol within an enterprise VoIP network.

---

20. *The DTP state on a trunk port may be set to auto (default mode), on, off, desirable, or non-negotiate.*

21. *Yersinia. www.yersinia.net*

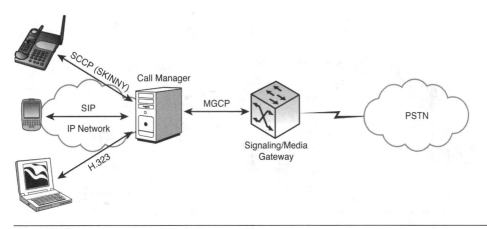

FIGURE 3.24 MGCP integration in VoIP networks.

Other protocols, such as SIP, H.323, or proprietary (for example, Cisco SCCP or "Skinny") protocols, may be used between the edge devices and the call agent (or call manager) to initiate, modify, and terminate sessions. It is important to understand that if the proper controls are not enforced to protect the signaling and media gateway, an attacker can manipulate connections using the MGCP protocol to carry out attacks, including premature termination, call diversion, and eavesdropping.

An attacker can send MGCP signaling messages to the PSTN gateway to change the state of an existing call and force the PSTN gateway to divert RTP traffic to the attacker's host or conference themselves into the conversation without the participants' knowledge and in essence eavesdrop on their conversation.

Figure 3.25 shows the sequence in which the attacker sends MGCP signaling messages to the PSTN gateway to divert RTP traffic to his host. The following five messages take place in the attack:

1. The attacker sends a request to get a list of all active calls.
2. The gateway responds with a list of active connections (calls).
3. The attacker queries a specific connection to get the corresponding details.
4. The gateway responds with the information.
5. The attacker sends a modify connection request to change the state of the connection and to divert the traffic to his host.

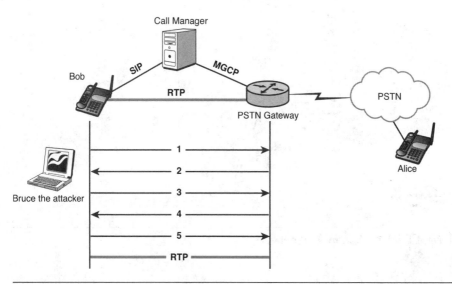

FIGURE 3.25 Real-time eavesdropping by manipulating the MGCP gateway.

The initial step in performing this attack is identifying existing connections on the PSTN gateway. Although the MGCP protocol is text based, it is not as intuitive as SIP. The following message requests the MGCP gateway to list all available end points:

```
AUEP 1500 *@mgcp.gateway MGCP 0.1
```

The AUEP (Audit End-Point) message includes a transaction (1500) and the end point to audit. In this case, the message is using an asterisk as a wildcard to request all available end points on the target host (mgcp.network.com).

The response from the gateway includes all the end points (ports) available on this gateway. Where there is an end point, there is likely to be a connection, too. The following is an actual listing from a gateway that lists 15 available end points:

```
200 1500
Z: S0/SU1/DS1-0/1@mgcp.gateway
Z: S0/SU1/DS1-0/2@mgcp.gateway
Z: S0/SU1/DS1-0/3@mgcp.gateway
```

```
Z: S0/SU1/DS1-0/4@mgcp.gateway
Z: S0/SU1/DS1-0/5@mgcp.gateway
Z: S0/SU1/DS1-0/6@mgcp.gateway
Z: S0/SU1/DS1-0/7@mgcp.gateway
Z: S0/SU1/DS1-0/8@mgcp.gateway
Z: S0/SU1/DS1-0/9@mgcp.gateway
Z: S0/SU1/DS1-0/10@mgcp.gateway
Z: S0/SU1/DS1-0/11@mgcp.gateway
Z: S0/SU1/DS1-0/12@mgcp.gateway
Z: S0/SU1/DS1-0/13@mgcp.gateway
Z: S0/SU1/DS1-0/14@mgcp.gateway
Z: S0/SU1/DS1-0/15@mgcp.gateway
```

The next step in the attack is to interrogate an individual end point and determine whether it supports an existing call or is idle. This interrogation is performed using the AUEP message:

```
AUEP 1000 S0/SU1/DS1-0/1@mgcp.gateway MGCP 0.1
F: R,D,S,X,N,I,T,O,ES
```

Note that in this message the end point is indicated as S0/SU1/DS1-0/1, and the F: header identifies the requested information to be returned. The following is a listing of the MGCP gateway's response:

```
200 1000
I: 2EDA
N: ca@10.96.1.51:2427
X: 1
R: D/[0-9ABCD*#](N)
S:
O:
T:
ES:
```

The response contains the connection ID I: 2EDA, which is needed to integrate the specific connection and identify the host to which the MGCP sends the RTP traffic associated with the call. Figure 3.26 displays the syntax of an MGCP and expands on the purpose of the corresponding fields.

3. THREATS AND ATTACKS

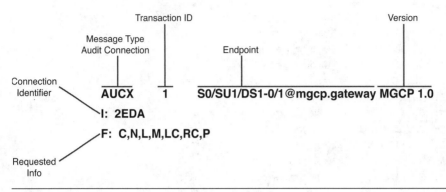

FIGURE 3.26 MGCP message syntax.

The message AUCX (Audit Connection) is sent to the gateway to audit a specific connection (in this case, S0/SU1/DS1-0/1@mgcp.gateway) with connection identifier of 2EDA and identifies additional information to be used to complete the attack. The following is the response received by the MGCP gateway:

```
200 1
C: D00000000200059400000F50000001d
N: ca@10.6.1.21:2427
L: p:20, a:PCMU, s:off, t:b8
M: sendrecv
P: PS=9817, OS=1570720, PR=9817, OR=1570720, PL=0, JI=60, LA=0
v=0
c=IN IP4 10.6.255.25
m=audio 18688 RTP/AVP 0 100
a=rtpmap:100 X-NSE/8000
a=fmtp:100 192-194
```

The response contains a lot of useful information, such as the call agent with which the MGCP gateway is communicating (ca@10.6.1.21:2427), indicated in the N: (Notified entity) header, and its mode, M:, send and receive (sendrecv). The SDP portion of the message contains the phone's IP address (10.6.255.25) and port (18688) to which RTP traffic is sent. This allows an attacker to monitor someone's call patterns by automating these steps as part of the process. Figure 3.27 depicts this method.

The next step is to modify the existing connection by sending an MDCX (Modify Connection) message to the gateway. The following sample message captures the MDCX request:

```
MDCX 1553 S0/SU1/DS1-0/1@mgcp.gateway MGCP 0.1
C: D000000002003e0e000000F580001f6d
I: 2EDA
X: 16
L: p:20, a:PCMU, s:off, t:b8
M: sendrecv
R: D/[0-9ABCD*#]
Q: process, loop

v=0
o=- 1334 0 IN EPN S0/SU1/DS1-0/1@mgcp.gateway s=Cisco SDP 0
t=0 0
m=audio 17994 RTP/AVP 0
c=IN IP4 10.6.158.178
```

This request instructs the MGCP gateway to modify the existing connection on the corresponding channel (S0/SU1/DS1-0/1) and start sending
RTP packets to the attacker's host at 10.6.158.178 on port 17794. When the
MGCP gateway executes this modification, the parties will lose the incoming or outgoing streams. So, the attacker has to identify and modify both
the inbound and outbound RTP streams before executing the attack to
eavesdrop on the conversation without suspicion. In the case where the
attacker taps into a conference bridge, the attacker may disrupt one
participant's RTP stream but be able to listen to the rest of the parties. The
participant who was interrupted may join the conference again as soon as
he realizes that he was "dropped."

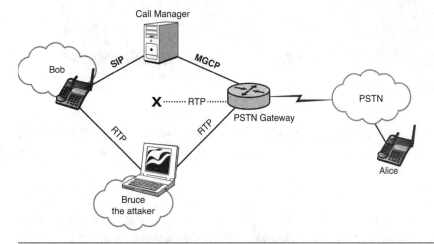

FIGURE 3.27 Relaying RTP traffic through the attacker's host.

In this case, the attacker instructs the MGCP gateway to start redirecting the RTP traffic to the attacker's host, and in turn the attacker can forward the traffic to the phone of the unsuspecting user. To redirect the RTP traffic to the legitimate user's phone, the attacker can use a tool such as RAT (Robust Audio Tool), which allows reception and transmission of RTP streams, as shown in Figure 3.28.

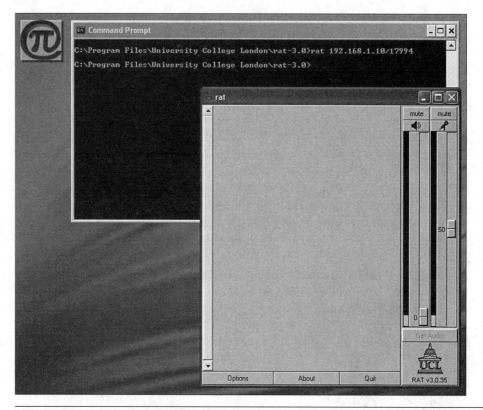

FIGURE 3.28 Relaying RTP traffic using RAT.

Using RAT, the attacker can set up a port to listen for an RTP stream and forward the traffic to a remote address and port (in this case, the victim).

This attack is independent of what operating system or RTP redirection tools the attacker may be using because the attacker needs to manipulate the signaling of the MGCP gateway to divert the RTP streams. Other tools that can receive and forward RTP packets can be used, too.

Masquerading

This section discusses masquerading and describes techniques that can be exploited at various levels of the protocol stack. Masquerading attacks have been around since ancient times. A famous example is the Trojan war, which was won with the use of an agent, the Trojan horse. In essence, the Greek army used a device to masquerade its entrance into the city of Troy. A team of skilled soldiers hid inside the wooden structure.

One special case of masquerading is subscriber impersonation. In this case, an attacker masquerades his identity by using previously captured credentials or gaining access to a device associated with a subscriber. The device is most likely under the attacker's physical or logical control. For example, Bruce (a malicious user) is working after hours and uses Alice's phone in the next cubicle to make fraudulent phone calls. Another example is where an attacker has logical control of the device by exploiting a vulnerability that allows her to gain unauthorized access remotely and generate various attacks (that is, inject messages to the network or probe for other vulnerabilities). In either scenario, the attacker's true identity is obfuscated using various methods. For example, the section "Presence Hijacking" describes the steps of hijacking a subscriber's registration, which allows attackers to perform several attacks (including intercepting calls by diverting them to the attacker's device). In this example, the SIP protocol is used to demonstrate this attack. The attack is not protocol specific and can be performed in VoIP networks that use other signaling protocols, such as H.323.

Application or service impersonation requires the coordination of various aspects, including replication of the application's or service's look and feel and synchronization of messages and events between the components and the end user's device. Depending on the sophistication of the application or service, an attacker can impersonate a service or an application using various attacks, including man in the middle or traffic diversion. Typically, an attacker may have gained control of the underlying components that support the application or taken advantage of vulnerabilities that impact the routing of the signaling protocols.

Another masquerading attack is device impersonation. The attacker may impersonate a device such as a phone, signaling gateway, media gateway, DNS server, SIP registrar, PSAP, or softswitch to impersonate a component or a network, depending on which component is impersonated, and carry out attacks that aim to collect and manipulate traffic. For example, an attacker may impersonate a DNS server that provides translation for SIP URLs and divert incoming calls to the attacker's desired target host.

Currently, several methods and vulnerabilities can be used to impersonate a user or a component in a VoIP network. Although traditional methods can be used to carry out a masquerading attack (that is, MAC or IP address cloning and IP packet spoofing), the methods associated with VoIP aim to manipulate the signaling messages to carry out the attack. In this case, the attacker has access to the VoIP network and has the knowledge and ability to craft signaling messages that impersonate a user or a device.

Caller ID Spoofing

Caller ID spoofing in VoIP can be carried out by manipulating the messages of the signaling protocol used (for example, SIP INVITE). Various methods have been discussed in literature, including manipulating the VoIP gateway (for example, Asterisk PBX) or crafting a spoofed INVITE request manually using a tool such as SIVuS. Although there a number of ways for configuring Asterisk PBX to spoof caller ID, the easiest way is to use the command SetCallerID(2015551212) in the extensions.conf file. The number 2015551212 is the spoofed telephone number that will be used for the call. Although this is simple, it requires that the entry is edited manually, and Asterisk has to be restarted for every call. Figure 3.29 displays an example of caller ID spoofing using the SIVuS tool.

The Message Generator tab in SIVuS can be used to craft several variations of SIP messages to demonstrate various attacks, including caller ID spoofing. Note that the depicted version of SIVuS does not support the ability to establish calls with spoofed caller ID information. It is used only for demonstration purposes.

Caller ID spoofing is also feasible in VoIP provider networks with enterprise customers. Typically, VoIP service providers route VoIP traffic from enterprise customers by establishing a point-to-point configuration between the provider's VoIP gateway and customer's VoIP gateway (for example, SBC, SIP proxy, H.323 gatekeeper). In this scenario, the VoIP provider accepts any VoIP traffic without having the ability to verify caller ID information from the originating enterprise network. Therefore, a malicious user who resides in the enterprise network can spoof caller ID information through the service provider's network.

The caller ID spoofing attack can be used against systems that use caller ID information to identify users. For example, some mobile telephone companies use caller ID to authenticate subscribers to their voice mailboxes. If the caller ID matches the user's voice mailbox, it will not prompt the caller for a password because it assumes that the call is originating from the user's cell phone.

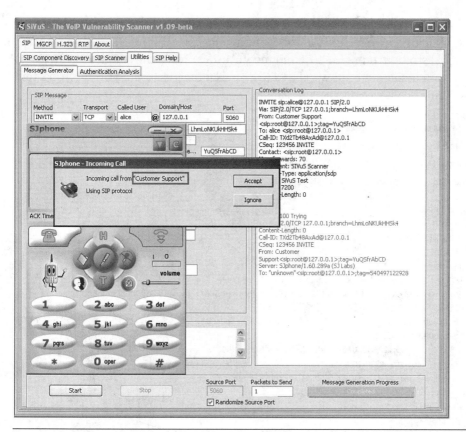

FIGURE 3.29 Caller ID spoofing using SIVuS.

Currently, some companies provide caller ID spoofing services (for example, SpoofTel,[22] NuFone,[23] and VoicePulse[24]).

Presence Hijacking

Hijacking a user's presence can have adverse implications in certain environments, such as health care or the military. Therefore, it is encouraged to define appropriate security requirements during the design phase of the VoIP network and enforce the proper security controls and countermeasures to minimize the impact from attacks.

3. THREATS AND ATTACKS

An example that demonstrates the mechanics of a presence hijacking attack is provided in the following paragraphs. Figure 3.30 shows a valid registration message to announce a user's availability and IP address to send incoming requests (INVITE). This indicates to the VoIP network that the user device can accept calls.

Frame 1 (611 bytes on wire, 611 bytes captured)

Ethernet II, Src: 00:12:17:e5:7e:00, Dst: 00:05:00:e5:6b:00

Ethernet Protocol, Src Addr: 192.168.10.5 (192.168.10.5), Dst Addr: 192.168.10.2 (192.168.10.2)

User Datagram Protocol, Src Port: 5061 (5061), Dst Port: 5061 (5061)

Session Initiation Protocol
  Request-Line: REGISTER sip:atlas4.voipprovider.net:5061 SIP/2.0
    Method: REGISTER
    Resent Packet: False
  Message Header
    Via: SIP/2.0/UDP 192.168.94.70:5061;branch=z9hG4bK-49897e4e
    From: 201-853-0102 <sip:12018530102@atlas4.voipprovider.net:5061>;tag=802030536f050c56o0
      SIP Display info: 201-853-0102
      SIP from address: sip: 12018530102@atlas4.voipprovider.net:5061
      SIP tag: 802030536f050c56o0
    To: 201-853-0102 <sip:12018530102@atlas4.voipprovider.net:5061>
      SIP Display info: 201-853-0102
      SIP to address: sip: 12018530102@atlas4.voipprovider.net:5061
    Call-ID: e4bb5007-b7335032@67.83.94.70
    CSeq: 3 REGISTER
    Max-Forwards: 70
    Contact: 201-853-0102 <sip:12018530102@192.168.10.5:5061>;expires=60
    User-Agent: 001217E57E31 Linksys/RT31P2-2.0.13(LIVd)
    Content-Length: 0
    Allow: ACK, BYE, CANCEL, INFO, INVITE, NOTIFY, OPTIONS, REFER
    Supported: x-sipura

Request to REGISTER and announce contact address for the user. In the REGISTER request the From and To headers must use the same user information.

Indicates that the registration will expire in 60 seconds. Another REGISTER request should be sent to refresh the user's registration.

The Contact header contains a SIP or SIPS URI that represents a direct route to the device, usually composed of a username at a fully qualified domain name (FQDN).

FIGURE 3.30 SIP REGISTER message.

The REGISTER request contains a Contact header that indicates the IP address of the user's device (that is, VoIP soft phone or hard phone). When a proxy receives a request to process an incoming call (INVITE), it performs a lookup to identify the IP address of the respective user's device and forwards the request. In this example, the user with the phone number 201-853-0102 can be reached at IP address 192.168.10.5. The proxy forwards the INVITE request to that IP address. You might notice that the advertised port is 5061. This port is reserved for SIPS, and in this implementation is in violation of RFC 3261.[25]

Frame 1 (611 bytes on wire, 611 bytes captured)

Ethernet II, Src: 00:12:17:e5:7e:00, Dst: 00:05:00:e5:6b:00

Ethernet Protocol, Src Addr: 192.168.1.3 (192.168.1.3), Dst Addr: 192.168.10.2 (192.168.1.2)

User Datagram Protocol, Src Port: 5061 (5061), Dst Port: 5061 (5061)

Session Initiation Protocol
  Request-Line: REGISTER sip:atlas4.voipprovider.net:5061 SIP/2.0
    Method: REGISTER
    Resent Packet: False
  Message Header
    Via: SIP/2.0/UDP 192.168.1.5:5061;branch=z9hG4bK-49897e4e
    From: 201-853-0102 <sip:12018530102@atlas4.voipprovider.net:5061>;tag=802030536f050c56o0
      SIP Display info: 201-853-0102
      SIP from address: sip: 12018530102@atlas4.voipprovider.net:5061
      SIP tag: 802030536f050c56o0
    To: 201-853-0102 <sip:12018530102@atlas4.voipprovider.net:5061>
      SIP Display info: 201-853-0102
      SIP to address: sip: 12018530102@atlas4.voipprovider.net:5061
    Call-ID: e4bb5007-b7335032@192.168.1.5
    CSeq: 3 REGISTER
    Max-Forwards: 70
    Contact: 201-853-0102 <sip:12018530102@192.168.1.3:5061>;expires=60
    User-Agent: 001217E57E31 Linksys/RT31P2-2.0.13(LIVd)
    Content-Length: 0
    Allow: ACK, BYE, CANCEL, INFO, INVITE, NOTIFY, OPTIONS, REFER
    Supported: x-sipura

> Modified IP address in the Contact header will force incoming calls to be diverted to the attacker's device.

FIGURE 3.31 Spoofed REGISTER request.

Figure 3.31 shows a modified version of the REGISTER request that is sent by the attacker. In this request, all the message headers and parameters remain the same except the parameters in the Contact header. The information that has been changed in the Contact header is the IP address (192.168.1.3), which points to the attacker's device rather than the actual user's IP address. The REGISTER request is sent to the SIP registrar at

25. See www.vopsecurity.org/Security_Issues_with_SOHO_VoIP_Gateways-052005.pdf for additional information.

3. THREATS AND ATTACKS

192.168.1.2. The tool that was used to generate this request is SIVuS, which is shown in Figure 3.32.[26]

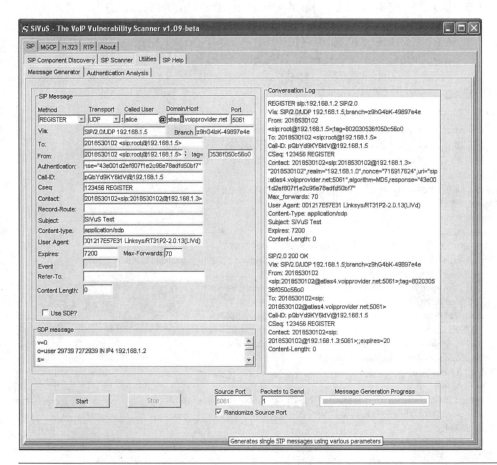

Figure 3.32 Spoofing a REGISTER request using SIVuS.

The hijacking attack works as follows:

1. Disable the legitimate user's registration. This can be done as follows:

   Perform a DoS attack against the user's device to prevent it from re-registering.

---

26. See www.vopsecurity.org/html/tools.html.

Deregister the user by sending a spoofed message for the same user setting the value of the expiration header to zero (Expires:0). This indicates that the user would like to terminate his presence with the corresponding registrar.

Generate REGISTER requests in a shorter timeframe (that is, every 15 seconds) to override the legitimate user's registration request. Typically, handsets are configured to update their registration every 60 seconds.

2. Send a REGISTER request with the attacker's IP address rather than the legitimate user's IP address.

Figure 3.33 demonstrates the attack approach. The following steps take place in the given scenario:

0. DoS attack.
1. User registration.
2. Caller, session initiation request.
3. Proxy, domain lookup, and routing.
4. Proxy, user lookup, where the SIP proxy now retrieves the attacker's IP address.
5. Proxy, contacts the user.
6. Callee answers.
7. Proxy forwards caller response. The connection has been established, and media is routed between the two phones.

This attack is possible for the following reasons:

- The example implementation does enforce message authentication to challenge registration requests (or INVITEs to control call origination).
- The signaling messages are sent in the clear, which allows attackers to collect, modify, and replay them as they want.
- The current SIP implementations do not support integrity of the message contents, and therefore modification and replay attacks are not detected.

To protect against this attack, implementations should authenticate REGISTER requests and use SIPS (SIP over TLS). One of the important parameters in the SIP authentication mechanism is the nonce, which is a random string of characters used in conjunction with the user's ID, secret password, realm, and URI to generate the MD5 digest for the

3. THREATS AND ATTACKS

authentication. The attacker has to know the secret password and the nonce to successfully authenticate to the SIP proxy. Therefore, using SIPS provides another layer of protection from someone attempting to intercept the contents of the signaling message.

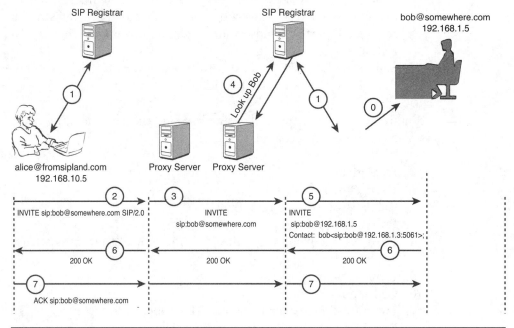

FIGURE 3.33 Registration hijacking example.

In some implementations, this attack can be successful even if the remote SIP proxy server requires authentication of user registration because the SIP server may not challenge every request, only the initial one. In other cases, the SIP server, erroneously, may reuse cached authentication information in REGISTER requests, and because they are transmitted in the clear, they can be captured, modified, and replayed (for example, using the same nonce and thus generating the same digest). This attack can be launched against enterprise or residential users. For example, a home network that uses a poorly configured wireless access point without encryption can be compromised by an attacker who can then intercept and replay registration requests. The attacker can perform various attacks, including making fraudulent calls or redirecting communications. In an enterprise environment, an attacker can divert calls to unauthorized parties. (For example, calls from stockholders can be diverted to an agent who is not authorized to handle certain trade transactions for customers.)

This attack can be suppressed by implementing SIPS and authenticating SIP requests and responses (which can include integrity protection) using new pseudo-random nonce values in every message. In fact, the use of SIPS and authentication of responses can suppress many associated attacks, including eavesdropping and message or user impersonation.

Impersonating a Call Manager and Diverting All Calls

Another attack vector in VoIP is impersonation of a network element, such as a call manager. The call manager is deployed between the VoIP phone and the voice gateway and manages all inbound and outbound calls for the network (see Figure 3.34). The call manager is responsible for contacting the user's VoIP phone and allocating resources (voice channels) on the voice gateway to support inbound and outbound calls. All communications between the call manager and the voice gateway are performed using MGCP.

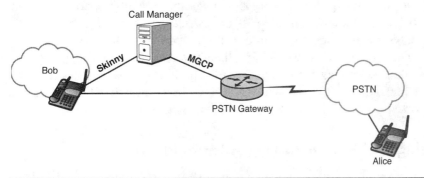

FIGURE 3.34 Call manager and PSTN gateway configuration.

An attacker can take advantage of the "redirect" package in MGCP to impersonate a call manager and instruct the MGCP to route incoming calls to a rogue call manager. RFC 3991, "Media Gateway Control Protocol (MGCP) Redirect and Reset Package," defines a set of signaling messages that allow the call agent to redirect a group of end points without affecting the end point or connection state. These signaling messages allow a call agent to pass a new NotifiedEntity or NotifiedEntityList to a collection of end points specified by an "all of" wildcard. This is useful if a new call agent takes over from a previous one and wants to redirect end point(s) to send messages to it from now on. At the same time, this "feature" can be used by an attacker to instruct the voice gateway to redirect signaling traffic to a new call manager. The following message demonstrates this attack:

```
EPCF 1200 *@gw1.whatever.net MGCP 1.0
RED/N: ca1@ca1234.whatever.net
```

The EPCF (End Point Configuration) message is sent to the voice gateway on port 2427. The message uses an asterisk in front of the domain as a wildcard to instruct the voice gateway to apply this change to all the available end points. The RED/N header indicates where the traffic should be sent (in this case, ca1@ca1234.whatever.net). The following message is another variation and indicates a backup call manager:

```
EPCF 1200 *@gw1.whatever.net MGCP 1.0
RED/NL: ca1@myca.whatever.net, a2@mybackupca.whatever.net
```

Because MGCP does not provide any security controls, one approach to protect against such an attack is to restrict connections to the MGCP port (2427) from untrusted sources. In other words, a one-to-one mapping should be configured between the call manager(s) and the voice gateway(s) to exchange signaling MGCP messages. Another approach is to configure IPSec between the call manager and the voice gateway if such a feature is supported on the call manager and the voice gateway.

Listing of Masquerading Attacks in VoIP

In VoIP, a number of elements can be impersonated to gain unauthorized access, commit service fraud, or disrupt services. Table 3.2 provides a list of components that can be impersonated by an attacker, along with the objective and attack method that can be used.

Table 3-2 Possible Masquerading Attacks against VoIP

Target Entity/Component	Objective for Impersonation	Attack Method
User	Deception Fraud	Obtain user credentials through another attack and use them to sign on to the device Gain physical access to the user's device Gain remote access to the user's device Manipulate signaling messages at the signaling gateway or registration server SIP proxy or signaling server reconfiguration to route traffic to a new location
Edge device	Commit fraud To be used as an eavesdropping mechanism To be used as incriminating evidence for another crime Launching point for new attacks	Gain physical access to the device Gain remote access to the device
DNS	Redirect session requests to unauthorized devices	Cache poisoning Unauthorized access with intent to modify the network element's configuration
Signaling gateway	Divert signaling traffic and ultimately calls to unauthorized parties	Remote manipulation of signaling to divert traffic to other destinations (for example, attack on MGCP protocol) Unauthorized access with the intent to modify the network element's configuration

(continues)

Table 3-2 Possible Masquerading Attacks against VoIP (*continued*)

Target Entity/Component	Objective for Impersonation	Attack Method
Media gateway	Divert media traffic to unauthorized parties	Remote manipulation of signaling to divert traffic to other destinations (for example, attack on MGCP protocol) Unauthorized access with the intent to modify the network element's configuration
SIP proxy	Collect user credentials Divert signaling traffic and ultimately calls to unauthorized parties	Remote manipulation of signaling to divert traffic to other destinations (for example, manipulating sessions by spoofing signaling messages such as REFER and INVITE to divert a call) Unauthorized access with the intent to modify the network element's configuration
SIP registrar	Collect user credentials	Spoof registration requests Unauthorized access with the intent to modify the network element's configuration
H.323 gatekeeper	Collect user credentials Collect call traffic information	Spoof registration requests Unauthorized access with the intent to modify the network element's configuration
Soft switch	Divert signaling traffic and ultimately calls to unauthorized parties Collect call traffic information	Unauthorized access with the intent to modify the network element's configuration

Fraud

As technology evolves, fraud schemes are also made easier to carry out at a higher frequency. In addition, the convergence between circuit-switched and packet-based networks will increase the opportunities for fraud. In 2004, the FBI reported an increase in online fraud from 2003 by 64 percent. The total loss amounted to $68.14 million, with Internet auction fraud being "by far the most reported offense."[27] Telecommunications fraud has been one of the primary concerns of telecommunications carriers and service providers for many years. Generally, fraud in telecommunication networks (that is, wireline and cellular) has an annual growth of about 10 percent on average. A worldwide telecom fraud survey that was conducted by the Communications Fraud Control Association in 2003 identified telecom fraud losses to be $35 to $40 billion. It has been reported that the average loss for a service provider is estimated to be between 3 percent and 8 percent annually. In addition, it is estimated that there are a little more than 200 variants of telecom fraud, and it is anticipated that this number will increase with the growth of next-generation networks including VoIP and IMS.

Today, network providers that maintain a reasonable IP backbone can offer competitive VoIP services. This includes not only incumbent telcos, but also cable operators and Internet service providers. Therefore, deployment of packet-based multimedia applications such as VoIP, IPTV, and others has become a priority to maintain competitiveness. The demand to market quickly inhibits the implementation of adequate security controls. In addition, the network architecture changes dynamically to accommodate new services, applications, and billing methods. All these variables (new and complex technology, new services, new billing methods, and time to market) provide a fertile ground for fraud and criminal activity that will propagate at a higher rate compared to the past.

Generally, one factor that aids in accelerating fraud activity is the availability of tools (software, hardware, or the combination of both) that lessen the technical competence required to carry out the fraud and provide the means to easily and continuously replicate the process.

---

27. *2004 IC3 Annual Internet Fraud Report, National White Collar Crime Center and the Federal Bureau of Investigation.*

VoIP fraud introduces a new challenge for the service providers because of many factors, including the following:

- Complexity of the technology increases the opportunity for security inconsistencies and oversight.
- New technology, and therefore new security limitations and vulnerabilities, are introduced.
- Time to market to remain competitive suppresses the need to deploy proper security controls.
- Billing methods may vary based on multimedia content, QoS, usage, or other matrixes, which expands the room for error and opportunity to manipulate billing codes or processes.

Fraud introduces socioeconomic issues by affecting the health of the provider's business and operations, which in turn may affect operating costs and to some extent consumer pricing. Although fraud has been a telecommunication provider issue, with the general increase of VoIP deployments, it will expand to enterprise network owners, too. External and internal attackers will try to gain access to critical components such as the IP-PBX or signaling gateways to make fraudulent calls, reroute calls to support money-making schemes, or methodically disrupt communications for extortion.

An attacker may use traditional methods to defraud VoIP services, such as social engineering or identity theft. For example, one of the methods used by criminals to defraud telecommunication services is to impersonate an existing subscriber by obtaining personal information of a subscriber (for example, name, address, and Social Security number) and requesting new services, which are abused and later abandoned.

The more technically savvy attacker can use a single vulnerability or a combination of vulnerabilities to obtain services fraudulently. These vulnerabilities may exist because of poor security controls on infrastructure components (that is, SIP proxy servers, H.323 gatekeepers, SBCs), insecure software implementations, or protocol limitations. The topic of VoIP vulnerabilities is discussed in more detail in the next chapter.

Types of Fraud

There have been various ways to defraud telecommunication services, which are discussed next. It is necessary to understand the types of fraud methods that exist to place them in the context of VoIP and essentially in NGN and derive possible new fraud scenarios. According to historical data, there are approximately 200 types of known telecommunication fraud. Some of these include subscription fraud, dial-through fraud (manipulation of the PBX), freephone fraud, premium-rate service fraud, handset theft, and roaming fraud.[28] Generally the types of fraud can be categorized as fraud that targets the process (that is, subscription, superimposed)[29] and fraud that targets the technology (that is, auto-dialers, unauthorized access). Here we discuss some of the most commonly experienced.

Subscription fraud is committed by purchasing services using falsified identity information. There are numerous ways that subscription fraud can be carried out. The purchased services may be sold to others or used by the criminals to run up high toll charges and collect the money from the targeted telephone company. The objective of the perpetrator is to use the service and run up high charges and later abandon the account or use the subscription to collect toll money from the telco. For example, someone can subscribe to a telephone service at a company in the United States using falsified or stolen identity information. At the same time, the perpetrator may have set up an account in another country for which he charges $5 per minute for incoming calls. This allows making calls from the United States and getting charged outrageous tolls on the U.S. account. The perpetrator collects the money from the local telco for the incoming calls, but obviously doesn't pay the charges on the U.S. account (thus leaving the telco in debt). Although this scheme has been very costly for telcos, it provides several indicators that can be used in fraud detection, which are discussed in later sections.

Superimposed fraud is caused by fraudsters using another user's subscription without authorization. All the toll charges are billed to the account of the unsuspecting victim. The fraud is committed by having access to the user's stolen equipment (for example, cell phone), equipment cloning, or the use of personal-identifiable information such as a calling card or subscription plan information with the telco. Detecting this type of

28. J. Shawe Taylor, et. al. Novel techniques for profiling and fraud in mobile telecommunications. In P. J. G. Lisboa, B. Edisbury, & A. Vellido (eds.), Business Applications of Neural Networks. The State-of-the-Art of Real World Applications (pp. 113–139). World Scientific, Singapore.

29. R. J. Bolton, and D. J. Hand. Statistical Fraud Detection: A Review. Statistical Science, Vol. 17, No. 3 (August 2002), pp. 235–249

activity is difficult but not impossible. Anomaly-detection methods can be used in fraud management, which we discuss below.

Unauthorized access is one of the fundamental techniques used for many attacks, including committing fraud. Gaining access to billing systems, telephone switches, or other infrastructure components allows an attacker to manipulate the configuration or data (that is, call detail records) to avoid charges. Unauthorized access takes advantage of vulnerabilities that may exist in the software that runs on the infrastructure components, poor configuration, or lack of proper security controls.

Auto-dialers are programs designed to make automated calls to a list of phone numbers or a telephone exchange. The auto-dialers are used by telemarketers to call potential customers and sell their services and by phreakers to identify toll-free numbers or modems attached to systems and ultimately attempt to gain unauthorized access. Auto-dialers are also used as a mechanism to carry out fraud. The perpetrator claims to be a customer-owned coin-operated telephone (COCOT) vendor. He then connects an auto-dialer to what should have been a payphone line and initiates war dialing on an assorted list of toll-free numbers (that is, 1-800 in the United States). Because the calls are made to 800 numbers, the charges are reversed, and therefore the called parties (companies that own the 800 number) are forced to reimburse the fraudulent COCOT provider for "calls received from a payphone."

Other fraud schemes include pre-paid calling cards that use passcodes that can be stolen and then used to make fraudulent calls, telemarketing that attempts to sell services to vulnerable victims (for example, elderly), and forced calls to service numbers (for example, 809, 876-HOT, 900) that are purposefully overpriced (and the owners reside in countries where such practice is not legally restricted; for example, the Caribbean, Jamaica, and elsewhere).

Fraud in VoIP

It is expected that VoIP providers will experience new types of fraud.[30] Some schemes will be able to be listed under the known categories, but there will be others that will require new categorization and probably new detection and mitigation techniques. Although the scope of this book does

---

30. *Fraud Analysis in IP and Next-Generation Networks. The International Engineering Consortium.* www.iec.org/online/tutorials/fraud_analysis/

not include predicting the future, there is enough evidence to help speculate about what technical vulnerabilities can be exploited by future fraud schemes.

One of the fundamental issues is the fact that the signaling in VoIP is in-band. This means that voice and control messages are not isolated. Although this practice was performed in the older days of the PSTN, when CAS (Common Associated Signaling) was used, it was terminated and a new system emerged, the CCS[31] (Common Channel Signaling), in which control messages are sent out of band. In the older system (CAS), it was possible to place fraudulent[32] calls because of the ability to send voice and generate control signals over the same line. In CCS when someone makes a call, he receives only a dial tone, without having any control over the signaling. All the control messages to set up and tear down the call occur within the network separately from the user's communication line.

Another area of concern is the architecture of VoIP. Typically, VoIP components (that is, SIP proxies, DNS servers) reside on networks accessible from the Internet and therefore exposed to attack. VoIP service providers may not necessarily manage the Internet connection of their subscribers, and therefore all signaling and voice traffic from the end user's device will traverse one or more foreign networks. This exposes the subscriber and the service provider to various threats, including eavesdropping and unauthorized access, which can support fraud activities. For example, an attacker may exploit a vulnerability in the subscriber's residential VoIP gateway that will allow capturing credentials that can be used to gain access to the provider's network and make fraudulent calls.

Fraud Through Call-Flow Manipulation

Figure 3.35 shows an example in which implementation vulnerability can be used to defraud a VoIP service. The vulnerability takes advantage of how SIP signaling messages are processed by the SIP proxy and the billing

---

31. *Also known as CCS7, Common Channel Signaling System 7 or SS7.*

32. *A popular exploit was used in the late 1960s to place long-distance calls for free by generating the 2600Hz supervisory signal, which indicates the status of a trunk, on hook (tone) or off hook (no tone). The caller would usually dial an 800 number and then generate the 2600Hz frequency, which indicated to the other end that the caller hung up. At that point, the far end is forced to an off-hook condition waiting for the routing digits. The attacker then generated a key pulse (KP, the tone that starts a routing digit sequence), followed by a telephone number with a start tone (ST).*

system. Typically, a SIP proxy considers that a session between two users has been set up when the three-way handshake is completed (INVITE, OK, ACK messages). Figure 3.35 depicts a typical SIP handshake.

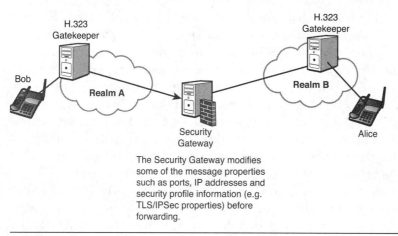

The Security Gateway modifies some of the message properties such as ports, IP addresses and security profile information (e.g. TLS/IPSec properties) before forwarding.

FIGURE 3.35 Typical three-way SIP handshake.

Bob wants to talk to Alice, and when he dials the digits, his phone generates an INVITE message that is sent to his local SIP proxy. Bob's proxy performs a lookup to determine to which proxy it needs to send the INVITE to reach Alice's proxy. Upon determining the IP address of the proxy that serves Alice, it forwards the INVITE, and Alice's proxy forwards the INVITE to Alice's phone. When Alice answers the phone, an OK response is sent to Bob's phone to indicate that Alice has accepted the call. At that point, Bob's phone sends an ACK response, which indicates that the session has been established and the two users can communicate. Notice that all the messages are propagated through both proxies A and B, and therefore there is a record of the messages that have traversed the proxies. The records that are created on the proxies are critical for providing billing and service-usage information. If this information is corrupted or not recorded accurately, it impacts the service provider's billing process.

One way to defraud a VoIP service provider is by manipulating the call flow between the two end points. It is possible to establish a call between two end points and avoid toll charges by manipulating the SIP message sequence. Let's assume that Bob has the ability to manipulate the message flow of his SIP phone (for example, by manipulating the runtime code or proxying the SIP messages through another device). In this case, he will send the SIP INVITE to contact Alice. The INVITE request will propagate through the intermediate SIP proxies A and B and eventually will reach Alice. When Alice answers the phone, an OK response is sent back to Bob's SIP phone. At this point, Bob knows that Alice has answered. In essence, Bob can start sending voice to Alice's phone without having to send the ACK response. Figure 3.36 demonstrates this scenario.

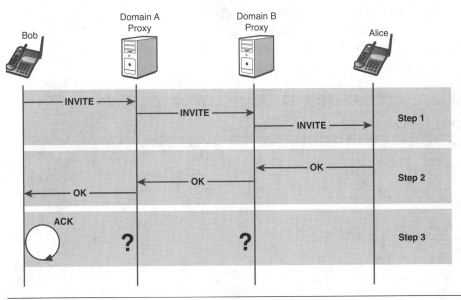

FIGURE 3.36 SIP message-suppression attack used for service fraud.

In this case, the ACK response is suppressed and the intermediate proxies (A and B) assume that the call was not established and therefore do not record it (see Figure 3.36). Therefore, it will not be reflected in the billing records either. Depending on the implementation, Alice's phone may have to be programmed to ignore waiting for an ACK and to accept media streams on the preallocated ports that were indicated in the OK response.

One approach that service providers take to protect against this attack is to start billing when the OK is sent back from the called party. Although this provides some protection, it might not stop emerging attacks that manipulate the call flow or signaling messages to bypass billing.

Phishing

The term *phishing* refers to an attacker sending masqueraded email messages to unsuspecting users to lure them into disclosing confidential or personal information, such as account credentials. The email message has the same look and feel of a legitimate message originating from an organization that the user has a prior relationship with, typically a financial institution or online merchant (for example, Bank of America, IRS, eBay, Amazon.com).

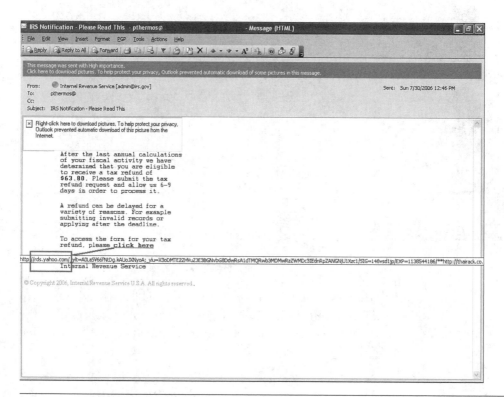

FIGURE 3.37 Sample "phishing" email message.

Figure 3.37 shows an email message that appears to originate from the IRS (Internal Revenue System).[33] The email message can be crafted to appear as if it originates from a specific organization that maintains private user information such a financial institution. The message urges the user to visit the institution's online system to verify credentials, claim a balance, or dispute a charge. The content of the message is formatted using HTML, which helps the attacker to obfuscate the real URL that the user is asked to follow to verify his or her credentials. The highlighted "click here" text appears as an HTML link as a convenient way for the user to connect to the online system and proceed with the verification of credentials. In Figure 3.37, the highlighted link indicates that the actual URL resolves to the rds.yahoo.com domain, which is clearly not an IRS system. In addition, the URL contains the path to a script that prompts the user to enter his or her credentials, such as Social Security number, user ID and password, credit card number, and so on). When the user follows the URL, he is prompted to enter his credentials, which will be captured by the attacker. The credentials may be logged in a file, sent to an email account, or posted to another Web site or IRC channel.

The same approach can be using VoIP communications. An attacker can lure unsuspecting victims into calling a number managed by the attacker. The email message can be sent to users asking them to call an 800 number.

Figure 3.38 shows the steps used in this attack. The first two steps can be performed simultaneously or in either order. In our example, the attacker has first analyzed the target company's interactive voice system and creates an exact replica. In the next step, an 800 number is obtained by a VoIP service provider (it provides a layer of believability to the spoofed message being sent because users are accustomed to calling toll-free numbers to contact customer service). In addition, the cost for a VoIP toll-free number is relatively insignificant. The next step is to craft and send an email message that instructs recipients to call the 800 number and verify their credentials for the targeted institution. If recipients are convinced to call the 800 number, they will go through the prompts and disclose their credentials. The spoofed system can terminate the victim's call by responding with a polite message such as "Thank you for verifying your information with Big International Bank!" and hanging up the call. And the attacker will have recorded the information on his or her system. It is expected that VoIP-related phishing attacks will become apparent during 2008 or 2009.

---

33. *IRS is the tax-collection agency of the United States.*

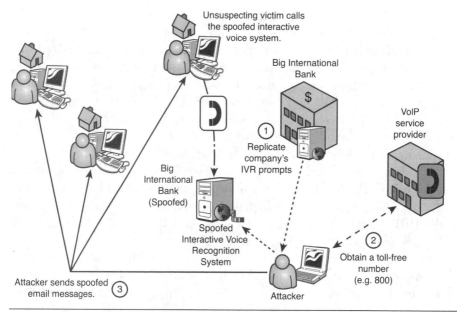

FIGURE 3.38 VoIP phishing attack.

Another variation of this attack is to embed a SIP URL rather than an HTTP URL in the email message. This will work only in cases in which the user's system has the ability to place VoIP calls using SIP URLs. Another attack is to invoke the soft phone that resides on a victim's system by using a command in the URL link, such as the following (see Figure 3.39):

```
C:\Program Files\CounterPath\X-Lite>x-lite.exe --help -
dial=sip:7325551212
```

FIGURE 3.39 Invoking a soft phone from a command line or an attack script.

The first line of defense is user awareness. Organizations should educate their users of the potential of such attacks. From a technological perspective, a mutual caller ID authentication mechanism should be established. Such an enhancement will require the development of an ITU or IETF standard. The proposed standard will require that the called institution authenticates itself to the user by announcing to the user a piece of information that will be known to the institution and the user only. For example, the institution can prompt the user to select from a list of choices a private piece of identifying information such as the last four digits of the respective account or Social Security number (for example, "Does your account number with us end in 6789, 1111, 4343, or 3232?"). The user can select the correct response, which is already known to the user and institution.

Although this attack has several technical parameters, it is categorized under fraud because it is mainly used to obtain a user's credentials for identity theft and to perform fraudulent transactions such as unauthorized purchases, money transfers, or withdrawals.

Fraud Management

Fraud management in VoIP requires a multidimensional approach because of the complexity of the technology and the variation in applications and services. To effectively combat fraud in VoIP networks, the following should be considered:

- Incorporate fraud control requirements in new service offerings as part of the product development life cycle.
- Define fraud control requirements in the early stages of a product offering to minimize potential loss due to fraud and help streamline the fraud management system to detect behaviors that violates the defined requirements. This proactive measure helps minimize costs associated with later efforts to manage service fraud at the time of occurrence.
- Deploy a VoIP fraud management system to assist in recognizing suspicious activity patterns. Several vendors offer fraud management systems for VoIP. Before selecting and deploying such as product, consider the following:

  Security features offered by the system, such as role-based access controls (that is, administrator, analyst, manager), secure remote access (that is, SSL/SSH), and data integrity

Pattern-matching capabilities (that is, granularity of configurability, elimination of false positives)

Detection and pattern-recognition capabilities (that is, event- or rule-based detection)

Integration and maturity curve (that is, the amount of time it takes for the analysis engine to "learn" network traffic behavioral patterns)

Alert mechanisms (that is, console, pager, remote management station)

Performance capabilities and limitations (that is, analyzing large data sets within a reasonable amount of time)

Reporting capabilities (that is, categorizing and prioritizing events)

Training and learning-curve requirements

It is important to note that deploying a fraud management system will not guarantee minimization of fraud losses unless the deployment of the fraud system has been appropriately planned and implemented. A critical aspect for deploying a fraud management system is to identify requirements for managing and administering the system, along with integrating it into the current infrastructure. Telecommunication service providers purchase fraud management systems without performing proper evaluation, which leads to poor implementation and higher maintenance costs.

Identifying an infrastructure's capabilities and integrating associated control mechanisms in the fraud management plan can help manage and suppress fraud activity. For example, enforcing bandwidth limiting for specific subscribers, performing message inspection to identify suspicious activity, and implementing access control mechanisms (that is, authentication servers, session border controllers, firewalls).

Some large telcos have established fraud management and reduction teams that focus on defining and implementing the company's strategy for fraud management. The team is responsible for defining requirements to manage fraud, coordinating data collection and analysis, and promoting awareness. For smaller organizations, such as enterprise networks, fraud management is an integral responsibility of the security or network engineering team, which may or may not possess the appropriate knowledge and skills to manage fraud and therefore require the help of external subject matter experts. In either case, organizations of all sizes should maintain a mechanism for disseminating information about fraud activity to other organizations through various channels (for example, associations or online forums) or contacting the local and federal law enforcement agencies. This mechanism helps raise awareness and minimize the propagation of fraud activity.

Summary

This chapter discussed VoIP threats, including eavesdropping, masquerading, service disruption, unauthorized access, and fraud, and outlined examples of attacks in each category. Although there can be many ways to carry out an attack (for example, manipulating signaling messages, exploiting a software vulnerability), the attacker's ultimate objective can be categorized under the aforementioned areas. These attacks, along with the discussion of VoIP vulnerabilities in the next chapter, demonstrate the weaknesses that exist in VoIP networks and help you understand the applicability of the protection mechanisms discussed later in this book. Later chapters help you build a foundation for understanding the inner workings of the protection mechanisms, their strengths and weaknesses, and their applicability to addressing security issues in a VoIP environment.

## CHAPTER 4

VoIP Vulnerabilities

Chapter 3, "Threats and Attacks," discussed threats and attacks in VoIP networks, and this chapter focuses on the actual vulnerabilities, meaning the flaws that allow a threat agent to take advantage. When explaining the vulnerabilities, we will again use some example attacks that are the real-life realizations of the more abstract threats. Security vulnerabilities in networks, in devices, and in software are the underlying reason behind security compromises. It is possible for a threat to exist even without vulnerability in the system. The attacks are still always bound to a specific vulnerability, which they exploit. When the vulnerability is fixed, the attack is mitigated. The exploit, or the attack script, would not work anymore. The best way to eliminate security threats is to find and fix the vulnerabilities. This is the ultimate purpose of vulnerability analysis.

Categories of Vulnerabilities

First we need to understand the different categories of vulnerabilities. There is no single best categorization for all the vulnerability assessment purposes, and you might want to create your own grouping that best fits into your own system requirements. Vulnerabilities can be categorized based on different criteria. Therefore, we start by explaining some traditional vulnerability profiles before going deeper into our own VoIP specific categorization.

When the Vulnerabilities Are Created

The simplest categorization is based on the time of introduction of the vulnerability, divided in specific phases of the software development life cycle.[1] The main categories are design flaws, implementation flaws, and configuration flaws. The threats discussed in Chapter 3 can be realized with attacks that exploit vulnerabilities that exist in the following areas:

- **Flaws in the design—protocol design problems and network architectures**
  With regard to network architectures, inadequate security controls include the following:

  –Traffic monitoring, filtering, and management

  –Device and user authentication and authorization

  –Network segmentation

  –Policy-enforcement components

- **Flaws in software implementation—bad-quality software implementations of**
  –Operating system services or functions and other platform service interfaces used for management, administration, provisioning, or operations (for example, SSH, FTP, SNMP, HTTP)

  –Application logic, application interfaces, or application control interfaces (for example, signaling and media SIP, H.323, RTP)

- **System configuration—poor system configuration, including**
  –Default settings

  –Use of poor passwords

  –Lack of auditing and logging

  –Improperly configured network access controls and so on

The following sections discuss vulnerability and attack categories in further detail and provide applicable techniques and methods as examples, and in some cases for demonstration purposes.

---

1. *This was the starting point for the research of the Oulu University Secure Programming Group (OUSPG), since 1996 conducted at the University of Oulu, Finland. Their focus in research was, and still is, implementation-level (that is, programming-related) security flaws and the proactive discovery of those flaws in quality-assurance processes.*

Attack Categories and Security Requirements

A good starting point for vulnerability analysis is understanding attacks and vulnerabilities from a security requirements perspective. There are more than ten basic security principles, including everything from authenticity and nonrepudiation to accountability, but the industry accepted security requirements are confidentiality, integrity, and availability (CIA). Vulnerabilities can be categorized according to these three objectives. This type of categorization can never be a taxonomy because many vulnerabilities can belong to several categories at the same time.[2] A chart that maps attacks with these three security principles is available in Table 4.1. This is based on work by NEC[3] and the University of Colorado,[4] with some modifications.

Table 4-1 Mapping of Attacks Based on Whether They Violate Confidentiality, Integrity, or Availability Goals

Attack Name	Confidentiality	Integrity	Availability
Malformed messages	X[5]	X[6]	X
Message flooding			X
Session teardown			X
Session hijack	X	X	X
RTP SSRC collision		X	X
Forged reception reports		X	X
DHCP impersonation	X	X	X
TFTP impersonation	X	X	X

(continues)

2. *A taxonomy is always unique; like in biology, you cannot be a fish and a mammal at the same time.*

3. *Modified from a presentation at NMRG meeting in 2005 by Saverio Niccolini, Jürgen Quittek, Marcus Brunner, and Martin Stiemerling: "VoIP Security Threat Analysis." NEC, Network Laboratories, Heidelberg. http://www.ibr.cs.tu-bs.de/projects/nmrg/meetings/2005/nancy/voip-sec.pdf*

4. *Shawn McGann, Douglas C. Sicker. "An analysis of security threats and tools in SIP-based VoIP systems." University of Colorado at Boulder. Presented at 2nd VoIP Security Workshop. June 2005. https://www.csialliance.org/news/events/voip/Jun2_session2_pres1_McGann.ppt*

5. *Malformed message attacks enable changing memory structures and the execution of code on the system, enabling total control and stealing of any information, including installation of eavesdropping software. This is why we have added this category, although it was not in the original presentations.*

6. *Malformed messages and buffer-overflow problems were not categorized as integrity problems. We added this because these attacks allow total control of the target system, enabling attacks such as worms and viruses.*

Table 4-1 Mapping of Attacks Based on Whether They Violate Confidentiality, Integrity, or Availability Goals *(continued)*

Attack Name	Confidentiality	Integrity	Availability
Message modification	X	X	X
Replay attack		X	X
Proxy impersonation	X	X	X
False caller ID		X	X
False capabilities		X	X
SPIT		X	X
Eavesdropping	X		
Media injection		X	X
Man in the middle	X	X	X
Key manipulation	X	X	X

CWE Vulnerability Categories

Common Weakness Enumeration (CWE) is a recent academic attempt (first released in March 2006) to create a taxonomy of flaws.[7] It is based on the Common Vulnerabilities and Exposures (CVE) database that has been created during the past several years. CWE forms a dictionary of vulnerabilities. As a starting point to our analysis of VoIP vulnerabilities, a subset of the categories from CWE is explained next. We give a short description of the selected categories with examples of vulnerabilities included in them. We name these categories with CWE-## for later referencing in the related VoIP vulnerability categories.

CWE-01 Insufficient Verification of Data

All data needs to be verified for correctness before processing it further. Lack of data verification can introduce several types of vulnerabilities in the software, and therefore data verification is performed for various purposes. Most important, the integrity of the messages needs to be validated. Validation of the origin and authenticity of the data is also sometimes

---

7. *Common Weakness Enumeration (CWE) is a community-developed dictionary of common software weaknesses hosted by Mitre. http://cwe.mitre.org/*

necessary. The best data-verification measures can be provided through cryptographic tools. Because strong hash algorithms can be too time-consuming, simple checksums will be used because they provide adequate protection from data corruption and random modifications. If you do not check all available integrity checks in data, the software can become prone to attacks that alter data on transit or impersonate valid messages, injecting unexpected data in the streams of data.

A typical mistake is to implement data validation checks into client software. Data verification should never be done in the client software because attackers can circumvent these client-side checks by building their own clients that will not do the validation. If data encoding is needed, for example, it is good to check in the server side that the client has used approved data encoding, or simply reject everything that is not encoded correctly.

The data itself needs to be reviewed even if the data is coming from a trusted source and all the checksums and data-verification algorithms are passed. This is because the attackers will also use correct encodings and checksums in the attack packets. All communication interfaces have rules regarding allowed content. For a simple interface such as a username, the validation rule can be very simple. Verification of data should always be done by "white-list" principle—that is, only a set of approved characters or symbols are accepted. A "black-list" principle would search for restricted characters and deny them, but the problem is that in many communication protocols, there are several ways to describe any character. For example, %20 can be used as an encoded form of the white space character in URLs.

CWE-02 Pointer Issues

Data received from an external source is eventually copied to some location in the memory. Secure programming practices are extremely important when implementing software with programming structures that allow references to memory or other data structures. Insecure handling of memory pointers in C and C++ programming languages creates flaws that enable buffer-overflow attacks. This means that a programming structure is copying data delivered by the attacker directly into memory structures, allowing the attacker to overwrite critical data such as executable areas of the memory.

Similar types of flaws can also exist in other programming languages with data structures such as indices and arrays.

CWE-03 Resource Management Errors

DoS situations take place when the software or service runs out of critical resources. Those resources can be anything from memory, processing power, hard drive, and network sockets. Any modification of these resources can threaten the reliability of the entire system and the integrity of the data.

Programmers have to be cautious when memory is allocated, used, and finally freed. Flaws in these operations enable buffer-overflow attacks and DoS conditions (due to running out of memory resources, or other memory exceptions, during the memory management routine). Another potential attack against memory handling is related to leakage of the data contained in the memory blocks. Memory-related resource management flaws are similar to pointer issues. Any low-level resource-handling issue typically results in a crash.

Besides memory, other resources can also be limited. For example, network sockets are a limited resource in a networked operating system. With only about 65,000 possible available ports for both TCP and UDP, extensive traffic through a networked system can reserve all potential ports. When software reserves (binds) a port, no other software can reserve that resource (thus denying service for the subsequent network requests).

The limits of processing power can be attacked with extensive floods of network traffic. A request should always be more expensive for the client than it is for the server to check the validity of the request. Even with such limitations, however, the attacker can have hundreds of times more bandwidth and processing power to render the system or network useless. A distributed denial-of-service (DDoS) is an example of such an attack.

CWE-04 Race Condition

CWE identifies race conditions as one of the vulnerability categories, although race conditions can also arguably be an attack category. Race conditions can happen with, for example, file handling, signal handlers, switch operations, and certificate-revocation checks. A race condition basically means that in between a validity check of a resource and the time a resource is used, there is a time window during which someone can change the resource. Atomic operations protect against race condition attacks by preventing context switch or access to the resource during the time window when it is open for unprivileged change.

CWE-05 Temporary File Issues

When critical data is stored in a temporary file, it is important to make sure that nobody can access that file. Another attack is enabled when a file is created with a high-priority process and an attacker can abuse the temporary file to elevate his user privileges in the system. This vulnerability is one of the potential causes of race condition attacks.

CWE-06 Password Management

Passwords stored in plain text, weak cryptography, and any recoverable (reversible hash) format enable attackers to harvest passwords. Typical places to store passwords include user databases and configuration files. Empty or preset—sometimes even hard-coded—passwords enable easy compromise of the system. If the password is a hard-coded secret in an embedded device, it can be difficult or even impossible to fix.

CWE-07 Permissions, Privileges, and ACLs

Sometimes it is necessary to limit access to some data or to some resources. Insecure default permissions on objects enable resources to be accessed by unauthorized people. Besides those permissions that are set during the installation process, insecure permissions can also be inherited by newly created objects or by objects copied from external sources. Vulnerabilities from adjusting and assigning permissions during runtime can result in race condition attacks, in which the attacker tries to access the resource before access is restricted (for example, between the creation of the object and the initiation of the privileges). Failure to manage privileges and failure to have audit trails of such changes can result in unnoticed attacks. Failure to drop privileges can create a false sense of security, where the attacker can still regain the higher privileges. In computer science, the principle of least privilege requires that in a particular abstraction layer of a computing environment everyone must be able to access only such information and resources that are necessary to his or her legitimate purpose.[8]

---

8.   Wikipedia. http://en.wikipedia.org/wiki/Principle_of_least_privilege

CWE-08 Cryptographic Errors

Cryptography is a branch of information theory, the mathematical study of information and especially its transmission from place to place in secure manner.[9] Cryptography is not only about encryption. In cryptography, a cryptographic hash function includes certain additional security properties to make it suitable for use as a primitive in various information security applications, such as authentication and message integrity.[10] Proprietary cryptography almost always fails, and reversible hash functions are useless for security use.

The simplest vulnerability in cryptography is using weak encryption for critical data stored on the system or transmitted over the network. Failure to comply with cryptographic standards and failure to use the right steps and initialization vectors for the standards can also make the attempt to encrypt void.

Hash algorithms are frequently used incorrectly. It is important to understand how hash algorithms work. The most commonly used hash algorithms are MD4, MD5, and SHA. An example of generating an SHA hash for a string "password" is shown here:

```
$ echo password | openssl sha
6cd692675e3eb61e2f0a7a31d5911267f33f009b
```

It should also be very difficult to brute force a hash of confidential data. An offline brute-force attack of a hash created with a broken or weak algorithm is always extremely easy to implement and fast to break. The preceding example would break in less than a second using a simple dictionary attack. Cryptographic errors also include flaws in the key management, such as the use of hard-coded cryptographic keys or inadequate authentication during key exchange.

CWE-09 Randomness and Predictability

Using a small space of random values, insufficient entropy, noncryptographic pseudo-random number generators (PRNGs), or weak values for seeding the PRNG typically results in a vulnerable system with predictable

---

9. Wikipedia. *http://en.wikipedia.org/wiki/Cryptography*

10. Wikipedia. *http://en.wikipedia.org/wiki/Cryptographic_hash_function*

or guessable random numbers. Randomness in software is rarely truly random but usually uses pseudo-random algorithms. For example, according to MSDN,[11] the Excel spreadsheet software uses the following iterative algorithm for the RAND function. The first random number is generated with the following equation:

```
random_number=fractional part of (9821 * r + 0.211327), where
r = .5
```

Successive random numbers are generated then based on the earlier random numbers:

```
random_number=fractional part of (9821 * r + 0.211327), where
r = the previous random number
```

For the attackers, it is fairly easy to guess such pseudo-random number sequences.

CWE-10 Authentication Errors

Authentication is used to validate the identity of a user/device. It is also best practice to limit access to functionality that consumes a significant amount of resources. Single-factor authentication, such as relying only on passwords, does not always suffice. The state of the authentication should be kept in the authenticating side and not rely on data assumed immutable. No data in the communications that the user can control and change, such as Ethernet addresses, IP addresses, or domain names, should be used for authentication because spoofing can attack those types of authentication mechanisms. Trusted paths and channels, or alternative names for the same resource, that do not require authentication or that only require simple authentication add the potential that the attacker uses this alternate path/channel to attack.

A sample vulnerability against single-factor password authentication is to allow password guessing by not preventing or limiting multiple failed authentication attempts. Most network-based services allow hundreds of attempts to guess the correct passwords, and local attacks such as breaking stored hashes can be calculated in tens of thousands per second with unlimited parallel calculation possibilities enabled by offline processing.

---

11. *MSDN Article ID 86523. Random Number Generation. http://support.microsoft.com/default.aspx?scid= kb;en-us;86523*

Another example vulnerability is the use of either IP addresses or Ethernet (MAC) addresses for identifying devices. MAC table flooding is one attack against identifying devices based on Ethernet addresses. Although valid users are guaranteed to have unique MAC addresses, an attacker can easily spoof both the MAC addresses in his attacks. A network switch protects from hijacking connections by using an address table that identifies which MAC addresses are located at which physical device port. Similar attacks also apply for packet authentication based on the IP address. ARP flooding and ARP poisoning attacks operate so that these IP address tables that map the addresses to MAC addresses are filled and the spoofed IP address will replace the stored entry in the table. The attack can be combined with a DoS attack. As a result, traffic intended for the valid device is redirected to a different device. This will result in a man-in-the-middle attack. With critical applications, application-level protocols or strong authentication protocols need to be used for authenticating the users and devices. In addition, legacy protocols such as DNS are vulnerable to authentication errors. Without reliable trust built between different servers, proxies, and clients, an attacker can fake responses to DNS clients, replacing the IP address of a domain name in the cache. New revisions of these protocols, such as DNSSEC, aim at correcting these flaws in the protocols.

Reflection, replay, and impersonation attacks are some additional examples of attacking authentication vulnerabilities.

CWE-11 Certificate Issues

This is a subcategory of authentication vulnerabilities. When digital certificates are used,[12] the failure to follow, verify, and validate the chain of trust in the certificates results in the trust of a given resource even if it is not certified by any commonly trusted third party. It is also important to check the references between the certificate and the resource or the origin of the resource. It is essential to verify that the certificate you received is for the data or person you want to check securely. A valid certificate is useless without this connection. A failure to validate the certification expiration date and to check for potential certificate revocation will also create a vulnerability that can be abused by attackers.

---

12. *A digital certificate is a proof of identity issued by a certification authority (CA). It can be issued to a device, service, company, or person. X.509 is a commonly used standard for digital certificates.*

CWE-12 Error Handling

Any failure can result in an error, and that error situation can be processed insecurely. Unexpected return codes from software components, not correctly checking for error conditions, or not processing errors correctly can result in DoS. In addition, if a subcomponent crashes, the software can implement an exception-handling routine, or a watchdog routine, which can make sure that the component is restarted and adequate alerts are issued. Any error condition can always be a sign of a potential attack, and therefore we need to consider what we want to do in case of critical errors. Two strategies for internal failures are "fail open" and "fail closed." Three possible responses are commonly seen when the error is caused by an erroneous input:

- Trying to tolerate the input
- Issuing an error message
- Ignoring the input

A vulnerability is created in error handling by insecurely handling error codes from memory-handling routines. When memory is allocated for new data structures, programmers must carefully check the return codes for any problems, such as out-of-memory situations. Blindly using the allocated memory without validating that the memory allocation was successful is extremely dangerous and can cause vulnerabilities that can be exploited with buffer-overflow attacks.

Another example of misusing error situations is related to password-guessing attacks. A fail-closed result in a password prompter means that if incorrect passwords are tried too many times, the software will deny any further attempts. This is a typical feature implemented to protect from brute-force attacks, but at the same time it can enable the attacker to use this feature to deny service for legitimate users by shutting down their authentication opportunities. Spoofing can enable attackers to fake attacks that seem to be coming from the intended victim and that are targeted at a critical service. A fail-closed mode in perimeter defenses can also result in the system closing its service to the victim.

For a critical service, the decision in a failure is usually fail open, meaning that the system is trying to recover from the error condition. The goal when engineering reliable communication systems is that the software will never crash. One way to ensure this is by using exception-handling routines that catch all possible error conditions and attempt to recover from them. From a security perspective, this does not ensure reliability. The opposite happens if all exceptions, such as pointer exceptions, are caught. An illusion of reliability is created while the memory of the process corrupts quietly. Fail open also enables the attacker to try again, refining his attack until he succeeds in completely penetrating the defenses. One example of this is buffer-overflow attacks. In buffer-overflow attacks, the attacker usually has to try several times to get all the memory addresses correctly, and when he fails the system usually crashes. If he succeeds, the hostile code provided by the attacker will be executed and the attacker can get access to the system.

Error codes from various communication protocols can be used to fingerprint a system and software versions. Error codes can also be used to assist in password brute-force attacks or for enumerating valid user accounts for further attacks against valid users. Error codes can also be used to map the boundary values in a server or to map the available features in the service. A sample indication of triggering a boundary value is the status code received from an Apache Web server when a long request is sent to it, as shown here:[13]

```
HTTP/1.1 414 Request-URI Too Large
Date:Thu, 25 Jan 2007 22:56:38 GMT
Server:Apache/2.0.54 (Fedora)
Content-Length:340
Connection:close
Content-Type:text/html; charset=iso-8859-1
```

Here is another example of mapping available features from the responses to any incomprehensible HTTP methods, again from an Apache Web server:

---

13. *Similar and many other error codes can be discovered when tested with any other Web fuzzing tool. These examples were received from an Apache Web server under test with the Codenomicon HTTP robustness test tool.*

```
HTTP/1.1 501 Method Not Implemented
Date:Thu, 25 Jan 2007 22:56:39 GMT
Server:Apache/2.0.54 (Fedora)
Allow:GET,HEAD,POST,OPTIONS,TRACE
Content-Length:292
Connection:close
Content-Type:text/html; charset=iso-8859-1
```

Web Security Categories from OWASP

The Open Web Application Security Project (OWASP) studies vulnerabilities in Web services and lists the top ten Web-related vulnerabilities with explanations.[14] Whereas CWE has a generic look at vulnerabilities, the OWASP is looking at the vulnerabilities with a very technology-oriented view. Although many of these vulnerabilities might not be directly applicable to VoIP services, there are numerous services provided over Web services and used over the VoIP network. For this reason alone, it is useful to study and understand at least the most critical flaws in Web applications. We have numbered the categories taken from the OWASP Web site with OWASP-## for later referencing when studying the VoIP-related vulnerability categories. Note that these categories are not in the original order, and the categories will change over time.

OWASP-01 Unvalidated Input Parameters

A typical vulnerability in a Web application is created when Web application developers do input sanitation in the client. An attacker bypasses the intended client and sends invalid input parameters to the server, which blindly trusts the data. Server-side implementations should never trust client-side validation for input sanitation, but always treat data as untrustworthy. Both communication entities have to check and validate all data they receive.

OWASP-02 Cross-Site Scripting Flaws

Cross-Site Scripting (XSS) is a security problem created when active content is mixed with media such as Web pages. A user submits an input that

---

14. Open Web Application Security Project (OWASP) Web pages are at www.owasp.org.

is used to create content on the server. This could be, for example, a visitor book in which the user can create content. Instead of writing text only, the attacker can submit a script that will be executed on the visitor's browser. User trust of a familiar portal enables many scripting-based attacks to work, even in browsers of security-critical users, who would never let that script be executed on any other third-party Web portal. In other XSS attacks, a link to a hostile operation is provided and the user is fooled into clicking that with his credentials.

OWASP-03 Injection Flaws

These include SQL and command-injection attacks. Instead of providing normal text and numbers as their parameters to Web forms, the attacker writes simple database and operating system commands in languages such as SQL and scripting languages. When the parameter is passed to the processing script in the server, this malicious piece of SQL is executed, resulting in basically full access to the database or operating system. Any script-based language can be prone to code-injection flaws through if user-provided data is used as a parameter for the executed scripting language.

OWASP-04 Buffer Overflows

Although a limited-size memory location is typically reserved for an input, the attacker can always write an unlimited amount of data. The result is a buffer overflow, where the data provided by the attacker will either overwrite critical memory sections or manipulate other data that follows the memory location. The resulting failure can either crash the system with a DoS attack or overwrite otherwise inaccessible data or even take full control of the victim's computer. Buffer overflows are one of the most common attacks used by worms and viruses to spread from one network-connected machine to another. Buffer overflows can happen in both Web applications and in the used client and server software. Buffer overflow is most commonly used to refer to an attack or to a failure mode.

OWASP-05 Denial of Service

Denial of service (DoS) is a very overloaded term, and typically refers to various attacks and crash-level failure modes. DoS situations can result from basically any flaws in the products that the user can ignite, including DoS from flooding the network perimeters and crash-level quality errors such as buffer-overflow vulnerabilities in software. In a Web environment with millions of users, DoS situations are difficult to protect from because it is very difficult to distinguish malicious traffic from valid Web requests.

OWASP-06 Broken Access Control

In some environments, users are anonymous or can impersonate someone else. A server process, or even an individual service, can run with higher privileges and can access files that other users in the same host or other services should not be able to access.

A directory traversal attack is an example where a file outside the intended Web root is accessed with the privileges of the Web server or the service by asking it to access a file directly in the following fashion:

```
"../../../secret-location/secret-file.db"
```

Another sample vulnerability is if the Web server does not have a user-level access control list (ACL) to see whether a requested file is an accessible file for the authenticated user. In such situations, a user can request files such as include files or server-side script source files. Some files, such as script files, can contain confidential data, such as passwords to database systems or other servers, and the source code should not be accessible by the users.

OWASP-07 Insecure Storage

Critical data such as keys, certificates, and passwords have to be encrypted when stored in databases, files, or memory. Typical mistakes include proprietary or bad usage of encryption algorithms and poor randomness that enables attackers to predict encryption keys.

OWASP-08 Broken Authentication and Session Management

The state of the authentication should always be maintained in the server. When there are millions of simultaneous users, the authentication state is often stored in cryptographically created cookies that only the server can create. It must be impossible for the client to re-create these cookies or to use other means to claim he is authenticated. Encryption should always be used when passwords are sent over the Internet.

OWASP-09 Improper Error Handling

When an error occurs in the operation, it has to be handled according to the requirements set for the service. A common mistake is that the Web server returns the name of the script file, the line where the mistake happened, and even the code itself. This will help the attacker to refine the attack and try again. Although security through obscurity always fails, it is still foolish to give out information about the internals of the service, especially when the software itself is of bad quality and easy to exploit by using this information.

OWASP-10 Insecure Configuration Management

Application developers do not always understand the requirements set by system administrators. Typical flaws include dependence on old Web servers or modules, which might be outdated or insecure. Servers need to be secured to prevent attackers from exploiting known flaws in typical server setups. Default accounts and services must be secured or removed, if not needed. In addition, encryption needs to be set up correctly.

VoIP Categories

In VoIP, we have all the same categories as were presented by CWE and OWASP, but in a different context. VoIP is not as simple an infrastructure as Web services, but depends on many communication services and platforms. Many non-VoIP-related attacks also threaten the VoIP infrastructure. Basically, any client, server, and proxy component has specific vulnerabilities that can be attacked. Later, when application servers are introduced to VoIP, all Web services-related vulnerabilities will apply also to VoIP. We first explain the basic categories of vulnerabilities, with cross-references to the more traditional vulnerability categories covered previously. As noted previously, several categories of vulnerabilities are very closely related. Many threats, attacks, and failure modes are sometimes easily misunderstood as vulnerabilities.

Various security requirements and threats are realized because of different vulnerabilities. Figure 4.1 maps the various types of security threats in VoIP to the basic requirements of CIA and QoS.[15] These and others threats were covered in Chapter 3.

---

15. *These VoIP threat categories and VoIP vulnerability categories are based on a series of VoIP security presentations by Ari Takanen, first presented at IP Voice Meeting 2005, 5-7 April 2005, Lisbon, Portugal. The presentations by Takanen are available at http://www.codenomicon.com/media/white-papers/.*

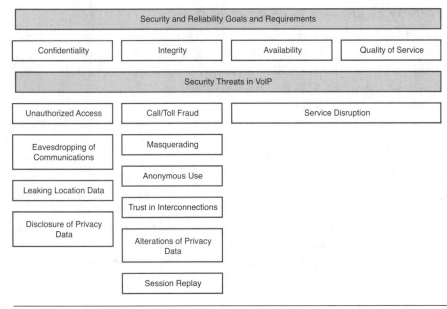

Figure 4.1 VoIP security threats against security and reliability goals and requirements.

Various VoIP design, implementation, and configuration vulnerabilities violate these security requirements. Figure 4.2 lists these, with explanations following later.

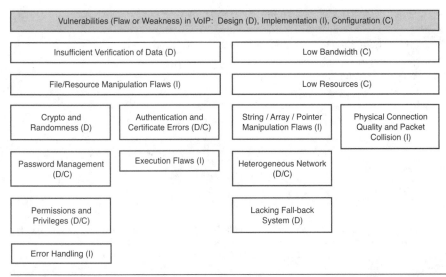

Figure 4.2 VoIP vulnerabilities divided into flaws compromising the confidentiality, integrity, availability, and quality of service.

VOIP-01 Insufficient Verification of Data

This category includes vulnerabilities that could also be categorized under the following classes defined earlier: CWE-01 (Insufficient Verification of Data), OWASP-01 (Unvalidated Input Parameters), and OWASP-02 (Cross-Site Scripting Flaws).

Insufficient verification of data in VoIP implementations enables man-in-the-middle attacks for both signaling and media. The origin and authenticity of data need to be verified when processing messages. Data verification also includes checks for protocol consistency. All inputs from the network should always be considered hostile and need to be validated against approved structures and character sets. Also, attackers can intentionally break encodings to crash the communication software.

An example of a man-in-the-middle attack is related to RTP traffic validation. The security researchers of the Oulu University Secure Programming Group (OUSPG) tried injecting RTP traffic into an existing call without knowing any details of the media traffic.[16] An example RTP packet is shown here:

```
msg-rtp0
 Header
  V: 0b1 0b0
  P: 0b0
  X: 0b0
CC: 0b0 0b0 0b0 0b0
  M: 0b1
  PT
   PCMU: 0b0 0b0 0b0 0b0 0b0 0b0 0b0
  sequence-number: 0x38 0x59
  timestamp: 0x00 0x00 0x00 0x00
  SSRC: 0x00 0x00 0x00 0x01
  CSRC: ()
 Header-Extension: ()
 Payload:
   0x41 0x41 0x3f 0x3f 0x3f 0x3f 0x3f 0x3f 0x3f 0x3f 0x3f 0x3f 0x40
```

---

16. Christian Wieser, Juha Röning, Ari Takanen. "Security analysis and experiments for Voice over IP RTP media streams." 8th International Symposium on Systems and Information Security (SSI'2006). Sao Jose dos Campos, Sao Paulo, Brazil. November 8–10, 2006. Available at www.ee.oulu.fi/research/ouspg/protos/sota/SSI2006-rtp/.

```
0x40 0x40 0x3f
   [...]
   0x40 0x40 0x3f 0x42 0x41 0x41 0x40 0x3f 0x40 0x40 0x41 0x40 0x41
0x40 0x3f 0x40
```

Relevant elements are the sequence number, timestamp, and synchronization source (SSRC). The results of injecting RTP messages into an existing media stream with different values for the validation parameters are detailed in Table 4.2

Table 4-2 RTP Message-Validation Examples

VoIP Phone	SSRC Checked	Timestamp Checked	Sequence Number Checked	Broadcast Rejected	Detects Source Address Change	Detects Source Port Change
#1	No	Partly	Partly	No	No	No
#2	No	No	No	No	No	No
#3	Yes	Partly	Partly	Yes	Yes	Yes
#4	No	No	No	No	No	No
#5	No	No	No	No	No	No
#6	No	No	No	Yes	Yes	Yes

To interpret this table, we can note that implementations #2, #4, and #5 basically had no verification of data, meaning that the attacking media stream sent to them can have any SSRC, timestamp, and sequence number. Because the transport typically is UDP, the data can be broadcast to the network with all phones accepting it as a valid RTP media packet, and the attack can appear to originate from any spoofed domain name, IP address, source port/socket, and MAC address. The injected media would still play on top of the existing phone call by the vulnerable VoIP phone. Also, increasing the SSRC, timestamp, or the sequence number will, with some implementations, replace the original media stream where messages will be appear to be too old for the new media stream.

Another vulnerability of this category is found when signaling messages are broadcast (or multicast) to the network. In SIP, for example, at least INVITE and NOTIFY messages are known to cause annoying situations when broadcast. An INVITE message sent to a broadcast address would make all phones ring in the same broadcast area. Again, if UDP is used as a transport, the message can seem to originate from any source IP address. No broadcast messages should be accepted, especially with signaling messages. Avoiding broadcast attacks can be difficult if the application protocol does not see the IP layer details.

Attackers can attack the VoIP devices with various malformed requests. One single message can disturb the operation of the software by crashing it or forcing it to execute commands or code inserted by the attacker into the messages. Careful input validation is required to prevent this. Sample attacks include boundary value conditions, broken syntax or semantics of the protocol, buffer overflows, and execution attacks. These are covered in more detail in following categories (VOIP-02 and VOIP-03). A good input validation defines a set of allowed characters and structures and verifies that each input element conforms to the requirements and specifications. Blacklisting various attacks always fails because many character sets and encodings can be used to describe different strings of characters.

When VoIP-aware perimeter defenses are used, it is important to understand that few of these products actually validate that the RTP streams contain the media types negotiated in the signaling. In many cases, the perimeter defense, such as the firewall, does not even have access to the content of the media streams. VoIP can therefore also be called EoIP ("Everything over IP"). For example, SIP can be used to signal any media streams, and the payload of those media streams can be desktop sharing, network games, videoconferences, file sharing, and any other data service imaginable. Even many session border controllers do not actually check the entire media stream but perhaps only the initial session to see what is actually being transmitted in the RTP stream. In an enterprise environment, this places even higher importance on only using accepted hardware and software configurations. Nonauthorized devices should not be able to connect to the network.

VOIP-02 Execution Flaws

This category includes vulnerabilities that can also be categorized under OWASP-03 (Injection Flaws), defined earlier.

Standard databases are typically used as the backbone of VoIP services and registrations. Implementation has to be paranoid in filtering out active content such as SQL queries from user-provided data such as usernames, passwords, and SIP URIs. This becomes extremely important with

VoIP middleware solutions and development platforms such as application servers. The majority of problems related to execution flaws result from bad input filtering and insecure programming practices when subroutines are called with tainted parameters.

VOIP-03 String/Array/Pointer Manipulation Flaws

This category includes vulnerabilities that can also be categorized under the following classes defined earlier: CWE-02 (Pointer Issues), CWE-03 (Resource Management Errors), and OWASP-04 (Buffer Overflows).

Malformed packets with unexpected structures and content can exist in any protocol messages, including SIP, H.323, SDP, MGCP, RTP, SRTP, RTCP, TLS, SCTP, H.248, UPnP, RTSP, RSVP, STUN, TURN, DCCP, Sigtran, SigComp, and any other platform-related protocols. Most typical malformed messages include buffer-overflow attacks and other boundary-value conditions. A buffer-overflow attack typically consists of a long string of characters that is copied by the software into a memory location that is too small to store it. The result is that the input given by the attacker is written over other internal memory content, such as registers and pointers, which will enable the attacker to take full control of the vulnerable process. The C programming language is extremely vulnerable to buffer overflows. Good secure programming practices should be used to avoid string-manipulation flaws. With binary protocols such as H.323, the TLV (Type, Length, Value) structures will create another opportunity for array-handling mistakes. When the length element is inconsistent with the actual value of the structure, a buffer overflow can happen.

Examples of buffer overflows in text-based and binary protocols can be found from PROTOS research from the University of Oulu. PROTOS researchers have provided free robustness testing tools for numerous protocols since 1999, including tests for SIP and H.323.[17] One PROTOS test case description in which the SIP method has been replaced with an increasing string of *a* characters is shown here:

```
aaaaaaaaaaaaaaaaa sip:<To> SIP/2.0
Via: SIP/2.0/UDP <From-Address>:<Local-
Port>;branch=z9hG4bK00003<Branch-ID>
```

---

17. For access to the various PROTOS test tools, see www.ee.oulu.fi/research/ouspg/protos/, and for more complete test coverage, see the spin-off company Codenomicon at www.codenomicon.com, which is continuing the development of fuzzing tools for SIP, H.323, MGCP, RTP, H.248, SigComp, and more than 200 other critical interfaces used in VoIP and other communication networks.

```
From: 3 <sip:<From>>;tag=3
To: Receiver <sip:<To>>
Call-ID: <Call-ID>@<From-Address>
CSeq: <CSeq> INVITE
Contact: 3 <sip:<From>>
Expires: 1200
Max-Forwards: 70
Content-Type: application/sdp
Content-Length: <Content-Length>

v=0
o=3 3 3 IN IP4 <From-Address>
s=Session SDP
c=IN IP4 <From-IP>
t=0 0
m=audio 9876 RTP/AVP 0
a=rtpmap:0 PCMU/8000
```

The PROTOS c07-sip-r2 test suite contains more than 4,500 individual test cases that systematically break different header elements of the protocol. Test cases can be configured with command-line options, and some dynamic functionality has been implemented for protocol elements, such as Content-Length, as shown previously. First released in 2002, the PROTOS SIP tests were generated using a proprietary Mini-Simulation technology, which basically is a general-purpose robustness testing platform. Although it is easy to implement millions and millions of semi-random test cases for any communication protocol,[18] the effectiveness of the optimized PROTOS approach has been proven over time. Very few buffer overflow problems in SIP and H.323 have been reported publicly, besides those that PROTOS found. The PROTOS SIP test tool is still actively used by the industry to test any SIP-enabled communication devices.

On the standardization side, the IETF has defined a set of tests for testing different anomalous inputs in SIP[19] and SigComp. IETF calls these test specifications *torture tests*. Many test tools implement these tests, but the test coverage in these specifications is limited. An example test description is shown here:

---

18. *Security testing based on randomness is known as fuzzing.*

19. *R. Sparks et al. RFC 4475, "Session Initiation Protocol (SIP) Torture Test Messages."*

3.1.2.4. Request Scalar Fields with Overlarge Values

This request contains several scalar header field values outside their legal range.

o The CSeq sequence number is >2**32-1.

o The Max-Forwards value is >255.

o The Expires value is >2**32-1.

o The Contact expires parameter value is >2**32-1.

An element receiving this request should respond with a 400 Bad Request due to the CSeq error. If only the Max-Forwards field were in error, the element could choose to process the request as if the field were absent. If only the expiry values were in error, the element could treat them as if they contained the default values for expiration (3600 in this case).
Other scalar request fields that may contain aberrant values include, but are not limited to, the Contact q value, the Timestamp value, and the Via ttl parameter.

As you can see in the preceding example, the IETF approach is rather different from the PROTOS approach. In the torture test suite, the correct responses to error situations are defined, whereas PROTOS ignores the responses and does not try to define the correct behavior under corrupted or hostile situations. The approach of defining the responses to attacks limits the possible test coverage of torture tests.

VOIP-04 Low Resources

This category includes vulnerabilities that can also be categorized under the following classes defined earlier: CWE-03 (Resource Management Errors) and OWASP-05 (Denial of Service).

Especially in embedded devices, the resources that VoIP implementations can use can be scarce. Low memory and processing capability could make it easy for an attacker to shut down VoIP services in embedded devices. An attacker can also send tens of thousands of signaling messages that open media sessions to the target system until no more sockets are available for valid connections. The resulting failure is DoS. The common attack is to reserve or open UDP ports in a gateway by sending a flood of INVITE messages in SIP over UDP and requesting varying port numbers for the RTP streams. SIP over TCP is more difficult to attack because it requires more resources from the attacker and because TCP is challenging to spoof.

VOIP-05 Low Bandwidth

This category includes vulnerabilities that can also be categorized under the OWASP-05 (Denial of Service) class, defined earlier.

A common flaw resulting in DoS is that when implementing the service, or the network architecture, the designers do not take into account that someone might intentionally flood the network with requests to shut down the service. A standard performance limitation in telephony is the so-called Mothers' Day traffic. The service has to be built so that it will withstand the load even if every subscriber makes a call at the same time. While the number of subscribers to a VoIP service is low, this is not a big problem. But when the service is intentionally flooded with thousands of (ro)bot clients, or when there is an incident that results in a huge load by valid subscribers, the result might be a shutdown of the whole service.

Any open communication interface can be flooded. The best targets for flooding are static ports such as 5060 (TCP and UDP) for SIP and port 1720 (TCP) for H.323/H.225 initial signaling. Although RTP has dynamic port numbers, there usually is an implementation listening to every RTP port, especially behind a busy proxy or gateway. A media gateway can be completely driven down with extensive and perhaps even random RTP traffic. Not much can be done to protect from flooding attacks. Perimeter defenses can eliminate some of the simplest attacks, such as repeating or replaying exactly the same simple sequences over and over again, and rejecting connections from hostile clients.[20] Load balancers and QoS techniques can limit the damage and maintain an acceptable service even under heavy attack.

One attack against low bandwidth is flooding a SIP-enabled server or proxy with INVITE messages. Besides reserving extensive resources in processing power and memory to retain all state information, and with the limits in possible open sockets, SIP INVITE flooding can also be easily spoofed and will result in the server or proxy generating more data outward than was sent inward. This can be used for amplification attacks. And

---

20. A *"fail-closed"* solution is often impossible to implement because it could be used for DoS by itself.

when the spoofed originator of the attack and the final destination of the call can be other proxies, the amplification attack can grow into enormous traffic with only a few provoking packets.

VOIP-06 File/Resource Manipulation Flaws

This category includes vulnerabilities that can also be categorized under the following classes defined earlier: CWE-04 (Race Condition) and CWE-05 (Temporary File Issues).

File-manipulation and resource-manipulation flaws are typical implementation mistakes, programming errors from using insecure programming constructs that result in security problems. Several file-handling categories of attacks have been introduced in the past, but when the actual reasons behind these attacks are studied, they can easily be categorized under one single vulnerability category. Almost all race condition flaws are also related to file-handling functions in code. This category of vulnerabilities applies to any file-like resources such as the Windows Registry and file systems, but also to databases.

File- and resource-manipulation flaws include any insecure access to files. For example, file-transfer services for SIP have been proposed,[21] and such file-sharing capabilities are already implemented in multimedia applications such as instant messaging. When the other endpoint can request a file, this has to be implemented carefully; otherwise, an attacker can request any file from the system. Also, when handling temporary files with critical data, such as authentication details for the session, the implementation has to make sure that good protection measures such as encryption and file permissions are used to store that data temporarily.

A code example of a race condition vulnerability with temporary file handling is shown here:

```
if (do_exist("/tmp/tmp-1")) {
exit(-1);
}
f =fopen("/tmp/tmp-1", "w");
fwrite(f, "secret");
/* Do some processing */
fclose(f);
remove_file("/tmp/tmp-1");
```

---

21. M. Isomaki. *Requirements and Possible Mechanisms for File Transfer Services Within the Context of SIP Based Communication*. http://tools.ietf.org/id/draft-isomaki-sipping-file-transfer-01.txt

The problem here is that the existence of the temporary file is checked first, but later it is not verified that the file we actually opened for writing was the same file that was checked. The attacker can create the file or a symbolic link to a file after the validation on first line.

Input validation can also prepare for various file-manipulation flaws. When a string of characters is used in combination with file-manipulation functions in the source code, input-validation algorithms need to carefully verify that only alphanumeric characters are allowed. Special characters like the colon (:) and the slash (/) can have unexpected results when the input is passed to the subroutines. If special characters are required, all special characters should be escaped or encoded before using them in combination with filenames. For example %20 should be used rather than the white-space character in URLs and URIs.

Simple tools for analyzing file-manipulation flaws in Windows environment are FileMon and RegMon from SysInternals.[22] These and similar applications for other platforms monitor the file and Registry access by applications, revealing insecure handling of those resources.

VOIP-07 Password Management

This category includes vulnerabilities that can also be categorized under the CWE-06 (Password Management) class, defined earlier.

User identification in PSTN has traditionally been done when subscribing to a telephone line. In VoIP, users are often anonymous. The only identifier a VoIP consumer has is the telephone number (or SIP URI) and a possible password for the service. The passwords are stored in both the client and server. When a client stores the password, it means that anyone using that device is authenticated as the owner of that device. Also, anyone with access to that device can potentially recover the password from the device. If passwords are saved in the server in a format that can be reversed, anyone with access to that server (or proxy or registrar) can collect the username and password pairs.

When hash functions are used and the passwords are saved in one-way hashes only, you should save those hash files carefully. A common method to break hash algorithms is by brute forcing the hashes by systematically going through all possible passwords and hashing them and comparing those hashes until a match is found.

---

22. *Microsoft acquired SysInternals in July 2006. www.microsoft.com/technet/sysinternals/default.mspx*

VOIP-08 Permissions and Privileges

This category includes CWE-07 (Permissions, Privileges, and ACLs) and OWASP-06 (Broken Access Control).

Resources have to be protected both from the operating system and platform perspective and from the network perspective. Installation of the software has to take the platform file security into consideration to protect confidential material. System auditing should be used to monitor access to critical resources.

VoIP services running on the platform have to consider the privileges they run with. A VoIP service does not necessarily require administrative or "root" privileges to run. A security flaw in such a service would not then endanger all the critical services running on the same platform.

VOIP-09 Crypto and Randomness

This category includes vulnerabilities that can also be categorized under the following classes defined earlier: CWE-08 (Cryptographic Errors), CWE-09 (Randomness and Predictability), and OWASP-07 (Insecure Storage).

In VoIP signaling, we need to handle confidential data that needs to be protected from eavesdropping attacks. Confidential data sent over the network includes authentication data whether it is in the signaling protocols or in DTMF signals,[23] location and privacy related data, and media such as voice. Randomness is required, for example, when setting up port numbers for consequent communications and for setting one-time session keys that are difficult to guess by the attackers.

The most common vulnerability in this category is to fail to encrypt at all, even if the encryption mechanisms are available. Both signaling and media in VoIP are confidential data, and anyone in between the different communication parties can potentially access the data. A simple network analyzer can decode the network packets to reveal the identity and location of recipients and listen in to the conversation.

In addition, when encryption is used, it has to be used carefully to maintain the security brought by encryption. Encryption algorithms are not trivial to implement. Both commercial and open source stacks are available. You should never do any proprietary cryptography; but if you

---

23. *DTMF (Dual Tone Multi Frequency) signals are used to transmit PIN codes and other confidential data (for example, in banking applications).*

need it, a thorough mathematical crypto-analysis is required to prove that the created encryption algorithm is secure.

Key exchange is critical in setting up secure communications. During the first communication attempt, when keys are exchanged and verified, thorough user and device verification is required, and this can sometimes be time-consuming. For example, in H.323, the initial H.225 negotiation is critical because the security parameters for H.245 are negotiated there, and finally the security parameters for the media streams are negotiated in H.245. The entire key-exchange sequence must be solid against third-party eavesdropping

Cryptographic key escrow systems also pose a threat to the communication systems because hard-coded and difficult-to-change escrow keys can be stolen or reverse-engineered. It is close to impossible to have fixed secrets in hardware- or software-based solutions. They can always be recovered from the products and misused to crack all encryption easily with a master key.

With well-deployed cryptography, message integrity can also be guaranteed. In VoIP, many elements in the various messages require protection from modification, whereas some elements in the protocols need to be changeable by network elements such as proxies or firewalls. The integrity of some elements should be guaranteed from end to end, and some elements need protection only hop to hop. Note that encryption without message signing does not ensure message integrity, only the confidentiality. A hop-to-hop encryption using TLS will still enable all devices that have access to the contents to also alter all the content in the messages.

One of the most problematic areas of confidentiality is the protection of calling patterns and other calling behaviors. Access to the message streams can reveal the existence of a call even if the actual media is encrypted. In some locations, any organization that is providing telephony services has to always maintain all call records. This is confidential data and can easily be tracked on the network. This is both a good thing and a bad thing. On the one hand, regulatory requirements can be fulfilled; on the other hand, however, that data will be available for other people who have access to the data network. Usually, the only way all the calling behavioral patterns can be protected is a completely physically or logically separate network for telephony. But, when too much security is added, monitoring of the services becomes difficult.

Chapter 5, "Signaling Protection Mechanisms," and Chapter 7, "Key Management Mechanisms," explore the protective measures on these issues.

VOIP-10 Authentication and Certificate Errors

This category includes vulnerabilities that can also be categorized under the following classes defined earlier: CWE-10 (Authentication Errors), CWE-11 (Certificate Errors), and OWASP-08 (Broken Authentication and Session Management).

Users and devices in VoIP networks need to be authenticated. Also, other services, such as device management, exist in VoIP devices that need user authentication. Most messages transmitted over the network also need to be authenticated if there is a chance that someone can spoof the messages, faking the identity of a valid device/user.

The device itself can have administration accounts that need to be secured. In a vulnerability analysis of numerous VoIP devices, the following authentication vulnerability findings were uncovered:[24]

- Default accounts with default passwords in HTTP and SNMP services
- Inability to change credentials
- Development debug access with no authentication

These types of authentication flaws enable attackers to contact your VoIP device and reconfigure it to use different VoIP proxies and servers and hijack communications or shut down the systems.

Registration hijack in SIP is a flaw in which the registrar system does not authenticate the user or the device, but enables attackers to spoof registration messages and reregister themselves as the valid user.

Another authentication-related attack is a deregistration attack in which spoofed REGISTER messages are used to expire the users' registration by setting the "Expires" element to zero. Yet another authentication vulnerability is a spoofed BYE, CANCEL, or Temporarily Unavailable message to reset the call with SIP signaling or sending an RTCP message

---

24. From a presentation in January 2006 by Shawn Merdinger titled "VoIP WiFi Phone Handset Security Analysis: We've met the enemy ... and they built our stuff?!?" presented at SchmooCon 2006. Available at www.shmoocon.org/2006/presentations/shmoocon_preso_voip_wifi_phone_merdinger.pdf.

to terminate the media flow. Even a simple "Moved Permanently" message can hijack an existing session if no authentication is performed.

Registration and other critical messages in VoIP cannot depend on the IP address or any other easily spoofed mechanism for authentication. The implementation also has to be careful not to elevate the used hashes into passwords; so if a "digest authentication" is used, it must be based on some secret key that the attacker cannot access and must be time-stamped and re-created every time, so that the attacker cannot just replay the packet for the desired effect. This type of vulnerability is easy to test for by capturing and resending authenticated packets. At least all signaling (SIP, H.323) and media control (RTCP) messages should be authenticated because these messages can be used to change the call properties and quality.

One attack against MGCP network elements is to send an MGCP message to the gateway and reconfigure it to start sending signaling and media traffic to a new call agent of your choosing. For example

```
EPCF 1200 *@gw1.whatever.net MGCP 1.0
RED/N: ca1@ca1234.whatever.net
```

The first line indicates that EndPointConfiguration (EPCF) command is used to modify all available endpoints (*=wildcard) on the gateway (gw1.whatever.net). The second line indicates the new call agent to which the control should be transferred. There appears to be no authentication of who can divert calls and where they can be diverted to. This is more of a call agent masquerading attack because you move the control to an unauthorized network element, but the standard (RFC 3991) indicates that this should be done without affecting the state of any calls. In essence, you can selectively divert calls to another host that you have control over. Someone can connect remotely to the MGCP gateway on port 2327 and perform the attack. RFC 3991 discusses the NotifiedEntity MGCP package in detail. The attack shown previously is similar to the MGCP eavesdropping attack, but it is using a different mechanism.

VoIP also depends on security certificates to validate and authenticate service providers and, in some cases, the users of VoIP services. Validation of the chain of trust for the used certificates is essential. These mechanisms are explained in later chapters.

Any password-based system can always be broken into by dictionary or brute-force attacks. In a dictionary attack, a set of passwords is tried based on a collection or "dictionary" of commonly used passwords. In brute-force attacks, all alphanumeric values are tried for passwords. Several incorrect attempts for the password should always trigger alerts or be rejected automatically. Note also that if several password guesses trigger the user account to be locked, the attacker can use this to deny service to valid users by shutting down their accounts. The IP address of the attacker cannot be used as an identifier of the attacker in UDP-based protocols because the attacker can spoof the source address of the attack.

A known method of breaking into a database where there are hundreds of thousands of users is to take a common password and brute force the username because in a large database of users there commonly are at least some users with bad passwords. It will be much more difficult to notice attackers who are doing username guessing because there will not be several tries to any single account, and if UDP is used as the transport, all attacks can come from different IP address. The only protection typically is to prevent users from using simple and easy-to-guess passwords.

In most TLS implementations, digital security certificates are issued to the devices and signed by the organization deploying the signaling/media encryption. Without this process, no authentication is involved with TLS. Both client and server should have valid and authenticated certificates for device or user authentication. Without constant verification of security certificates and monitoring of certificate revocation lists, any attacker can do a man-in-the-middle attack by proxying the encrypted communications.

The Internet is always anonymous. The identity and location of the attackers will be difficult if not impossible to trace. Without the use of certificates, caller IDs can always be forged in Internet-based communications. Caller IDs should never be trusted. However, the same also applies already for any traditional telephony services. Different Internet-based services can already be used to forge any originating telephone number, and short messages (SMS) are already used for phishing attacks. When a call or an instant message is free, it will also be exploited for phishing attacks and telemarketing, and faking or hiding the identity is commonly used.

VOIP-11 Error Handling

This category includes vulnerabilities that can also be categorized under the following classes defined earlier: CWE-12 (Error Handling) and OWASP-10 (Improper Error Handling).

One example of error handling in SIP implementations is how incorrect registration is handled. The error codes from REGISTER messages can be used to scan different usernames or telephone number extensions. A REGISTER message with an invalid telephone number can result in a "404" error code, whereas a valid telephone number would result in a "401" error. This will enable the attacker to narrow down the attack to try a brute-force attack on valid accounts only, or to harvest for valid accounts for SPIT attacks. For example, Asterisk software has been updated so that the system administrator can force the software to always return a "401" error, even if the account does not exist (the "alwaysauthreject" option in sip.conf). Simply refusing traffic from a host brute-forcing user accounts or passwords is not feasible in SIP because UDP can be used to fake the origin of the attack or a proxy can be used in the attack, and both of these would result in denying service to authorized users.[25]

VOIP-12 Homogeneous Network

An unpredicted vulnerability in many network infrastructures is a wide dependence on a limited number of vendor brands and device variants. If the entire network depends on one specific brand of phone, proxy, or firewall, one automated attack such as a virus or worm can shut down the entire network.

VOIP-13 Lacking Fallback System

When the VoIP network is down, as it eventually will be, there has to be backup systems that the users can fall back to. Users of telephony are sometimes very critical concerning the availability of telephony services. Although in many countries cellular phones have already replaced landline communications, and will provide a backup for VoIP, the availability criteria can be much higher than what traditional data network engineering is used to. Even one hour of outage per year can be unacceptable for telephony. Telephony should also work in case of power blackouts. This requires careful planning for the infrastructure.

---

25. *A real attack based on this technique was analyzed in the "Attacks in the wild: brute force password hacking" message thread on the VOIPSEC email list. See www.voipsa.org for the archives.*

VOIP-14 Physical Connection Quality and Packet Collision

Many of the voice-quality issues are related to the quality of the physical connections. Packet loss and distortion in IP connectivity is usually due to bad infrastructure and physical wiring. Wiring and packet infrastructure has to be planned for future traffic. Packet loss should not happen, except in very rare occasions. If you have packet loss in your data infrastructure, you probably are not ready for VoIP. Network latency and jitter should be minimal. All bottlenecks in the communications will immediately be revealed when VoIP is introduced, even if those were not apparent with traditional data communications. VoIP is real time, and the quality of the call will be extremely bad if the network is not adequate for real-time communications.

For a well-designed network infrastructure, packet collision is an extremely rare event and can be handled by the transport layer. Also, for VoIP infrastructures depending on unreliable transport such as UDP, a missing packet or loss of quality might not be discovered. A slight problem in the network infrastructure can cause bad quality in the voice connectivity and sometimes even DoS.

Configuration Management Vulnerabilities in VoIP

The OWASP also focuses on discussing configuration management, which includes many different critical tasks that the system administrators need to ensure are under control, and the feedback loop back to the developers who might not have the latest and most secure platform in their development environment.[26] Servers and clients need to be configured correctly and securely. Default passwords and sample configurations need to be changed. The latest updates and upgrades from device vendors need to be in place, and all changes need to be regression tested prior to deploying them to production networks. In addition, all recent publicly exposed security problems (both vulnerabilities and existing attacks) need to be mitigated until the responsible vendor releases a security update to fix the vulnerability.

Also, all client software requires careful management, and device management is a fast-growing market. In June 2005, Carmi Levy, a senior

---

26. See the OWASP-10 category described earlier in this chapter.

research analyst from the Info-Tech Research Group, said, "VoIP handsets are simply Internet-capable computers disguised as telephones. They are subject to the same security threats as other Web-connected devices. Until the VoIP world gets serious about security, industry growth risks being stunted." All the security problems that plague network devices also apply to any client software. VoIP endpoints are typically running standard operating systems, such as Linux, and are affected by viruses and worms targeting that specific platform. The operating system and the communication software used on the VoIP phones must be regularly updated, and the configuration on those phones needs to be protected from tampering.

Security configuration management and vulnerability management solutions analyze and monitor the network and validate the configuration of client and server software from a security perspective. Configuration management consists of four simple tasks or phases:[27]

- **Identification**—Specifying and identifying all "configuration items," which consist of the hardware, software, documentation, and personnel related to each IT component and system
- **Control**—Management processes and management responsibilities for each configuration item
- **Status**—Maintenance processes and monitoring processes for the development and current status of each configuration item
- **Verification**—Review and audit processes to validate the data in the database

An up-to-date configuration management database will increase the response time to released security updates and enable a fast correction of newly released vulnerabilities.

Approaches to Vulnerability Analysis

Whereas configuration management allows fast reactive practices to mitigate security problems, vulnerability-analysis processes take a proactive approach to finding the root causes in security compromises. In vulnerability analysis, the focus is on identifying the vulnerabilities in the systems.

---

27. *ISO 20000 / BS15000 Directory: Configuration Management. www.bs15000.org.uk/config.htm*

When analyzing vulnerabilities, you start by studying the network and the interfaces. When there is an understanding of the tested systems, it is important to map the used software systems and applications. After understanding the critical components and their exposed communication interfaces that need further analysis, we can study the vulnerability of those systems in more detail.

The easiest method of vulnerability analysis in the enterprise environment is using products called security scanners. Security scanners are automated tools that do many of the vulnerability-analysis techniques explained in more detail below. The problem with security scanners is that they do reactive analysis. They only look for known issues. For VoIP, this means that only after we know real existing vulnerabilities can we implement security scanners to look for these problems. The best-known security scanner is a free tool called Nessus.[28]

For a more proactive approach, it is good to understand how hackers look for vulnerabilities and how they find them. There are several ways to find vulnerabilities depending on whether you have access to the source code or if you have to use black-box methods to find the issues in software.

With access to the source code, vulnerabilities in software are "easy" to find as long as you know what vulnerabilities look like in the code. Auditing code can be done either manually or automatically. Manual review is always the most efficient, as long as the people conducting the auditing are professionals in writing secure code. The use of automated code-auditing tools improves the software development process by automatically looking at the source code during the build process. A code-auditing tool contains, for example, a library of fingerprints and models for finding vulnerable constructs, vulnerable functions, and insecure programming interfaces in source code. The problem with automated code-auditing tools is the number of false positives, findings that the tool thinks are security related but when studied further are revealed not to be security-related problems at all.[29]

When there is no access to source code, we need to study the software through the external interfaces, or by reverse-engineering the software. In

---

28. *Note that Nessus might not be free anymore. See www.nessus.org for the latest status update.*

29. *An example analysis of code-auditing efficiency was written by Robert O'Callahan. Out of the 611 defects and 71 vulnerabilities found by one of the code-auditing tools, the Mozilla developers found only two or three were indeed security flaws. A more complete analysis is available on his blog at http://weblogs.mozillazine.org/roc/ archives/2006/09/static_analysis_and_scary_head.html.*

reverse-engineering, the binary is changed back to something that is close to the source code format that can be analyzed further. But, thorough reverse-engineering is not necessarily needed. It is usually enough to debug or instrument the binary by analyzing its internal operations for anomalous or suspicious behavior.

With black-box testing tools, the communications product is tested without access to the internals of the software. Robustness testing, or negative testing, is a method of analyzing a product from a security perspective. In negative testing, the product is tortured through the communication interfaces by sending corrupt, broken, and hostile messages to the communication software to crash it. This has also been called fuzz-testing or fuzzing, referring to the random nature of tests in many used tools.

The focus of code auditing and robustness testing is to find software vulnerabilities in the source code. The majority of security problems are created during the programming phase, and all possible development tools are used to proactively eliminate these problems during the early phases of the software life cycle. Because the network design and system configuration also create risks to the VoIP infrastructure; however, let's next focus on the flaws in deployment of VoIP.

Human Behavior Vulnerabilities

The final category of vulnerabilities involves the usability aspect of software. In VoIP, people expect that the devices are easy to use and might not consider the security aspects of their actions.

The human factor in communications opens opportunities for exploitation, and these are so called social-engineering vulnerabilities. One example of social engineering is posing as a maintenance person and asking for confidential data. In VoIP, this could include details such as device settings and PIN codes used for authenticating the user. *Dumpster diving* is a term used for searching thrown-away papers and files for confidential data. Any confidential data from the telephony network, including printed customer records and network architecture blueprints, should be handled as confidential information and destroyed when not needed. In addition, disgruntled employees can leak confidential data or destroy critical information.

Both training and physical security can be used as a solution for social-engineering vulnerabilities. The different ways of people actually physically stealing or destroying critical data in VoIP usage scenarios are beyond the scope of this book, but they should be prepared for.

Summary

The enablers of VoIP attacks are the vulnerabilities in software or in the network architecture, or even in how the telephony devices are used. Eliminating the vulnerabilities is the best way to close the security holes in the network. Understanding the different categories of vulnerabilities will make it possible to proactively defend the network by implementing good development practices and integrating adequate security mechanisms into the products and the resulting VoIP networks.

Various categories of vulnerabilities have been created for different communication networks, but they all share similarities that provide important lessons for VoIP technologies. This chapter covered the categorizations based on the phases of software life cycle from design to implementation, and finally to the deployment and network configuration. Another type of categorization is used in the Common Weakness Enumeration (CWE) scheme, and a similar categorization has been created for Web-related vulnerabilities. Learning from both of these, we compiled a simplified categorization of VoIP vulnerabilities, explaining the different types of weaknesses in relation to the other categories.

Configuration management is focused on keeping the different setups and software versions up-to-date. A failure in maintaining a network after it has been deployed will result in a growing number of known open security problems being present in the system. Whereas configuration management is a continuing process of keeping the system updated, vulnerability analysis takes a snapshot look at the security of the system. In vulnerability analysis, the system is thoroughly studied and new vulnerabilities are sought after. The security experts constantly uncover new vulnerabilities, and the vulnerability analysis can either look for these new, known issues or can even take a deeper look and attempt to find new previously unknown issues in the system. A proactive vulnerability assessment can consist of white-box methods, which depend on the availability of the source code, or black-box methods, in which the external interfaces are studied through systematic robustness testing or even random testing such as fuzzing.

Finally, even the most secure communication network can have vulnerabilities through how people use the network and the available services. Similar to how viruses are distributed through email attachments, the applications on VoIP can be exploited by fooling people to accept connections from untrusted sources and by attracting people to services hosted by attackers. If a service advertises something entertaining, such as pink dancing elephants, a majority of people will be curious enough to view that, for example.

SIGNALING PROTECTION MECHANISMS

One of the core issues in VoIP security is protecting the signaling messages being exchanged between participants and components. Signaling messages are used to set up communications, and in order to also exchange and manage cryptographic keys to secure media streams. Signaling messages may traverse networks that maintain security policies of questionable quality and standards, which creates an opportunity for attack. The proper protection of signaling messages plays an important role in defending against threats and attacks, including unauthorized access of the control plane, fraud, eavesdropping, call diversion, and others. Therefore, it is critical to understand the importance of defining a set of fundamental security objectives to protect signaling messages. These security objectives include authenticity, integrity, and confidentiality of the messages. This chapter identifies ways to support these security objectives.

A challenging area for carriers, service providers, and enterprise network owners is vendor support of security protocols to protect VoIP and Internet multimedia communications. For example, adoption of SRTP or TLS with session border controllers is almost nonexistent. In some cases, vendors are reluctant to address the threats and attacks associated with converged networks which results in developing insecure products. So, one of the recommendations of this book to engineers, architects, consultants, and CEOs is "trust but verify."

SIP Protection Mechanisms

Several protocols can be used to provide integrity and confidentiality of SIP signaling (RFC 3261[1]) messages against various attacks. These recommendations include the use of security protocols such as IPSec, S/MIME, TLS, and recently, DTLS. These recommendations have had variable success of industry adoption. Two fundamental measures for adopting security protocols are the ease of implementation and scalability. For example, TLS is preferred by vendors over S/MIME to protect SIP messages because TLS is ubiquitous and requires minimal alterations in software or firmware to support it. However, both have their strengths and weaknesses, as you will see in the next paragraphs.

Typically, when a SIP device such as a SIP hard phone is connected to a SIP network, it goes through the process of obtaining an IP address using DHCP, a configuration file through TFTP (or another similar mechanism) and announcing its availability to receive incoming calls by registering with a SIP registrar. The IP address of the SIP registrar can be discovered using three methods. First is by retrieving a configuration file (for example, retrieved during a TFTP file transfer), second is using the host part of the address of record (for example, sip:user@sip-domain.com) and third is using multicast (for example, sip.mcat.net or 224.0.1.75). The registration process is critical in SIP security. If adversaries can masquerade SIP register requests, they can perform various attacks such as call diversion. Therefore, it is strongly recommended that SIP registrations be authenticated to avoid registration hijacking attacks. In addition, requests to initiate calls (INVITEs) should also be authenticated to provide a level of protection against the initiation of unauthorized calls and DoS or annoyance attacks such as SPIT. The following section discusses authentication for registration and call establishment.

SIP Authentication

SIP uses HTTP digest authentication to provide authentication and replay protection of message requests for registration and session initiation and termination (for example, REGISTER and INVITE). Typically, SIP authentication credentials are meaningful within a specific domain. A

---

1. J. Rosenberg, H., et al. SIP: Session Initiation Protocol. RFC 3261, June 2002.

domain manages credentials of its users but cannot delegate user credentials to other domains unless there is a defined interdomain trust relationship. Figure 5.1 demonstrates a call flow that uses message digest to authenticate a REGISTER request and a subsequent INVITE request to initiate a phone call.

SIP Registration and Call Authentication

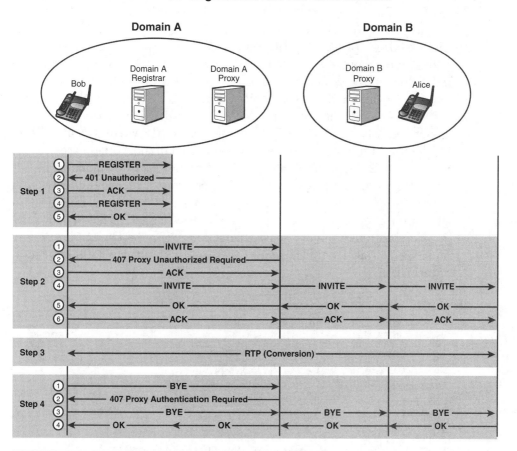

FIGURE 5.1 Authentication of SIP registration and call initiation.

Figure 5.1 demonstrates authentication for device registration, call initiation, and termination. Note that provisional responses, such as 180

Ringing, are omitted for brevity. Note that the device had to authenticate during call initiation (INVITE) in Step 2.1 and during termination (BYE) in Step 4.2.

In Step 1, the SIP phone registers with the local registrar (domain A). During registration (substeps 1–5), the SIP registrar uses challenge-authentication to authenticate the SIP phone by responding with a 401 Unauthorized message (sending a nonce) (Step 1.2) answering the REGISTER request in Step 1.1. The device sends a new REGISTER request (in Step 1.4) that includes the MD5 digest. If the authentication is successful, the registrar updates its internal records to reflect the necessary information about the user and the device (for example, the user's URI, the IP address of the device, and so on) and responds with OK (Step 1.5). The message format and challenge-authentication mechanism is the same for all SIP methods. The only variation is that a 401 Unauthorized message is generated when a REGISTER request is used, whereas a 407 Proxy Authentication Required message is generated in most other cases.

In Step 2, the user initiates a call to another user in domain B. In this step, the local SIP proxy (domain A) performs challenge-authentication before proceeding with the call by sending a 407 Proxy Authentication Required (Step 2.2) message to the initial INVITE (Step 2.1). The following demonstrate the messages exchanged between the UA and proxy.

The initial INVITE request is sent without any authentication information:

```
NVITE sip:alice@domain-b.com:5060 SIP/2.0
Via: SIP/2.0/UDP 192.168.1.3:5060;branch=z9hG4bK-5ef661a9
From: alice<sip:bob@domain-a.com:5060>;tag=aed516f97e1da529o0
To: <sip:alice@domain-b.com:5060>
Call-ID: ceab1739-db25a1e9@192.168.1.3
CSeq: 101 INVITE
Max-Forwards: 70
Contact: bob<sip:bob@192.168.1.3:5060>
Expires: 240
User-Agent: 001217E57E31 Linksys/RT31P2-3.1.6(LI)
Content-Length: 313
Allow: ACK, BYE, CANCEL, INFO, INVITE, NOTIFY, OPTIONS, REFER
Content-Type: application/sdp
```

The local SIP proxy (domain A) challenges the user's device to supply the proper credentials:

```
SIP/2.0 407 Proxy Authentication Required
Via: SIP/2.0/UDP 192.168.1.3:5060;branch=z9hG4bK-5ef661a9
From: bob<sip:bob@domain-a.com:5060>;tag=aed516f97e1da529o0;
To: <sip:alice@domain-b.com:5060>
Call-ID: ceab1739-db25a1e9@192.168.1.3
CSeq: 101 INVITE
Proxy-Authenticate: Digest realm="domain-a.com",
domain="sip:domain-a.com", nonce="969467834", algorithm=MD5
Max-Forwards: 15
Content-Length: 0
```

407 PROXY AUTHENTICATION REQUIRED The local SIP proxy's response contains a Proxy-Authenticate header that includes the realm, domain, nonce, and digest algorithm to be used to generate the challenge response (MD5 in this case):

```
Proxy-Authenticate: Digest realm="domain-a.com",
domain="sip:domain-a.com", nonce="969467834", algorithm=MD5
```

The SIP phone acknowledges the SIP proxy's message by sending an ACK:

```
ACK sip:alice@domain-b.com:5060 SIP/2.0
Via: SIP/2.0/UDP 192.168.1.3:5060;branch=z9hG4bK-5ef661a9
From: bob<sip:bob@domain-a.com:5060>;tag=aed516f97e1da529o0
To: <sip:alice@domain-b.com:5060>
Call-ID: ceab1739-db25a1e9@192.168.1.3
CSeq: 101 ACK
Max-Forwards: 70
Contact: bob<sip:bob@domain-a.com:5060>
User-Agent: 001217E57E31 Linksys/RT31P2-3.1.6(LI)
Content-Length: 0
```

The SIP phone sends a new INVITE request that includes the user's credentials in the Proxy-Authorization header. In addition, the CSeq has been
incremented from 101 to 102 to indicate that this INVITE message
belongs to a new dialogue:

```
INVITE sip:alice@domain-b.com:5060 SIP/2.0
Via: SIP/2.0/UDP 192.168.1.3:5060;branch=z9hG4bK-d04dcaa1
From: bob<sip:bob@domain-a.com:5060>;tag=aed516f97e1da529o0
To: <sip:alice@domain-b.com:5060>
Call-ID: ceab1739-db25a1e9@192.168.1.3
CSeq: 102 INVITE
Max-Forwards: 70
Proxy-Authorization: Digest username="bob",realm="domain-
a.com", nonce="969467834",uri="sip:alice@domain-
b.com:5060",algorithm=MD5,response="72f370515acd0b878bce1e9e788
99ad2"
Contact: bob<sip:bob@domain-a.com:5060>
Expires: 240
User-Agent: 001217E57E31 Linksys/RT31P2-3.1.6(LI)
Content-Length: 313
Allow: ACK, BYE, CANCEL, INFO, INVITE, NOTIFY, OPTIONS, REFER
Content-Type: application/sdp
```

When the remote user picks the phone, her device sends an OK
response:

```
SIP/2.0 200 OK
Via: SIP/2.0/UDP domain-a.com:5060;branch=z9hG4bK-f7bb35c3
Via: SIP/2.0/UDP 192.168.1.3:5060;branch=z9hG4bK-d04dcaa1
From: bob< sip:alice@domain-b.com:5060>;tag=aed516f97e1da529o0;
To: <sip: sip:bob@domain-a.com:5060>;tag=2027561073
Call-ID: ceab1739-db25a1e9@192.168.1.3
CSeq: 102 INVITE
Contact: <sip:alice@domain-b.com:5060>
Max-Forwards: 15
Content-Type: application/sdp
Content-Length:  217
```

At this point, the originating phone completes the session setup by
sending an ACK, which includes the authorization information:

```
ACK sip: alice@domain-b.com:5060 SIP/2.0
Via: SIP/2.0/UDP 192.168.1.3:5060;branch=z9hG4bK-6ee04695
From: bob<sip:bob@domain-a.com;5060>;tag=aed516f97e1da529o0
To: <sip:alice@domain-b.com:5060>;tag=2027561073
Call-ID: ceab1739-db25a1e9@192.168.1.3
CSeq: 102 ACK
Max-Forwards: 70
Proxy-Authorization: Digest username="bob",realm="domain-
a.com",nonce="969467834",uri="sip:alice@domain-
b.com:5060",algorithm=MD5,response="28909c2f5b3f682b2d8bc6a36ab
a572c"
Contact: bob<sip:bob@domain-a.com:5060>
User-Agent: 001217E57E31 Linksys/RT31P2-3.1.6(LI)
Content-Length: 0
```

Note that the RFC does not mandate SIP implementations to challenge an ACK because it does not require a response. In other words, when the SIP proxy receives the ACK, it should not respond with a 407 Proxy Authentication Required message. It is left up to the SIP device that originates the request to reuse the same authorization information used in previous messages.

When the conversation between the two users is completed and they hang up, a BYE message is generated. In our example, the BYE request was originated by Alice and is authenticated by the local proxy (domain A):

```
BYE sip:alice@domain-b.com:5060 SIP/2.0
Via: SIP/2.0/UDP 192.168.1.3:5060;branch=z9hG4bK-304dbcd
From: bob<sip:bob@domain-a.com:5060>;tag=aed516f97e1da529o0
To: <sip:alice@domain-b.com:5060>;tag=2027561073
Call-ID: ceab1739-db25a1e9@192.168.1.3
CSeq: 103 BYE
Max-Forwards: 70
Proxy-Authorization: Digest username="bob",realm="domain-
a.com",nonce="969467834",uri="sip:alice@domain-
b.com:5060",algorithm=MD5,response="96645bfe26e2a5b64803041948b
ba38d"
User-Agent: 001217E57E31 Linksys/RT31P2-3.1.6(LI)
Content-Length: 0
```

In our example, the local SIP proxy for domain A requires the user's device to authenticate the BYE request, and it responds with a 407 Proxy Authentication Required message:

```
SIP/2.0 407 Proxy Authentication Required
Via: SIP/2.0/UDP 192.168.1.3:5060;branch=z9hG4bK-304dbcd
From: bob<sip:bob@domain-a.com:5060>;tag=aed516f97e1da529o0
To: <sip:alice@domain-b.com:5060>;tag=2027561073
Call-ID: ceab1739-db25a1e9@192.168.1.3
CSeq: 103 BYE
Proxy-Authenticate: Digest realm="domain-a.com",
domain="sip:domain-a.com", nonce="35921938", algorithm=MD5
Max-Forwards: 15
Content-Length: 0
```

The user's SIP phone regenerates the BYE message and includes the appropriate authentication information:

```
BYE sip:alice@domain-b.com:5060 SIP/2.0
SIP/2.0/UDP 192.168.1.3:5060;branch=z9hG4bK-1be1b199
From: bob<sip:bob@domain-a.com:5060>;tag=aed516f97e1da529o0
To: <sip:alice@domain-b.com:5060>;tag=2027561073
Call-ID: ceab1739-db25a1e9@192.168.1.3
CSeq: 104 BYE
Max-Forwards: 70
Proxy-Authorization: Digest username="alice",realm="domain-
a.com",nonce="35921938",uri="sip:alice@domain-
b.com:5060",algorithm=MD5,response="f17f737430b236c73121ecf6a10
31518"
User-Agent: 001217E57E31 Linksys/RT31P2-3.1.6(LI)
Content-Length: 0
```

Finally, the remote user's phone responds with an OK message, and the session ends:

```
SIP/2.0 200 OK
Via: SIP/2.0/UDP 192.168.1.3:5060;branch=z9hG4bK-1be1b199
From: bob<sip:bob@domain-a.com:5060>;tag=aed516f97e1da529o0
To: <sip:alice@domain-b.com:5060>;tag=2027561073
Call-ID: ceab1739-db25a1e9@192.168.1.3
CSeq: 104 BYE
Max-Forwards: 15
Content-Length: 0
```

SIP implementations may enforce challenge-authentication at various degrees, which may not provide optimal security. For example, an implementation may authenticate REGISTER requests only, without requiring authentication for INVITEs. Another implementation may require authentication for REGISTER and INVITEs but not for BYE or CANCEL requests. These inconsistencies introduce opportunities for attacks, such as unauthorized call initiation or termination.

To protect against replay or message-masquerading attacks, challenge-authentication should be used for all messages that are intended to create, modify, or terminate a session. Such messages include INVITE, BYE, ACK, and REFER. The SIP RFC 3261 notes that the CANCEL method should not be challenged by proxies because this method cannot be resubmitted. It is left up to the SIP proxy that receives the CANCEL request to verify that the request was originated by a source (for example, SIP proxy) for which there is an associated SIP session. This directive assumes that there is a transport or network layer security association in place, such as IPSec or TLS. This assumption creates an opportunity for abuse in SIP implementations that use UDP as transport and don't use IPSec. If attackers collects the properties of a SIP dialogue (for example, using eavesdropping to collect information such as caller ID, CSeq, branch ID, and tag), they can masquerade a malicious CANCEL request to disrupt the setup of a call. Currently, most products support authentication of SIP INVITE and REGISTER methods but not BYE or CANCEL. Note that there are discussions in IETF to consider the idea of protecting final and provisional responses (for example, 183, 180) that are sent over UDP using cryptographic mechanisms to maintain the integrity of the message.[2] The objective is to protect against masqueraded provisional responses that may impact the state of a SIP session.

The mechanism used to generate a message digest in SIP messages is applied to all SIP messages (for example, REGISTER, INVITE, and so on) and is captured in Figure 5.2.

2. F.Cao. *Response Identity in Session Initiation Protocol, IETF 2006.*

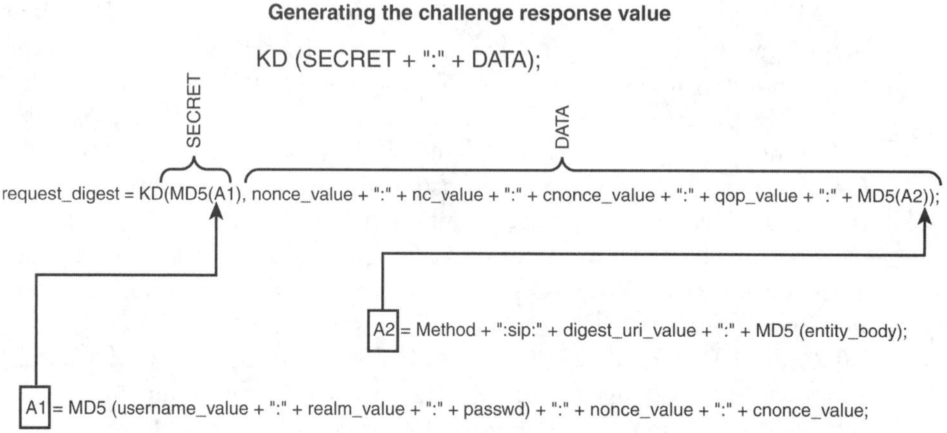

Generating the challenge response value

KD (SECRET + ":" + DATA);

SECRET

DATA

request_digest = KD(MD5(A1), nonce_value + ":" + nc_value + ":" + cnonce_value + ":" + qop_value + ":" + MD5(A2));

A2 = Method + ":sip:" + digest_uri_value + ":" + MD5 (entity_body);

A1 = MD5 (username_value + ":" + realm_value + ":" + passwd) + ":" + nonce_value + ":" + cnonce_value;

FIGURE 5.2 Process for generating the SIP challenge response for SIP authentication.

The purpose for each of the variables displayed is as follows:

- **nonce_value**—A server-specified data string that is uniquely generated each time a request is made.
- **nc_value (nonce count)**—This is a hexadecimal count of the number of requests that the client has sent with the nonce value within a corresponding request. For example, when the client sends the first request in response to a given nonce value, it includes "nc=00000001". The nonce count is required if qpop is used.
- **cnonce_value**—This is an opaque quoted string that is provided by the client and used by both client and server to avoid chosen plaintext attacks and to provide mutual authentication and a level of message-integrity protection
- **qpop_value**—Indicates the quality of protection. Two values are currently defined. See RFC 2617. The value "auth," which indicates authentication, and the value "auth-int", which indicates authentication with integrity protection.
- **A1**—The MD5 digest of username value, realm value, password, nonce value, and cnonce value:

    username_value. The user's name in the specified realm

realm_value. A string that contains the name of the host performing the authentication and the associated domain (for example, sipserver.domain.com)

passwd. The respective user or device password associated with username

nonce_value. See the previous description.

cnonce_value. See the previous description.

- **A2**—The MD5 digest of method, digest URI value, and entity body:

  Method. The SIP method indicated in the corresponding SIP message

  digest_uri_value. The URI from Request-URI of the Request-Line; duplicated here because proxies are allowed to change the Request-Line in transit

  The result is a string of 32 hex characters stored in the Response field of the Proxy-Authorization header, as shown here:

```
Proxy-Authorization: Digest
username="alice",realm="domain-
a.com",nonce="35921938",uri="sip:alice@domain-
b.com:5060",algorithm=MD5,response="f17f737430b236c73121e
cf6a1031518"
```

Although SIP message digest provides a level of protection for INVITE and REGISTER messages exchanged between SIP entities, it does not protect other SIP methods, such as CANCEL, BYE, and provisional or final responses (for example, 486 Busy Here). This weakness can be taken advantage of by an attacker to spoof SIP methods or provisional or final responses to perform an attack. One way to protect against a message or call-flow manipulation attack is to encrypt the signaling messages using a security protocol such as TLS, S/MIME, and IPSec or authenticate SIP responses.

Another area of concern is SIP authentication across domains that may maintain different policies or no policies at all. The question to be answered is "how do we properly authenticate a user from domain A to domain C through domain B?"

Common Pitfalls to Avoid When Implementing SIP Authentication

Although the SIP challenge-authentication mechanism offers protection against replay attacks, several SIP implementations maintain weak properties and may allow someone to replay SIP messages and successfully bypass security controls. To avoid some of these pitfalls, follow these recommendations:

- Generate nonce strings using cryptographic pseudo-random functions.
- Support SIP challenge-authentication for SIP messages that initiate, modify, or terminate a session.
- Avoid caching or reusing user authentication credentials.
- Use network or transport security protocols to protect signaling messages (for example, IPSec, TLS, DTLS, or S/MIME). See also Chapters 8, "VoIP and Network Security Controls," and 9, "A Security Framework for Enterprise VoIP Networks," for additional architectural and configuration security recommendations.

Transport Layer Security

One of the industry-accepted protocols for supporting transport layer confidentiality is TLS. The Transport Layer Security version 1.1 protocol is defined in RFC 4346,[3] and it provides the ability to perform mutual authentication (client and server), confidentiality, and integrity. The protocol is composed of two layers: the TLS Record Protocol and the TLS Handshake Protocol.

The TLS Record Protocol aims to maintain a secure connection between two end points (for example, client and server). The negotiation of the cryptographic properties (for example, cipher suites, encryption keys) for the corresponding connection is performed by the TLS Handshake Protocol, which is encapsulated within the TLS Record Protocol.

---

3. T. Dierks, E. Rescorla, *The Transport Layer Security (TLS) Protocol Version 1.1*, IETF RFC 4346.

The TLS Handshake Protocol is used for mutual client/server authentication and to negotiate cryptographic properties (for example, encryption algorithms and keys) of the respective session. The TLS Handshake has to be completed successfully before transmitting any data. Figure 5.3 shows the TLS client/server handshake.

TLS Handshake

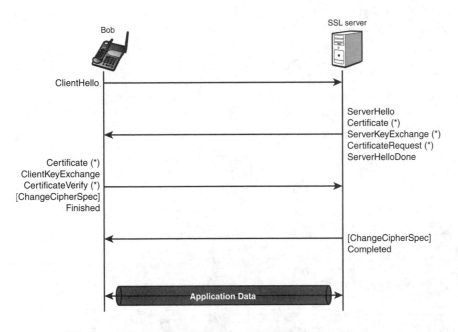

(*) Indicates optional or situation-dependent messages that are not always sent.

FIGURE 5.3 The TLS handshake as defined in RFC 4346.

TLS is designed to be used over a reliable transport such as TCP or SCTP. This introduces a limitation for implementations that use UDP as their transport protocol because TLS cannot be used with UDP to protect SIP messages. Recently, the IETF has published RFC 4347, "Datagram Transport Layer Security," to address this limitation, and it is discussed later in this chapter.

SIP and TLS

SIP RFC recommends the use of TLS to provide the necessary protection against attacks such as eavesdropping, message tampering, message replay, and so on. When users want to place a call and maintain a level of privacy, they can use SIPS URI (secure SIP or SIP over TLS) to guarantee that a secure, encrypted transport is used to protect the signaling messages between the two users. Figure 5.4 demonstrates a simple call flow that uses SIPS. Although the figure does not depict the initial TLS handshake, it is assumed that the SIP messages are exchanged using TLS.

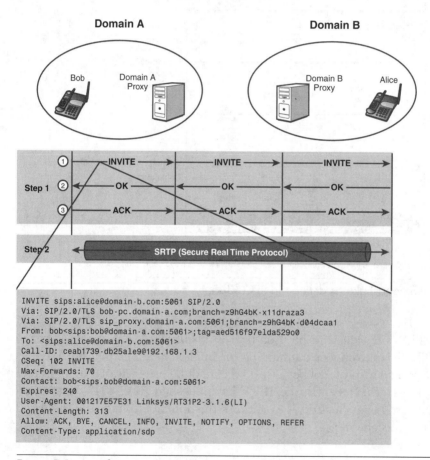

Secure SIP (SIPS)

```
INVITE sips:alice@domain-b.com:5061 SIP/2.0
Via: SIP/2.0/TLS bob-pc.domain-a.com;branch=z9hG4bK-x11draza3
Via: SIP/2.0/TLS sip_proxy.domain-a.com:5061;branch=z9hG4bK-d04dcaa1
From: bob<sips:bob@domain-a.com:5061>;tag=aed516f97elda529o0
To: <sips:alice@domain-b.com:5061>
Call-ID: ceab1739-db25ale9@192.168.1.3
CSeq: 102 INVITE
Max-Forwards: 70
Contact: bob<sips.bob@domain-a.com:5061>
Expires: 240
User-Agent: 001217E57E31 Linksys/RT31P2-3.1.6(LI)
Content-Length: 313
Allow: ACK, BYE, CANCEL, INFO, INVITE, NOTIFY, OPTIONS, REFER
Content-Type: application/sdp
```

FIGURE 5.4 Use of Secure SIP (SIPS).

The SIPS message is similar to a SIP (unencrypted) message that is transported over UDP, TCP, or STCP. The major differences are as follows:

- The URI syntax is defined as sips:alice@domain-b.com.
- The transport is TLS, instead of UDP or TCP.
- The SIPS port is 5061, instead of 5060, which is reserved for UDP and TCP.

When SIPS is used, all SIP messages are transported over TLS, which provides an adequate level of protection against attacks such as eavesdropping, replay, and message manipulation. In addition, TLS provides the means for mutual authentication using certificates to protect against "man-in-the-middle" attacks. The device can authenticate itself to the network, but it can also verify the authenticity of the SIP proxy (or SIP registrar). The recommended cipher suite to be used with SIPS is AES, using a 128-bit key in CBC (Cipher Block Chaining) mode, and the message authentication code is SHA-1 to provide integrity.

Another added benefit of using SIPS is the ability to exchange encryption keys to encrypt the media stream using SRTP (Secure Real Time Protocol). For example, SDescriptions can be used within a SIPS INVITE message to exchange the master key between two participants. The encryption key is provided in the SDP portion of the SIPS INVITE in the a=crypto attribute. Figure 5.5 provides an example.

The SDescriptions is one of the several key-exchange mechanisms currently being discussed in the IETF, including ZRTP and MIKEY. You can find a more detailed discussion about these key-management mechanisms in Chapter 7, "Key Management Mechanisms."

Although TLS provides confidentiality between two end points (client/server relationship), it does not support direct end-to-end confidentiality between two users that are connected through intermediate SIP proxies. For each segment, a distinct TLS connection has to be established. Figure 5.6 demonstrates this relationship.

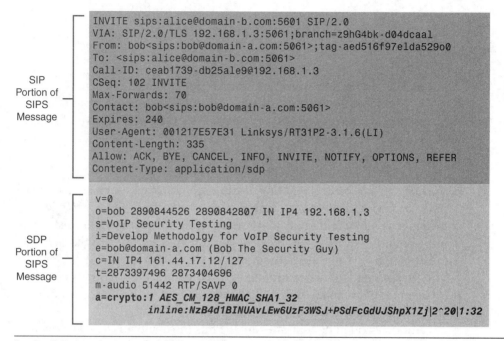

```
INVITE sips:alice@domain-b.com:5601 SIP/2.0
VIA: SIP/2.0/TLS 192.168.1.3:5061;branch=z9hG4bk-d04dcaal
From: bob<sips:bob@domain-a.com:5061>;tag-aed516f97elda529o0
To: <sips:alice@domain-b.com:5061>
Call-ID: ceab1739-db25ale9@192.168.1.3
CSeq: 102 INVITE
Max-Forwards: 70
Contact: bob<sips:bob@domain-a.com:5061>
Expires: 240
User-Agent: 001217E57E31 Linksys/RT31P2-3.1.6(LI)
Content-Length: 335
Allow: ACK, BYE, CANCEL, INFO, INVITE, NOTIFY, OPTIONS, REFER
Content-Type: application/sdp
```

SIP Portion of SIPS Message

```
v=0
o=bob 2890844526 2890842807 IN IP4 192.168.1.3
s=VoIP Security Testing
i=Develop Methodolgy for VoIP Security Testing
e=bob@domain-a.com (Bob The Security Guy)
c=IN IP4 161.44.17.12/127
t=2873397496 2873404696
m-audio 51442 RTP/SAVP 0
a=crypto:1 AES_CM_128_HMAC_SHA1_32
        inline:NzB4d1BINUAvLEw6UzF3WSJ+PSdFcGdUJShpX1Zj|2^20|1:32
```

SDP Portion of SIPS Message

Figure 5.5 SIPS message with the SDescriptions crypto attribute.

SIP and TLS

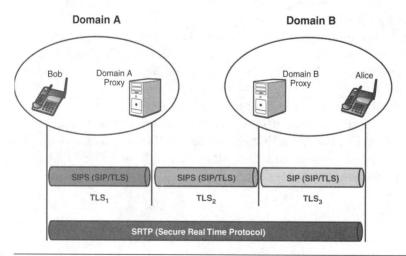

Figure 5.6 SIP message protection using TLS on a per-hop basis.

For this discussion, we refer to a connection between two consecutive components as a *hop*. Although SSL provides adequate protection for SIP messages, it has its limitations. Each intermediate SIP proxy needs to parse the SIP headers to route the message properly, and therefore the SSL connection is terminated and reestablished between hops. For each hop (for example, a connection between Bob and his domain proxy A), there is a distinct SSL connection established, SSL1. This connection may maintain a different security policy (for example, a stronger or weaker cipher suites) from the next hop between domain proxy A and domain proxy B, SSL2. The same can be said for connection SSL3. In some cases, it is not known whether an intermediate SIP proxy that is located beyond the user's domain can support the similar or stronger security policy or even support SSL. This situation can complicate call establishment with various outcomes, including the following:

- The attempt to establish the call may be unsuccessful depending on how the user's security policy is enforced.
- The connection may be established with a weaker strength of cipher suites than the ones defined in the user's policy.
- The connection may be established with no protection between the two proxies at the specific network segment.
- The connection may be established with no protection at all.

Whatever the outcome, the end user most likely may not be aware of the inconsistencies that occur and maintain a false sense of privacy. For example, when placing an international call, it cannot be guaranteed that all intermediate service providers will support SIPS either because of technological limitations or regulatory restrictions. This lack of end-to-end confidentiality will expose the encryption keys that are used with SRTP if key negotiation is established using SIP and not SIPS. On the other hand, the media stream does not need to pass through intermediate components as SIP does, unless it is configured to do so. Instead, a peer-to-peer connection is established, as depicted in Figure 5.6, for which confidentiality is achieved using SRTP.

Strengths and Limitations of Using TLS

TLS provides several features to protect SIP signaling messages and can be used as a mechanism for RTP key exchange. At the same time, some limitations need to be considered to evaluate its effectiveness in a particular environment.

- **Strengths**
  - Supports mutual authentication using certificates.
  - Provides message confidentiality and integrity, which can protect against attacks such as eavesdropping, message tampering, and replay.
  - Ubiquitous presence of SSL provides easier adoption and deployment.
  - It can protect the negotiation of cryptographic keys.
  - Proven protocol, widely used in Internet applications (Web applications, email, VPN).
  - Low performance impact compared to other security protocols such as IPSec.
- **Limitations**
  - Requires a PKI infrastructure to enforce mutual authentication at the SSL layer.
  - Does not provide direct end-to-end confidentiality. It requires the termination and creation of a new session at each hop (for example, between SIP proxies or session border controllers).
  - Can be used with TCP and SCTP but not UDP, which impacts SIP implementations that use UDP. Many SIP implementations in enterprise and carrier networks use solely SIP over UDP.
  - Susceptible to DoS attacks such as TCP floods and RSTs (connection reset). A TCP flood attack aims to consume system resources (for example, CPU cycles) performing RSA decryption. Also, an attacker may generate masquerade RST packets or TLS records to terminate a connection prematurely.

Datagram Transport Layer Security

The Datagram Transport Layer Security protocol, defined in RFC 4347[4], was developed to address the need for providing equivalent protection as TLS to application layer protocols that use UDP as their transport protocol, such as SIP. DTLS is similar to TLS in many ways, including the limitation of requiring a new session establishment between hops to protect SIP messages from one end point to another. One fundamental difference between TLS and DTLS is that DTLS provides a mechanism to handle the unreliability associated with UDP, such as the possibility of packet loss or reordering. If packet loss occurs during a TLS handshake, the connection fails. The TLS Record Layer, where data encryption is performed, requires that records are received and processed in consecutive order. If record n is not received, record $n + 1$ cannot be decrypted because the TLS traffic encryption layer is using CBC (Cipher Block Chaining), which requires knowledge of the previous record to decrypt the next record in the sequence. The latest version of TLS, 1.1, has added explicit CBC state to the records to alleviate this issue.

Another limitation of TLS is that it uses a MAC (Message Authentication Code) for each record to protect against replay and reordering. The MAC is generated using the sequence numbers in the records that are implicit for each record. Therefore, if packet loss is experienced, it renders replay detection useless.

DTLS is designed to overcome the limitations of TLS by providing the following:

- Reliability during the DTLS handshake (packet loss and reordering)
- Packet replay detection

To compensate for packet-loss conditions, DTLS provides a retransmission timer. When a client transmits the ClientHello message, it initiates a timer and waits for a HelloVerifyResponse message from the server. The server also maintains a message transmission timer. If the client's timer expires, he assumes that the either the ClientHello or HelloVerifyResponse was lost and retransmits the ClientHello message. Figure 5.7 depicts the packet-loss and -retransmission scenario.

4. E. Rescorla, N. Modadugu, *Datagram Transport Layer Security*, IETF RFC 4347.

5. SIGNALING PROTECTION MECHANISMS

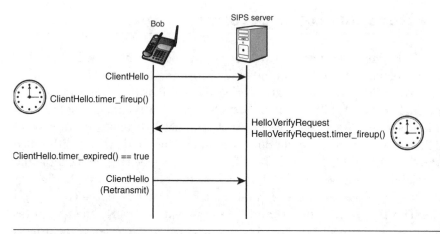

FIGURE 5.7 DTLS packet loss and retransmission.

On the other hand, the server will not retransmit the HelloVerifyResponse message prior to receiving the client's ClientHello retransmission.

For replay detection, the DTLS protocol recommends using a bitmap window of records that the client or server has transmitted, respectively. For example, using a bitmap window of 32 records means that the last 32 records will be processed. Anything prior to 32 records will be discarded, and anything higher will be verified. Figure 5.8 helps clarify this mechanism.

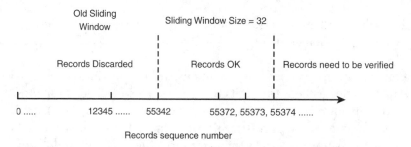

FIGURE 5.8 Protecting record replay attacks using the sliding window mechanism.

The receiver's packet counter is initialized to zero when the session is established, and for each received record, the receiver has to verify whether the record currently inspected is within the window boundaries. The right boundary of the window indicates the highest sequence number of records that has been verified within a session. Records with sequence numbers less than $n + 32$ (left boundary) are discarded.

Although the choice for the size of the window receiver is implementation dependent, the RFC mandates the support of a minimum window value of 32. The sliding window property is optional for implementations per RFC 4347 because packet duplication is not always malicious and can occur because of routing errors.

Another attribute of DTLS is the use of a stateless cookies technique to protect against DoS attacks. During the initial exchange of messages (for example, ClientHello and HelloVerifyRequest), the server includes a cookie in its response to verify that the request originated from the remote client and not from an impersonator. The legitimate client will have to calculate another cookie based on the information received by the server and generate a new ClientHello message that includes the client's cookie. The cookie is calculated using MD5 over a secret value, the client's IP address, and the client's parameters that were received in the ClientHello message. This mechanism helps mitigate against DoS reflection attacks where the attacker uses spoofed IP addresses to flood a victim with server responses.

Strengths and Limitations of DTLS

The DTLS protocol helps alleviate some of the issues associated with multimedia applications, such as early media and forking, while providing protection for signaling and media messages. The following list highlights its strengths and limitations that should be considered during an implementation or evaluation of the effectiveness to use DTLS in a specific environment.

- **Strengths**

  Easier to implement compared to S/MIME and IPSec.

  Inherits proven security properties from TLS.

  Provides mechanisms to compensate for limitations of TLS for handshake reliability and replay detection.

  The use of stateless cookies protects against DoS attacks.

- **Limitations**

  Requires the establishment of a new crypto session between intermediate hops, similar to TLS.

  Requires a PKI infrastructure to enforce mutual authentication.

  Does not provide direct end-to-end confidentiality. It requires the termination and creation of a new session at each hop (for example, between SIP proxies or SBCs).

S/MIME

The Secure/Multipurpose Internet Mail Extensions, defined in RFC 3851,[5] can provide end-to-end confidentiality, integrity, and authentication for application protocols such as SMTP and SIP. MIME defines a set of mechanisms to encode and represent complex message formats such as multimedia attachments (for example, graphics or audio clips) and linguistic characters (for example, Greek, Chinese) within other protocols such as SMTP or SIP. An S/MIME message is based on MIME, but it incorporates PKCS standards to meet its security objectives (for example, PKCS#7 Cryptographic Message Syntax standard, captured in RFC 3852). This combination (MIME and S/MIME) provides a great level of flexibility in supporting the exchange of complex messages along with preserving a set of security objectives, including confidentiality, integrity, and authenticity. At the same time, the ability to provide such granular protection adds a great level of implementation complexity.

S/MIME and SIP

S/MIME can be used to protect the headers of a SIP message, except the Via header, and provide end-to-end confidentiality, integrity, and authentication between participants. Unlike TLS and DTLS, S/MIME provides the flexibility for more granular protection of header information in SIP messages. As discussed in previous sections, TLS and DTLS provide adequate protection for SIP messages, but they encompass the entire message within their structure. S/MIME allows you to selectively protect portions of the SIP message. Furthermore, it can be used with UDP or TCP, which

---

5. *E. B. Ramsdell. S/MIME Version 3 Message Specification. RFC 2633, June 1999.*

overcomes the limitations experienced with IPSec, TLS, and DTLS, and provides end-to-end protection. Figure 5.9 displays a SIP message with an encrypted SDP portion using S/MIME.

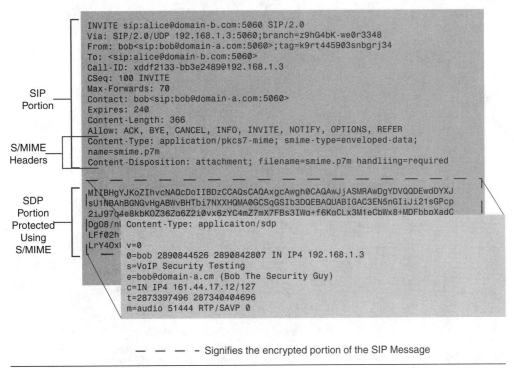

```
INVITE sip:alice@domain-b.com:5060 SIP/2.0
Via: SIP/2.0/UDP 192.168.1.3:5060;branch=z9hG4bK-we0r3348
From: bob<sip:bob@domain-a.com:5060>;tag=k9rt445903snbgrj34
To: <sip:alice@domain-b.com:5060>
Call-ID: xddf2133-bb3e2489@192.168.1.3
CSeq: 100 INVITE
Max-Forwards: 70
Contact: bob<sip:bob@domain-a.com:5060>
Expires: 240
Content-Length: 366
Allow: ACK, BYE, CANCEL, INFO, INVITE, NOTIFY, OPTIONS, REFER
Content-Type: application/pkcs7-mime; smime-type=enveloped-data;
name=smime.p7m
Content-Disposition: attachment; filename=smime.p7m handliing=required
```

SIP Portion

S/MIME Headers

SDP Portion Protected Using S/MIME

```
MIIBHgYJKoZIhvcNAQcDoIIBDzCCAQsCAQAxgcAwgh0CAQAwJjASMRAwDgYDVQQDEwdDYXJ
sU1NBAhBGNGvHgABWvBHTbi7NXXHQMA0GCSqGSIb3DQEBAQUABIGAC3EN5nGIiJi21sGPcp
2iJ97q4e8kbKOZ36Zq6Z2i0vx6zYC4mZ7mX7FBs3IWq+f6KqCLx3M1eCbWx8+MDFbbpXadC
DgO8/nl Content-Type: applicaiton/sdp
LFf02h
LrY4Oxl v=0
        O=bob 2890844526 2890842807 IN IP4 192.168.1.3
        s=VoIP Security Testing
        e=bob@domain-a.cm (Bob The Security Guy)
        c=IN IP4 161.44.17.12/127
        t=2873397496 287340404696
        m=audio 51444 RTP/SAVP 0
```

— — — - Signifies the encrypted portion of the SIP Message

FIGURE 5.9 Protecting SIP contents using S/MIME.

In this example, the SIP message remains the same except for the SDP portion, which is encrypted. This allows end users to protect information about their session, such as the UDP ports used to send and receive media, encryption keys to be used for media streams (for example, using SRTP), and properties about the scope of the session (for example, subject, participants, URLs to other resources, and so on).

Another approach is to encapsulate SIP messages using S/MIME. This provides an added level of privacy for the end user because it allows concealing the identity of the originator and provides a level of anonymity. Figure 5.10 demonstrates this approach.

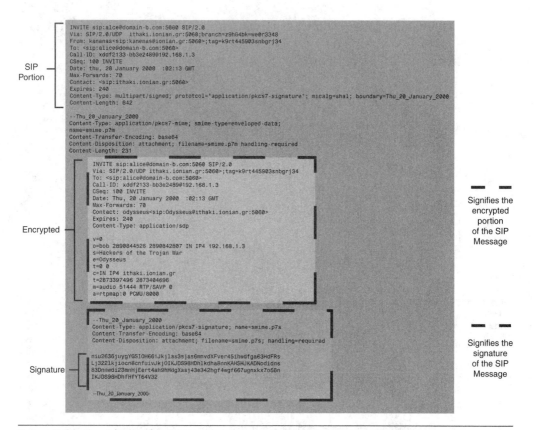

FIGURE 5.10 Providing integrity, anonymity, and confidentiality to SIP messages using S/MIME.

The outer portion of the SIP message contains information (for example, From, To, Contact, Via) that can be used by intermediaries to route the message to its destination. Note that the outer From header contains information that provides anonymity of the true sender of the message (for example, kanenas@ionian.gr). But the encapsulated SIP message contains the true identity of the originator (for example, Odysseus@ithaki.ionian.gr). In addition, the Contact header of the outer portion of the SIP message contains only the domain of the originator but not the exact location. The originator's location is contained in the inner SIP message, which is encrypted.

The recipient decrypts the S/MIME message and uses the value of the inner From field as an index to locate and verify the sender's identity by querying a certificate authority that maintains the remote user's certificate along with the sender's public key. And the integrity of the message can be validated by inspecting the attached signature. Obviously, for the edge devices (for example, hard phones or soft phones) to successfully process SIP messages with S/MIME objects, they have to support S/MIME. Unfortunately, many VoIP phones do not support S/MIME, except for some academic implementations that support S/MIME on soft phones. In addition, a PKI infrastructure is required to support S/MIME functions that require the use of certificates (for example, signing, verification, authentication, nonrepudiation, and so on).

The ability to selectively protect a SIP message overcomes the problem where SIP proxies need to inspect, or in certain cases modify, the SIP message headers to route it, whereas using TLS, DTLS, or IPSec requires terminating the encrypted session between intermediate hops for proxies to extract the contents of the encrypted message and make routing decisions. This allows the end users to achieve end-to-end confidentiality of the signaling messages they exchange.

SIP implementations that use S/MIME should support 3DES for the encryption algorithm and SHA1 as the digital signature algorithm, at a minimum. A recent IETF publication, RFC 3853, disuses the use of AES with S/MIME for SIP implementations. The AES algorithm is much more efficient in cryptographic calculations, and it has been designed to minimize resource consumption, which is ideal for mobile devices. Therefore, it is preferred to implement AES with minimum support of 128-bit keys. RFC 3261, in section 23, provides details about how to implement various protection mechanisms for S/MIME in SIP.

Certificates are a fundamental block for S/MIME to support security objectives such as confidentiality, integrity, and authentication properly. However, the investment and resource requirements needed to deploy a PKI infrastructure to support S/MIME to protect VoIP introduces a challenging proposition for organizations and most likely not one that will have much support.

Strengths and Limitations of S/MIME

The S/MIME protocol provides protection for signaling messages at a much more granular level than other protocols. At the same time, the complexity required to implement S/MIME to protect signaling messages can be a significant factor in limiting its implementations in most environments. The following list summarizes the strengths and limitations of S/MIME.

- **Strengths**

  It is transport independent and can be used with UDP or TCP.

  Provides great flexibility in the way it can protect portions of SIP messages.

  Provides end-to-end confidentiality, integrity, authentication, and nonrepudiation.

- **Limitations**

  Requires more effort to implement because of its complexity and infrastructure requirements (for example, PKI), compared to other protocols such as TLS or DTLS.

  Not widely deployed. Perhaps future developments in computing and network protocols will allow easier integration with existing infrastructures.

  Scalability is questionable because it requires a PKI infrastructure.

IPSec

IPSec[6] is a proven and widely deployed security protocol and provides protection to applications that use UDP or TCP as their transport. IPSec can be used in tunnel or transport mode to protect its payload. Because IPSec is covered extensively elsewhere, we focus only on how it affects SIP in this section. IPSec can provide confidentiality, integrity, and authentication for signaling and media messages by creating secure tunnels between end points. Figure 5.11 demonstrates the use of IPSec in a SIP environment.

---

6. S. Kent and R. Atkinson. *Security Architecture for the Internet Protocol (IPSec). RFC 2401, November 1998.*

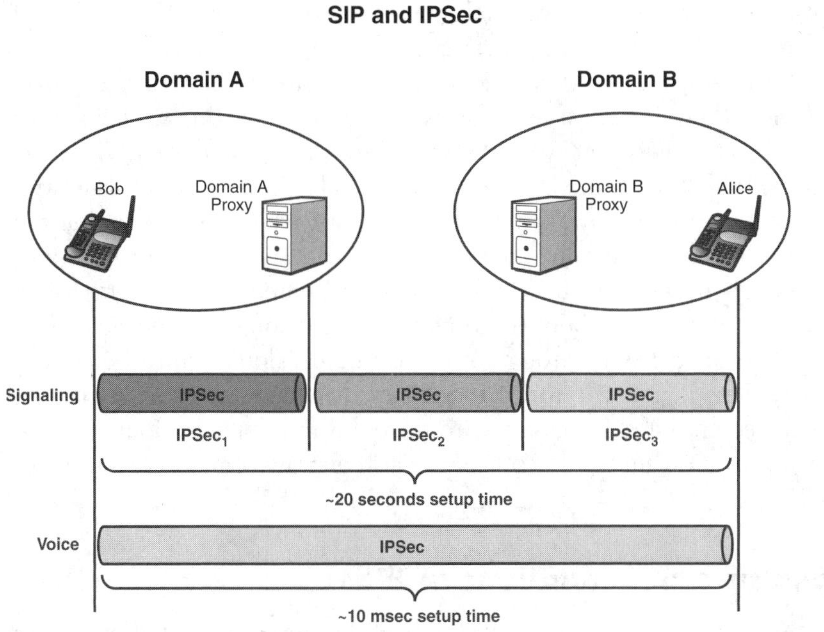

SIP and IPSec

Domain A   **Domain B**

Signaling	IPSec	IPSec	IPSec
	IPSec$_1$	IPSec$_2$	IPSec$_3$

~20 seconds setup time

Voice	IPSec

~10 msec setup time

FIGURE 5.11 Protecting SIP using IPSec.

5. SIGNALING PROTECTION MECHANISMS

In this example, Bob attempts to place a call to Alice. To protect the SIP signaling using IPSec, Bob's phone has to establish an IPSec tunnel with its corresponding SIP proxy (domain A). When the tunnel is established, the SIP proxy parses the message and forwards it to the appropriate destination. Before it sends the message, it has to establish another IPSec tunnel with the corresponding SIP proxy (domain B). When the tunnel is set up, Alice's SIP proxy parses the message and forwards it to Alice's phone. The creation of the three distinct IPSec tunnels may take on average ~2.7 seconds for each IPSec association to be established (approximately 5 to 6 seconds for the entire IPSec tunnel). A research study performed by Telcordia Technologies on behalf of NIST demonstrated that it takes ~20 seconds for a call setup (from Bob to Alice and back) when end-to-end IPSec is used. This is unacceptable because the industry-acceptable elapsed time for call setup should be no greater than 250ms. On the other hand, the media path (RTP) is set up directly between the two end points, and it takes on average ~10 milliseconds, which is negligible. This demonstrates it is not feasible to use IPSec for dynamically allocated sessions because the time it takes for signaling messages to traverse the intermediate hops is far greater than the average time a user will tolerate waiting for the call to be established. If the IPSec associations have already been established, there is almost no delay associated with routing signaling messages, which shows that VoIP over IPSec VPNs is feasible. In some instances, the IPSec tunnels need to be reestablished because of network errors, software or hardware failures, inactivity, or key renegotiation that may impact calls. Generally, however, IPSec can adequately protect VoIP traffic between networks in which the IPSec tunnels are pre-established. Typically, IPSec tunnels between remote sites remain stable because there is always traffic passing through and the tunnels don't expire because of inactivity. This is not true for VoIP phones that may use IPSec to protect the signaling and media messages. To solve this, implementations send frequent registration messages to their local registrar to maintain the IPSec tunnel.

Strengths and Limitations of IPSec

IPSec is effective in providing authentication and confidentiality of messages that carry signaling and media. At the same time, there are limitations that can impact the performance of multimedia communications. The following list summarizes the strengths and limitations of IPSec that should be considered during the design or implementation with a multimedia application:

- **Strengths**

  Proven security protocol and widely deployed

  Operates in the network layer, so it can support UDP, TCP, SIP, and RTP

  Provides string protection against various attacks such as eavesdropping, masquerading, DoS, and others

  Provides confidentiality, integrity, authentication, and nonrepudiation

- **Limitations**

  Requires more effort to implement because of its complexity and infrastructure requirements (for example, PKI), compared to other protocols such as TLS or DTLS.

Requires a PKI infrastructure to support edge-device authentication, integrity, and confidentiality, but not necessarily core VoIP element protection (for example, call manager and voice gateway or site-to-site VPN connection).

Intermediate components must be trusted.

Does not scale well for large distributed networks and distributed applications (for example, conferencing).

H.323 Protection Mechanisms

The H.323[7] is a series of ITU recommendations, from which H.225.0, H.245, and H.235.x are most relevant in our discussion. Recommendation H.225 has two subsets, one of which discusses RAS (registration, admission, and status) and the other call signaling. Call signaling is used between H.323 end points to establish and tear down connections, and it is similar to the ITU Q.931 recommendation. The RAS signaling recommendation is used by gatekeepers to manage end points within its zone. End points must use RAS to register with their corresponding gatekeeper and gain access to network resources and services. One architectural difference between RAS and call signaling is that RAS is transported over UDP, whereas call signaling can be supported over UDP and TCP. Therefore, different attacks are applicable to each with variable degrees of success. The H.245 specification is a control protocol used between two or more end points to manage media streams between session participants. Its main objective is to negotiate media parameters between end points, such as RTP IP address, ports, codecs (for example, G729, G.711), and so on. All three protocols, H.225 call control, RAS, and H.245, are used to establish, modify, and terminate sessions.

The H.235 recommendation discusses security services such as authentication and privacy (data encryption) for H.323 systems that use H.245 and H.225.0 to establish point-to-point or multipoint conferencing. The latest version of H.235 (v4) compartmentalizes the security recommendations into H.235.1 through H.235.9 sections. Earlier versions outlined security controls as Annexes A through F. Table 5.1 provides a listing of each of the recommendations and its corresponding objective.

---

7. *ITU-T Recommendations H.225, H.245, and H.235.0 through H.235.9.*

Table 5-1 H.235 Security Recommendations

Recommendation	Description
H.235.0	Security framework for H series (H.323 and other H.245 based) multimedia systems
H.235.1	Baseline security profile
H.235.2	Signature security profile
H.235.3	Hybrid security profile
H.235.4	Direct and selective routed call security
H.235.5	Security profile for RAS authentication using weak shared secrets
H.235.6	Voice encryption profile with "native" H.235/H.245 key management
H.235.7	MIKEY + SRTP security profile
H.235.8	Key exchange for SRTP on secure signaling channels
H.235.9	Security gateway support for H.323

One of the advantages of H.235 is the ability to incorporate keying material to protect the signaling and media streams through call setup messages. Mutual authentication and key exchange occur prior to the completion of the call setup. A typical H.323 setup using H.235 takes between 300 and 400ms depending on the implementation (H.323 hard phone or soft phone).

The following sections discuss each of the listed recommendations further.

H.235.0 Security Framework

The H.235.0 document defines its scope within H.323 and discusses the overall approach for areas such as RAS signaling procedures for authentication, mobility security, authentication signaling procedures, security error recovery, and so on. Each subrecommendation (1 through 9) is considered a profile of H.235.0.

Signaling protection is accomplished by using TLS (RFC 2246/3546) or IPSec (RFC 2401 using ESP mode). The use of security protocols in the network or transport layer provides the ability to authenticate and authorize calls. The feasibility of implementing IPSec with H.323 varies and depends on the environment and the security requirements. For example, IPSec might not be the appropriate method to authenticate subscribers in a VoIP service provider environment where millions of certificates may be required, whereas TLS can scale better. At the same time, depending on the environment, the H.235 profiles (1 through 9) may be implemented as required. The profiles are negotiated during the exchange of H.323 signaling messages (for example, RRQ message to a gatekeeper) and they are captured in *object identifiers*.

Proper user authentication is a critical component for robust security in any environment, and this includes VoIP using H.323. Authentication in H.235 is performed in three cases:

- During the initial call connection
- In the process of securing the H.245 channel and/or
- By exchanging certificates on the H.245 channel

As mentioned earlier, the authentication can be implemented as part of a network or transport security protocol, but it may be implemented by the H.323 application or service, too, for an added layer of protection. The recommendation discusses the following options for unidirectional or mutual authentication to receive or establish calls:

- Certificate-based authentication is based on using a mechanism for exchanging certificates in order to authenticate the user to the network (not just the device). But it does not specify any verification mechanism, and rather it is left up to the implementor.
- Shared secret authentication, which can be performed using the H225.0 signaling messages, as specified in the recommendation. Shared secret authentication can be established using the Diffie-Hellman key exchange to encrypt and exchange the shared secret.
- Security protocol authentication, using the properties of a separate security protocol such as TLS or IKE.

Authentication is considered the initial milestone in establishing trust between entities in H.323 environments. In addition, any entity that terminates an encrypted control channel or encrypted data channel is considered a *trusted element* of the corresponding connection.

The call control, H.245, should also be protected using one of the negotiated encryption algorithms to protect session information. Session information captured in the H.245 control channel may include encryption algorithms and keys to be used to protect the media stream. The initial negotiation of cryptographic algorithms and distribution of keying material is performed via H.245 using OpenLogicalChannel or OpenLogicalChannelAck messages. Furthermore, rekeying may be accomplished by the following H.245 commands:

- EncryptionUpdateCommand is used by the master to distribute session key material.
- EncryptionUpdateRequest is used by the slave to request a new session key from the master.
- EncryptionUpdate is used by the master to distribute a new session key.
- EncryptionUpdateAck is the slave response to acknowledge a new key.

The distribution of keying material is protected by operating the H.245 channel as a private channel (in band or out of band) or by protecting the keying material using certificates.

H.235.1 Baseline Security Profile

The baseline security profile recommendation provides support for message authentication and integrity of H.245, H.225.0 RAS, and call signaling messages. The integrity for H.225 call signaling and RAS messages is managed by hashing all the fields of the message. The recommendation also provides the option to implement authentication without integrity. This is helpful in cases where signaling messages traverse a NAT (Network Address Translation) device that causes the original message to lose its validity (because the NAT device alters its properties). The challenge-authentication is implemented using a HMAC-SHA1-96 to produce a 20-byte hashed password. The authentication between the end point and its gatekeeper is based on a distinct key, which may be different from the key used to protect call signaling. In some cases, it is required that there be two distinct keys used to protect RAS messages and call signaling messages. There are three ways discussed in the recommendation for which authentication of H.225 call signaling messages can be performed:

- **Gatekeeper routed**—The authentication key to be used by the end points to authenticate messages traverses their corresponding gatekeepers.
- **Direct**—The authentication key to be used by the end points to authenticate messages is conveyed directly between the end points.
- **Mixed**—Both points route the key through one corresponding gatekeeper.

Figure 5.12 provides an example in which the authentication key is exchanged through the corresponding gatekeepers.

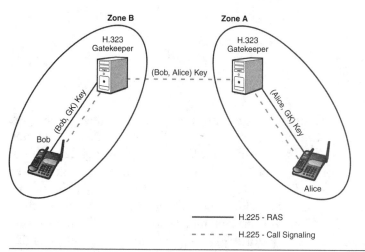

FIGURE 5.12 Gatekeeper routed authentication key.

The initial trust relationship between the end point (Bob's phone and the gatekeeper) is established using authentication through H.225 RAS. When this trust is established, the end point conveys the authentication key to Alice through the intermediate gatekeepers (for zone A and B). This scenario introduces opportunities for attack, especially if the signaling messages traverse other gatekeepers or networks for which security is questionable. To address this weakness, the use of a security protocol such as TLS or IPSec between intermediate hops is recommended.

Figure 5.13 provides an example in which the authentication key is exchanged directly between end points.

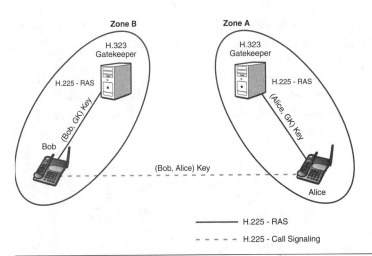

FIGURE 5.13 Directly routed authentication key.

Initially, Bob and Alice register with their corresponding gatekeepers using RAS and a distinct key to authenticate RAS messages. When Bob decides to place a call to Alice, Bob's H.323 device will use H.225 call signaling (Setup message), in which it will include a halfkey value generated using Diffie-Hellman. The halfkey is part of the dhkey field of the ClearToken header. The H.225 (RAS and call signaling) messages capture the authentication and encryption credentials within a more general structure named *cryptoTokens*. Figure 5.14 depicts the format of an H.225 Setup message that uses authentication.

Figure 5.15 provides an example in which the authentication key is exchanged through one of the two gatekeepers (mixed scenario).

The H.235.1 recommendation provides the additional details about how the fields are set in the H.225 messages. In addition, the H.235.1 profile can be used in conjunction with profiles 2 through 7 to provide additional protection of the H.225 and H.245 messages.

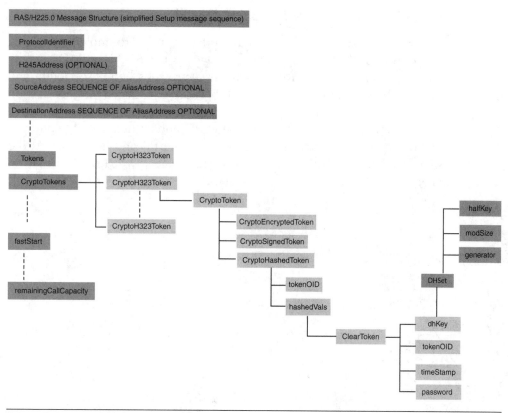

FIGURE 5.14 Simplified H.225.0 Setup message with authentication.

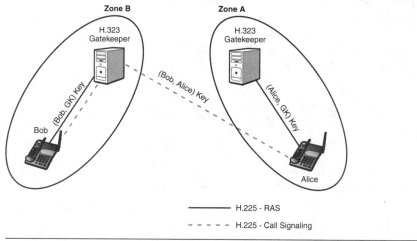

FIGURE 5.15 H.235 mixed mode authentication.

H.235.2 Signature Security Profile

The H.235.2 recommendation is an optional profile to implement digital signatures for H.225.0 signaling messages using SHA1 or MD5 as the hashing algorithm. This recommendation provides better scalability and manageability compared to H.235.1 because asymmetric authentication can be used for environments with many terminals (for example, large enterprise network). In addition to integrity and authentication, nonrepudiation can be supported because the use of certificates is feasible. At the same time, this mechanism can be used to exchange a shared secret key to encrypt RTP traffic (voice or video). Figure 5.16 demonstrates this method.

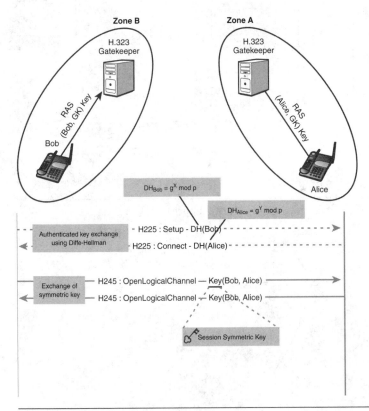

FIGURE **5.16** H.235 shared secret exchange using Diffie-Hellman.

This example demonstrates the negotiation of a shared secret through H.245. When the key is negotiated, it can be used with SRTP (Secure Real Time Protocol) to encrypt the media streams.

The recommendation specifies procedures for the following:

- Digital signatures using public/private key pairs
- Multipoint conferencing
- End-to-end authentication
- Authentication only
- Handling of certificates

These procedures can be used to protect H.225 (RAS and call signaling information) and H.245 messages.

H.235.3 Hybrid Security Profile

The hybrid security profile is using a combination of recommendations from H.235.1 and H.235.2 with the purpose of establishing a scalable profile based on PKI certificates. It combines the strengths from both of these profiles to support a large enterprise-grade VoIP deployment.

This profile mandates the use of a GK-routed model, where all messages are routed through the local gatekeeper instead of transmitting them directly to the end points. To accommodate user mobility and time-sensitive applications, the fast-connect call signaling method is used. Furthermore, it supports tunneling of H.245 call control messages within H.225.0 call signaling messages, which provides inherent security.
The procedures described in H.235.3 include the following:

- Hop-by-hop security (combining H.235.1 clause 7 and procedure II of H.235.2 clause 7).
- Security association for concurrent calls that are established between two entities (for example, conferencing) supports the use of a single key to handle encryption of all streams instead of separate keys.
- Key update to support renewal of keys.

Although this profile provides procedures to scale in large VoIP implementation, it imposes processing overhead through the use of the cryptographic functions on the gatekeeper. To alleviate some of the processing load, a separate Gate Keeper Security Processor (GKSP) is defined. Figure 5.17 depicts this component.

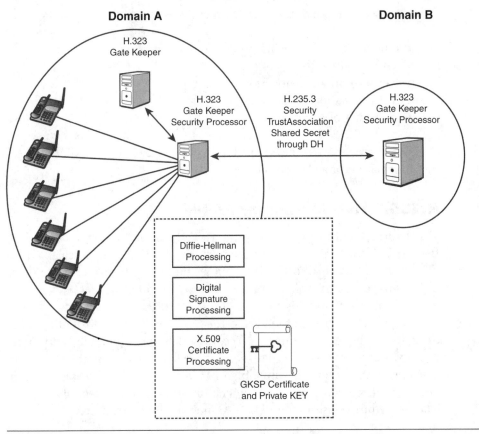

FIGURE 5.17 H.323/235 Gate Keeper Security Processor.

This figure demonstrates a decomposed gatekeeper for domain A, where all the security cryptographic functions such as Diffie-Hellman operations, digital signature computations and verifications, and X.509 certificate processing are performed by the GKSP. The gatekeeper is tasked with processing H.225 (RAS and call signaling) and H.245 messages. This approach is only a recommendation and has not been examined in detail by the ITU in terms of message flows and acceptable variations of the trust relationships required between gatekeepers and Gate Keeper Security Processors.

H.235.4 Directed and Selected Call Routing Security

The directed and selected call routing security profile attempts to provide a flexible alternative to the gatekeeper routed model for improved performance and scalability when handling multiple parallel channels. Figure 5.18 depicts this configuration.

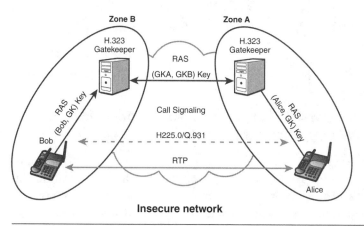

FIGURE 5.18 Directed and selected call routing security topology.

This configuration assumes that the end points are communicating across an insecure network. Each of the end points has established a trust relationship with its corresponding gatekeeper using RAS signaling, and sometimes the two gatekeepers have also established a trust relationship between them using RAS signaling. This relationship allows the two end points to negotiate a shared key across the insecure network to protect call signaling messages and media streams. This is ideal for environments in which direct call establishment is required between end points and the gatekeeper is concentrating on managing registration, admission, address resolution, and bandwidth control. The recommendation provides the following procedures for selected call routing:

- Corporate environment (DRC1)
- Interdomain environment I (DRC2)
- Interdomain environment II (DRC3)

In addition, the recommendation provides the following key derivation procedures:

- PRF-based key-derivation procedure
- FIPS 140-based key-derivation procedure

Both procedures define how to derive key material from the shared secret and other parameters in directed and selected call routing scenarios.

H.235.5 Framework for Secure Authentication in RAS Using Weak Shared Secrets

In certain implementations, the properties of the shared secret (for example, traditional static password) used to establish a trust relationship between two entities (for example, end point and gatekeeper) are not sufficient to withstand attacks that use exhaustive search (brute force).

Recommendation H.235.5 introduces a framework by which an end point and its gatekeeper, or between two gatekeepers, can use the initial RAS messages to negotiate a set of strong shared secrets between them, and use those secrets to encrypt and authenticate selected parts of subsequent RAS and call signaling messages. This method applies to gatekeeper-routed signaling only, not to direct routed signaling.

Two profiles are discussed within the framework:

- Specific security profile (SP1), which is used to construct a shared secret equivalent to an 80-bit random number (see also NIST SP 800-57)
- Improved Security Profile (SP2), which is based on SP1, but among other recommendations it provides improvements to protect against replay and dictionary attacks

The SP2 introduces the use of call signaling sequence numbers to protect against replay and reflection attacks. Although the mechanism does not alleviate this issue completely, it minimizes the chance for a successful attack. Protection against dictionary attacks is achieved by generating a new key that uses the original password and the end pointID as a salt using the following:

```
K = Trunc(SHA1(user_password || end pointID), 16)
```

Where Trunc(SHA1,16) truncates the resultant string of SHA1 to 16 octets.

The recommendation discusses additional extensions to provide additional security for establishing trust relationships and maintaining confidentiality of signaling messages such as using a master key to secure the call signaling channel over TLS and the use of certificates to authenticate the gatekeeper.

H.235.6 Voice Encryption Profile with Native H.235/H.245 Key Management

The voice-encryption profile is used in conjunction with the H.235.0 baseline security profile to provide confidentiality of media streams. The encryption profile is exchanged between the end points as part of the terminal security capability negotiation. It can use various encryption algorithms, including AES, RC2, DES, or 3DES using OFB mode (Output Feed Back mode, ISO/IEC 10116). The negotiation of the encryption algorithms is performed through H.245, where each encryption algorithm can be applied to a specific codec and together form a distinct capability for the end point. This granularity allows end points to scale their communications in large distributed environments with other end points as needed. Another architectural component of the recommendation is the establishment of a master role in which an end point is responsible for generating and promulgating encryption keys. This is especially applicable to a multicast controller for handling multiple channels.

To support mobile and delay-sensitive applications (for example, video, gaming, and voice), the use of fast-connect security is introduced. This is the same as the H.323 fast-connect mode, but it utilizes security mechanisms discussed in this standard to protect the signaling and consequently media messages. The recommendation also discusses encryption of DTMF

(Dual Tone Multi Frequency). Note that DTMF tones in H.323 can be carried within the signaling messages or RTP, whereas in SIP or MGCP implementations, DTMF is carried within RTP. In H.323 implementations, where DTMF tones are carried within RTP (by setting rtpPayloadIndication), it is recommended that the RTP payload also be encrypted because it is trivial to decode DTMF tones from unencrypted RTP traffic.

To exchange keys between H.323 entities, this recommendation provides two key transport mechanisms:

- Simple key transport to support end points with an earlier version of H.323 (version 1 and version 2) using the KeySyncMaterial field.
- Improved key transport to address weaknesses found in the simple key transport method in which the syntax of the KeySyncMaterial field and implementation of the ENCRYPTED operation provide adequate information (for example, the generalID of the master) to launch a brute-force attack.

The fast-start method is used to negotiate security capabilities between end points and establish a shared secret (Diffie-Hellman) at connection initiation. This Diffie-Hellman key is then used as the master key for the secure distribution of a secure key to encrypt the media (RTP) sessions.

VoIP conferencing is an essential application, and protecting it can be challenging because it requires coordination of security capabilities between several participants that may or may not support all necessary security requirements. The H.235.6 recommendation supports authentication in multipoint connections the same way it is established between two end points. For privacy, the multicast controller is the master and the participants are the slaves, so that the master can negotiate security properties, including keys and encryption algorithms as necessary. The media session keys can be protected by the protection mechanism used for H.245, using certificates (using the public key) or using another encryption mechanism, in which case the key is reflected in the sharedSecret field of the H.235 message.

A mechanism offered to mitigate DoS or annoyance attacks against media ports is the implementation of antispamming, in which the receiver authenticates the RTP packets using the message authentication code over specific fields of the RTP packet. The mechanism applies to media streams where packets are not encrypted or they are encrypted. If they are not encrypted, the receiving end calculates the MAC of the RTP header (including sequence number and timestamp) using the negotiated algorithm (in antiSpamAlgorithm field). Figure 5.19 illustrates this notion.

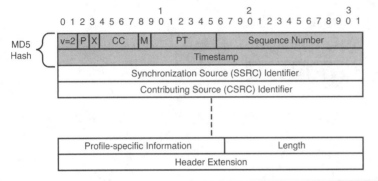

FIGURE 5.19 Example of H.235.6 RTP authentication for antispam.

If the RTP packet is encrypted, the antispam mechanism will have to verify the packet's authenticity prior to decrypting the payload. Although the RTP header is not encrypted, the headers of the audio and video codecs should be encrypted.

H.235.7 Usage of the MIKEY Key Management Protocol for the Secure Real Time Protocol Within H.235

The H.235.7 recommendation discusses the use of MIKEY with SRTP to negotiate encryption keys and protect the media stream. Because these two standards are covered in Chapters 6 and 7, respectively, in more detail, we discuss them only within the context of H.323/H.235.

The recommendation discusses the following two security profiles:

- Symmetric key-based security infrastructure supporting multiple gatekeepers
- Asymmetric key-based security infrastructure (PKI) supporting multiple gatekeepers

Figure 5.20 is a logical depiction of the use of MIKEY within a H.323 environment.

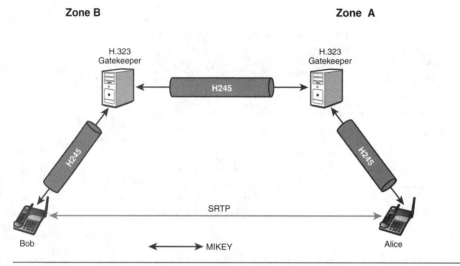

FIGURE 5.20 Use of MIKEY in H.323.

The MIKEY messages are carried within H.245 signaling handshake messages across to the end points, transparent to intermediate gatekeepers. The handshake messages include TerminalCapabilitySet, RequestMode, OpenLogicalChannel, and MiscellaneousCommand.

The MIKEY protocol can be applied at the session level within H.323 (multiple media streams) and media level (a specific logical channel).

In cases where a full-duplex channel is established and consequently the SRTP stream is instantiated twice for each direction, a single master key (TGK) is exchanged between end points.

In addition, the profile provides the ability to negotiate keying material through the use of symmetric and asymmetric techniques. In the case where pre-shared keys are used to support MIKEY, the H.235.1 baseline is implemented between hops, as shown in Figure 5.21.

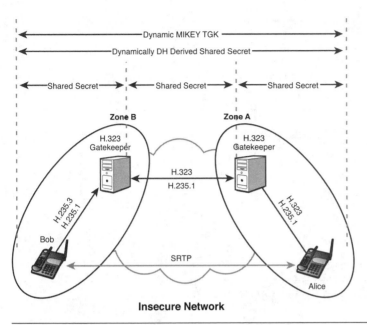

FIGURE 5.21 Use of pre-shared keys to support MIKEY.

In this scenario, a trust relationship has been established using shared secrets between each hop and using the H.235.1 baseline security profile. Although this configuration may be effective for small groups, it is not scalable for communications in large distributed environments. To support communications in large distributed environments, a scalable mechanism must be used that negotiates cryptographic keys dynamically. Figure 5.22 depicts this approach.

This configuration requires the use of a PKI infrastructure to negotiate shared keys dynamically. One important aspect for any key management protocol is time synchronization. The H.235 recommendation assumes that proper clock synchronization is automatically managed by the network.

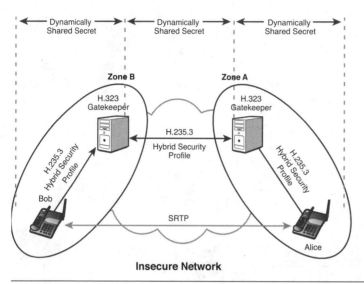

FIGURE 5.22 Dynamically allocated keys to support MIKEY.

H.235.8 Key Exchange for SRTP Using Secure Signaling Channels

The H.235.8 profile provides mechanisms to support key exchange along with authentication and encryption algorithm parameters for SRTP streams between H.323 terminals. The profile focuses on unicast communications and ITU plans to explore options for multicast in the future. The SrtpCryptoCapability field is used to advertise SRTP capabilities that are supported by the H.323 terminal and can be used during the negotiation phase. This subfield is located within the genericH235SecurityCapability field under the encryptionAuthenticationAndIntegrity branch of the H.245 message. The SrtpCryptoCapability contains a subfield SrtpCryptoInfo that contains the crypto-suite and session parameters to be used for the respective multimedia session.

The keying material to be used in SRTP is exchanged through the use of the SRTP crypto parameter SrtpKeyParameters, which is a subfield of SrtpKeys and conveyed through the H.245 OpenLogicalChannel message.

---

8. *Multicast is a mechanism to provide real-time network information to connected hosts.*

The authors of H.235.8 designed the SRTP crypto parameter to be able to establish the SRTP cryptographic parameters in a single message or a single round-trip message exchange. In addition, a single message can be used to exchange the SRTP crypto parameters, thus eliminating the negotiation phase.

For each unicast communication, two unidirectional channels maintain distinct SRTP parameters. For each direction, a distinct H.245 OpenLogicalChannel message is used to establish the SRTP crypto parameters. The originating H.323 terminal sends a crypto-offer to the remote terminal. The offer contains the SrtpCryptoCapability field, which contains one SrtpCryptoInfo structure and one *SrtpKeys* structure with one or more SrtpKeyParameters.

The default cryptographic transforms for H.235.8 are AES in counter mode and are using 128-bit length. The default message authentication code algorithm is SHA1, with either a 80-bit or 32-bit length. In addition, AES f8 is supported with 128-bit key and SHA1 with 80-bit length for UMTS (Universal Mobile Telecommunications System).

H.323 has similar problems to SIP with early media and forking of signaling requests. The problem with early media is that after the initial offer is sent to a remote terminal, the originating terminal may receive media (early media) from the called party's terminal before receiving an answer (for example, because of clipping or delay) about what crypto capabilities are supported by the remote H.323 terminal. Therefore, the originating terminal must be able to handle such a scenario because the originating terminal does not know which key the answerer is using for the media. In this case, the standard recommends using a mechanism such as H.460.11 delayed call establishment procedures. In the case where multiple offers have been generated (forking), the originating terminal does not know which offer was accepted by the answerer until the answer is received. At the same time, media may be received before receiving responses to all the offers. Similarly, a mechanism such as the H.460.11 delayed call establishment procedure should be used.

H.235.9 Security Gateway Support for H.323

The security controls defined in the H.235.x recommendations provide adequate support for protecting against various attacks and establishing secure communications between participants of an H.323 network. Some of the attacks include message manipulation and spoofing, eavesdropping, and SPIT. At the same time, these security controls hamper call flows that traverse network components, such as firewalls or ALGs (application layer gateways), that modify the signaling and media messages being exchanged. H.323 is not the only protocol affected by this condition. Similar issues are associated with SIP signaling, where message transport information such as IP addresses and ports is changed by an intermediate device (for example, NAT; see also Chapter 8's discussion on firewalls and NAT).

These modifications invalidate the integrity and authenticity of the messages, causing authentication and integrity controls to fail in such environments. Therefore, the ITU has introduced the H.235.9 recommendation, which describes ways to alleviate these issues by allowing the security gateway to manipulate signaling and media messages as needed.

Based on the definition of the standard, a security gateway is a "device installed between two or more IP network regions to perform security functions such as the validation or restriction of packet flows and the mapping of transport addresses between network regions."

The security gateway has to establish a trust relationship with the local gatekeeper it serves to receive, process, modify, and forward signaling and media messages. This relationship is established when the security gateway registers with the local gatekeeper. This trust relationship allows the security gateway to gain access to the authentication key negotiated between the gatekeeper and the end point that wants to transmit signaling or media messages. Having access to the authentication key allows the security gateway to manipulate nonprivate data (for example, transport addresses) in the signaling messages and regenerate the authentication information of the message before forwarding it to the destination. Figure 5.23 demonstrates the placement of the security gateway.

The ability to modify properties of security protocols (for example, TLS, IPSec) is vulnerable to bid-down attacks. For example, if an end point is capable of protecting media messages using a variety of mechanisms (for example, DES, AES, none) and properties (key lengths of 64, 128, 192, 256), a rogue security gateway might try to downgrade the length of the key size or request no encryption at all to gain access to the RTP traffic. It is recommended that the local security policy be enforced explicitly without room for deviation for negotiating weaker encryption mechanisms and properties under any conditions.

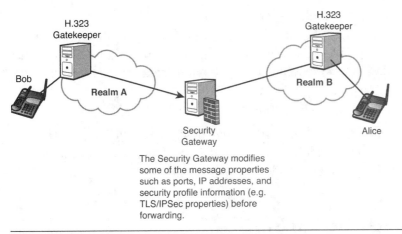

The Security Gateway modifies
some of the message properties
such as ports, IP addresses, and
security profile information (e.g.
TLS/IPSec properties) before
forwarding.

FIGURE 5.23 H.323 security gateway traversal.

In addition, having access to the negotiated key of the end device and the gatekeeper introduces an opportunity for an attack. For example, a rogue security gateway may register with a gatekeeper and use the negotiated authentication key to construct malicious messages by manipulating routing information (IP address, ports, originating phone number) to impersonate a user. Therefore, security gateways should be assigned passwords and follow challenge-response authentication procedures to enforce mutual authentication between the gatekeeper and the registering security gateway and follow the recommendations defined in H.235.1, H.235.2, H.235.3, and H.235.5.

Strengths and Limitations of H.235

H.235 provides several mechanisms to support authentication, confidentiality, and integrity, along with interfacing with key exchange protocols such as MIKEY to support distributed communications. The following list summarizes some of the strengths and limitations of H.235 that can be considered when designing a VoIP network or evaluating a VoIP deployment.

- **Strengths**
  Can provide end-to-end security, depending on the combination of security recommendations (profiles) that are used.

Can support multicast and unicast security.

It can protect against various attacks using combinations of the H.235 profiles, including DoS attacks, man-in-the-middle attacks, replay attacks, spoofing, connection hijacking, and eavesdropping.

- **Limitations**

Doesn't scale well for Internet communications.

Greater level of implementation complexity compared to SIP.

H.235 is not widely implemented, if at all, in products, and interoperability between vendors is questionable.

MGCP Protection Mechanisms

The Media Gateway Control Protocol (RFC 3435) is used by PSTN gateways to set up calls between IP networks or between IP networks and the PSTN. In some cases, the PSTN gateway may be decomposed into a signaling gateway and a media gateway. For our discussion, we will combine signaling and media gateway into one component and refer to it as a PSTN gateway. Figure 5.24 demonstrates the positioning of a PSTN gateway in the network.

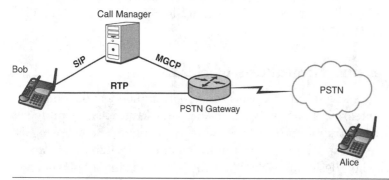

PSTN Gateway Positioning

FIGURE 5.24 Positioning of the PSTN gateway in a converged network.

In this example, the end user establishes a call through the call manager, which in turn instructs the PSTN gateway to allocate a channel for Bob's call. The call manager is responsible for coordinating call setup, modification, and termination between end devices and PSTN gateways. It converts signaling messages between various protocols, including SIP/H.323 and MGCP. After the PSTN gateway allocates the resources, it responds back to the call manager with the corresponding information that Bob's phone needs to use to send its RTP traffic (for example, UDP ports, the IP address of the PSTN gateway, codecs, and so on).

The MGCP protocol does not provide any security controls, but it recommends that security protocols such as IPSec be used to provide the necessary protection. Unfortunately, many vendors (if not all) do not support IPSec with MGCP. Various attacks can be launched against gateways that use MGCP. The openness of MGCP allows various attacks to be launched against a gateway that uses MGCP. An attacker can send signaling messages to disconnect calls, divert RTP packets to another host, or conference themselves into an existing conversation without the knowledge of the participants! These attacks are discussed in detail in Chapter 3, "Threats and Attacks."

Recommendations for Protecting Against MGCP Attacks

The following list provides recommendations that are effective in protecting against attacks on MGCP:

- Enforce network ACLs to restrict access to MGCP ports from unauthorized sources. This will protect against malicious attempts to manipulate existing sessions (see the section "Attacks on MGCP").
- Enforce one-to-one relationships between call managers (or call agents) and the PSTN gateways to exchange MGCP messages.
- If your PSTN gateway supports IPSec, enable it and encrypt traffic between the call managers and the PSTN gateways.

Strengths and Limitations of MGCP

MGCP is being used in many implementations to support signaling for setting up channels between IP and PSTN networks, but it lacks the proper security mechanisms to protect against attacks. The following list summarizes the strengths and limitations that should be considered when deploying MGCP in VoIP networks.

- **Strengths**

  Scalable for enterprise and carrier networks.

  In terms of security, there aren't any strengths other than the recommendation in the standard to use IPSec.

- **Limitations**

  Does not provide authentication, integrity, or confidentiality to protect its messages

  Uses UDP as transport, and therefore several attacks are applicable (for example, message masquerading)

Summary

In this chapter, the most popular signaling protocols were discussed, along with protection mechanisms that can be used to support confidentiality, integrity, and authentication of messages. By implementing these protection mechanisms, the risk is considerably minimized and even alleviated to successfully mount attacks such as eavesdropping, replay, call hijacking, unauthorized network access, and others. One critical aspect of securing a VoIP network is the configuration and implementation of the software that supports signaling and media streams. If a VoIP network is poorly configured and does not use confidentiality, integrity, and authentication for signaling and media messages, it will be vulnerable to attacks that may impact the organization's operations or profile or ultimately its strategic or financial stability. Therefore, designers of VoIP networks should consider developing a set of security requirements that must be supported by the VoIP network. Organizations that have already implemented VoIP should consider evaluating the security posture of their VoIP network to identify weaknesses that may impact operations or other areas of the organization.

## CHAPTER 6

MEDIA PROTECTION MECHANISMS

Any multimedia application—such as video, voice, or gaming—uses a distinct set of protocols to set up sessions between end points (for example, SIP, H.323) and a distinct protocol to transmit the media streams. The standard protocol used to exchange media streams is RTP[1] (Real Time Protocol), which is defined in RFC 3550. As discussed in Chapter 3, "Threats and Attacks," RTP streams can be intercepted and manipulated in order to perform various attacks. Although IPSec can be used to protect RTP, its limitations require a more scalable and versatile solution that alleviates the NAT traversal issue, dynamic allocation of sessions,[2] and the need for a PKI. This has led to the development of SRTP[3] (Secure Real Time Protocol). The use of SRTP requires a mechanism to exchange cryptographic keys before sending any media. Therefore, key management protocols such as MIKEY and SDescriptions[4] have been proposed to provide the necessary keying material and management mechanisms to maintain the security of multimedia sessions. Currently, there is not a single key-exchange mechanism considered to be the industry standard because each has strengths and weaknesses. The most logical approach: to combine SRTP with the appropriate key-exchange mechanism is to identify the requirements that need to be supported by the environment and evaluate the applicability of each of the existing key management mechanisms. Alternatives to using SRTP include DTLS (Datagram Transport Layer Security) and IPSec, which were discussed in Chapter 5, "Signaling Protection Mechanisms." The following sections describe SRTP and discuss its strengths and limitations.

---

1. H. Schulzrinne, et al. "RTP: A Transport Protocol for Real-Time Applications," IETF RFC 3550, July 2003.

2. P. Thermos, T. Bowen, J. Haluska, and Steve Ungar. Using IPSec and Intrusion Detection to protect SIP implanted IP telephony. IEEE GlobeCom, 2004.

3. M. Baugher, D. McGrew, M. Naslund, E. Carrara, and K. Norrman. "The Secure Real-time Transport Protocol (SRTP)," IETF RFC 3711, March 2004.

4. F. Andreasen, M. Baugher, and D. Wing. Session Description Protocol Security Descriptions for Media Streams, IETF draft draft-ietf-mmusic-sdescriptions-12.txt, 2005.

SRTP

The Secure Real Time Protocol (SRTP) is a profile for the Real Time Protocol (RTP, IETF RFC 3550) to provide confidentiality, integrity, and authentication to media streams and is defined in the IETF RFC 3711. Although there are several signaling protocols (for example, SIP, H.323, Skinny) and several key-exchange mechanisms (for example, MIKEY, SDE-SCRIPTIONS, ZRTP), SRTP is considered one of the standard mechanism for protecting real-time media (voice and video) in multimedia applications. In addition to protecting the RTP packets, it provides protection for the RTCP (Real-time Transport Control Protocol) messages. RTCP is used primarily to provide QoS feedback (for example, round-trip delay, jitter, bytes and packets sent) to the participating end points of a session. The RTCP messages are transmitted separately from the RTP messages, and separate ports are used for each of the protocols. Therefore, both RTP and RTCP need to be protected during a multimedia session. If RTCP is left unprotected, an attacker can manipulate the RTCP messages between participants and cause service disruption or perform traffic analysis.

The designers of SRTP focused on developing a protocol that can provide adequate protection for media streams but also maintain key properties to support wired and wireless networks in which bandwidth or underlying transport limitations may exist. Some of the highlighted properties are as follows:

- The ability to incorporate new cryptographic transforms.
- Maintain low bandwidth and computational cost.
- Conservative in the size of implementation code. This is useful for devices with limited memory (for example, cell phones).
- Underlying transport independence, including network and physical layers that may be used, and perhaps prone to reordering and packet loss.

These properties make the implementation of SRTP feasible even for mobile devices that have limited memory and processing capabilities. Similar design properties are found in MIKEY (Multimedia Internet KEYing). Therefore, the use of MIKEY for key exchange and SRTP for media protection is one combination of mechanisms to provide adequate security for Internet multimedia applications, including VoIP, video, and conferencing.

The application that implements SRTP has to convert RTP packets to SRTP packets before sending them across the network. The same process is used in reverse to decrypt SRTP packets and convert them to RTP packets. Figure 6.1 depicts this process.

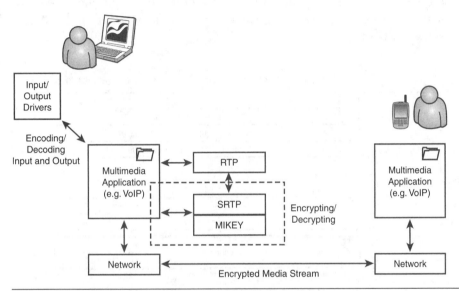

FIGURE 6.1 SRTP encoding/decoding.

After the application captures the input from a device (for example, microphone or camera), it encodes the signal using the negotiated or default encoding standard (for example, G.711, G.729, H.261, H.264) and creates the payload of the RTP packet. Next, the RTP payload is encrypted using the negotiated encryption algorithm. The default encryption algorithm for SRTP is AES (Advanced Encryption Standard) in *counter mode* using a 128-bit key length. This mode, along with the *null* mode,[5] is mandatory for implementations to be considered compliant with the IETF RFC (see RFC 3711 for additional requirements) and interoperate with other implementations. SRTP also recommends the use of AES in f8 mode to encrypt UMTS (Universal Mobile Telecommunications System) data. This mode also uses the same size for the session key and the salt as in counter mode. The use of AES in SRTP allows processing the packets even if they are received out of order, which is a desirable feature for real-time applications.

---

5. *The NULL mode can be used in cases where confidentiality is not desired.*

In addition to providing data encryption, the SRTP standard supports message authentication and integrity of the RTP packet. The default message authentication algorithm is SHA-1 using a 160-bit key length. The message authentication code (MAC) is produced by computing a hash of the entire RTP message, including the RTP headers and encrypted payload, and placing the resulting value in the *Authentication tag* header, as shown in Figure 6.2.

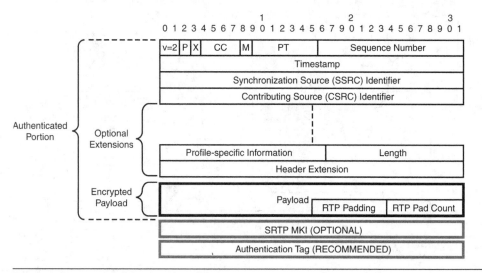

FIGURE 6.2 Format of the SRTP packet.

You might note that the SRTP message resembles the format of an RTP message with the exception of two additional headers: the MKI and the Authentication tag. The *MKI* (Master Key Identifier) is used by the key management mechanism (for example, MIKEY), and its presence is *optional* in implementations according to the SRTP standard (RFC 3711). The MKI can be used for rekeying or to identify the master key from which the session keys were derived to be used by the application to decrypt or verify the authenticity of the associated SRTP payload. The key-exchange mechanism generates and manages the value of this field throughout the lifetime of the session. The use of the Authentication tag header is important and provides protection against message-replay attacks.[6] In VoIP deployments, it

---

6. *J. Bilien, et al. Secure VoIP: Call Establishment and Media Protection. Royal Institute of Technology (KTH). Stockholm, Sweden, 2004.*

is recommended that message authentication be used at a minimum if encryption is not an option. Use of both is the optimal approach.

Note that the message headers are purposefully not encrypted (for example, sequence number, SSRC) to support header compression and interoperate with applications or intermediate network elements that might not be required to support SRTP but need to process the RTP headers (for example, billing). This limitation allows an attacker to perform traffic analysis by collecting information from the RTP headers and extensions, along with information from underlying transports (for example, IP, UDP). One area of interest is the future protocol extensions that will be developed for RTP and the sensitivity of the information that these extensions will carry.

Figure 6.3 shows an example of an application using SDescriptions (Security Descriptions) to transmit a cryptographic key for use with SRTP. The key is transmitted within the SDP portion of a SIP message. The SDP media attribute *crypto* defines the type of algorithm, the encryption mode, and the key length (AES_CM_128), along with the message digest algorithm and its length (SHA1_32).

```
SIP ⎧ INVITE ???: 5500@192.168.1.4:1707;line=ojn9itpa SIP/2.0
     │ ???: <SIP:192.168.1.60;ftag=xtt0pauad4;lr=on>
     │ Via: SIP/2.0/UDP 192.168.1.60;branch=z9hG4bKbd57.6311a6e7.0
     │ Via: SIP/2.0/UPD 192.168.15:3541;branch=z9hG4bK-cq11r2dqkncf;rport=3541
     │ From: "bruce" <sip:5500@192.168.1.60>;tag=xtt0paud4
     │ To: <sip:5500@192.168.1.60;user=phone>
     │ Call-ID: 7ce72e440287-zk8qfd509xr7@snomSoft-00413FFFFFF
     │ CSeq: 1 INVITE
     │ Max-Forwards: 16
     │ Contact: <sip:5501@192.168.1.5:3541;line=ojn9itpa>;flow-id=1
     │ P-Key-Flags: resolution="31x13", keys="4"
     │ User-Agent: snomSoft/5.3
     │ Accept: application/sdp
     │ Allow: INVITE, ACK, CANCEL, BYE, REFER, OPTIONS, NOTIFY, SUBSCRIBE, PRACK, MESSAGE, INFO
     │ Allow-Events: talk, hold, refer
     │ Supported: timer, 100 rel, replaces, callerid
     │ Session-Expires: 3600;refresher=uas
     │ Content-Type: application/sdp
     │ Content=Length: 362
     ⎩ P-hint: usrloc applied
```

```
SDP ⎧ Session Description Protocol Version (v): 0
     │ Owner/Creator, Session Id (o): root 28476 28476 IN IP4 192.168.1.5       SDESCRIPTIONS header
     │ Session Name (s): call
     │ Connect Information (c): IN IP4 192.168.1.5
     │ Time Description, active time (t): 0 0
     │ Media Description, name and address (m): audio 60662 RTP/AVP 0 8 3 101
     │ Media Attribute (a): crypto:1 AES_CM_128_HMAC_SHA1_32 inline:UlrbLIfNTNw3blKHQVLGze6oHsyFdjGj3NheKoYx
     │ Media Attribute (a): rtpmap:0 pcmu/8000
     │ Media Attribute (a): rtpmap:8 pcma/8000            Encryption key
     │ Media Attribute (a): rtpmap:3 gsm/8000
     │ Media Attribute (a): rtpmap:101 telephone-event/8000
     │ Media Attribute (a): fmtp:101 0-16
     │ Media Attribute (a): ptime:20
     │ Media Attribute (a): encryption:optional
     ⎩ Media Attribute (a): sendrecv
```

FIGURE 6.3 Key negotiation using SDescriptions in SIP.

The "inline" method indicates that the actual keying material is captured in the key-info field of the header. The syntax of the header is defined as follows:

```
a=crypto:<tag> <crypto-suite> <key-params> [<session-params>]
```

<crypto-suite> identifies the encryption and authentication algorithms (in this case, AES in counter mode using a 128-bit key length and SHA-1). The next attribute is <key-params>, where

```
key-params = <key-method> ":" <key-info>
```

In this case the <key-method> is inline

```
<key-info> = UlrbLlfNTNw3blKHQVLGze6oHsyFdjGj3NheKoYx
```

Another mechanism of exchanging cryptographic keys is through the use of MIKEY, as discussed in further detail in Chapter 7, "Key Management Mechanisms." Figure 6.4 shows a SIP INVITE that announces the use of MIKEY in the SDP portion of the message. The following message is a capture from communications that use the *minisip* implementation.[7]

The attribute header key-mgmt in the SDP indicates that MIKEY should be used to encrypt media during this session.

If the signaling message (in this case, SIP) is transmitted in the clear, the encryption key can be intercepted and the contents of the media streams can be decrypted by an adversary. Therefore, it is necessary that signaling messages that carry encryption keys are also encrypted using protection mechanisms discussed in Chapter 5. In this case, the SIP signaling was performed using UDP to exchange keying material. UDP does not offer any protection and thus the keying material are exposed to eavesdropping

After the keys have been negotiated, the application encrypts the RTP payload and sends the SRTP packets to the remote end. Figure 6.5 shows an example of the SRTP packet.

---

7. *Israel Abad Caballero. Secure Mobile VoIP. Master's thesis, Department of Microelectronics and Information Technology, Royal Institute of Technology, June 2003.*

```
Internet Protocol, Src: 192.168.1.35, Dst: 192.168.1.20                    IP

User ??? Protocol/ Src Port: 5060, Dst Port: 5060                          UDP

INVITE sip:bob@192.168.1.20 SIP/2.0                                        SIP
Route: <sip:192.168.1.20:5060;transport=UDP;lr>
From: <sip:slice@192.168.1.35>;tag=2029
To: <sip:bob@192.168.1.20>
Call-ID: 5872@192.1368.1.35
CSeq: 301 INVITE
Contact: <sip:alice@192.168.1.35:5060;transport=UDP>;expires=1000
Content-Type: application/sdp
Via: SIP/2.0/UDP 192.168.1.35:5060;branch=z9hG4bK19718
Content-Length: 3542

v: 0                                                                       SDP
o: - 3344 3344 IN IP4 192.168.1.35
s: Minisip Session
c: IN IP4 192.168.1.35
t: 0 0
a: key-mgmt:mikey AQQFgAATBcCAAAAAHK/AAAAAAAAAAAAAAAAAAAAoAx9bH01P3ztk
                   LAAAAJwABAQEBEAIBAQMBFAQBDgUBAAYBAAcBAQgBAQkBAAoBAQs
                   BCgwBAAcQrp33V4S04/yprsxz2nytcQMCBpMwggaPMIIEd6ADAge
                   CAgkA8+z1SAxBJE4wDQYJKoZIhvcNAQEFBQAwgYsxCzAJB
```

FIGURE 6.4 Use of MIKEY in SIP for key negotiation.

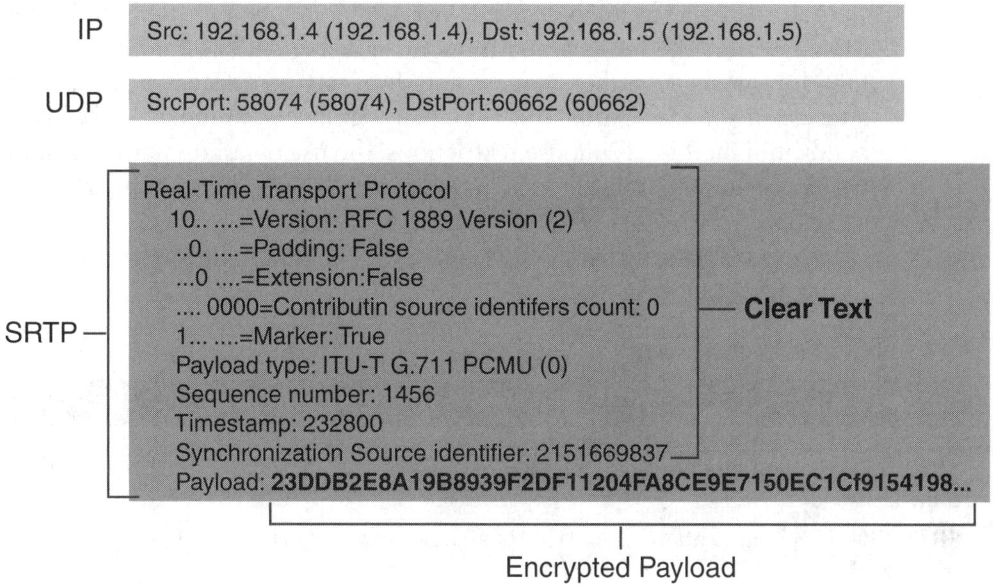

FIGURE 6.5 Contents of an SRTP packet.

All headers in the RTP packet are sent in the clear except for the payload, which is encrypted. Because SRTP uses AES by default, it provides protection against DoS attacks that aim to corrupt the encrypted media content. Typically, stream ciphers that rely on previous blocks to decrypt the next block (cipher block chaining) can be attacked by corrupting the data of one block and thus crippling the ability to successfully reassemble and produce the original content. AES does not suffer from this limitation because it can decrypt each block without requiring knowledge of previous blocks.

The use of authentication and integrity in SRTP messages is an important way to protect against attacks, including message replay and disruption of communications. For example, an attacker may modify the SRTP messages to corrupt the audio or video streams and thus cause service disruption. Another attack can be performed by sending bogus SRTP messages to a participant's device, thus forcing the device to attempt and decrypt the bogus messages. This attack forces the device application to impact the legitimate session by diverting resources to process the bogus messages. In cases where applications do not maintain session state, these attacks might not be as effective compared to stateful applications. Therefore, it is recommended that VoIP implementations use SRTP using SHA-1 with a 160-bit key length (and producing an 80-bit authentication tag) for message authentication and integrity to protect against such attacks. In some scenarios (for example, wireless communications) where bandwidth limitations impose restrictions, the use of a short authentication tag (for example, 32-bit length) or even zero length (no authentication) is an option.

Table 6.1 lists the parameters and corresponding values associated with key management in SRTP.

Table 6-1 SRTP Key Management

Parameter	Mandatory to Support	Default
SRTP/SRTCP cryptographic transforms	AES_CM, NULL	AES_CM, AES_F8 for UMTS
SRTP/SRTCP authentication transforms	HMAC_SHA1	HMAC_SHA1

Parameter	Mandatory to Support	Default
SRTP/SRTCP authentication parameters	80-bit authentication tag	80-bit authentication tag
Key derivation Pseudo Random Function	AES_CM	AES_CM
Session encryption key length	128 bit	128 bit
Session authentication key length	160 bit	160 bit
Session salt value length	112 bit	112 bit
Key derivation rate	0	0
SRTP packets max key-lifetime	2^{48}	2^{48}
SRTCP packets max key-lifetime	2^{31}	2^{31}
MKI indicator	0	0
MKI length	0	0

In addition, the following parameters are included in the crypto context for each session SSRC value: ROC (Roll Over Counter), SEQ (RTP sequence), SRTCP index, transport address, and port number.

Key Derivation

Although implementations may use a variety of key management mechanisms to manage keys, the SRTP standard requires that a native derivation algorithm be used to generate session keys. The use of the derivation algorithm is mandatory for the initial session keys.

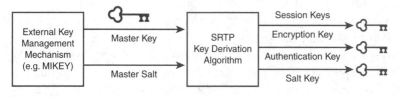

FIGURE 6.6 Key derivation algorithm.

The ability to derive keys through SRTP instead of using an external mechanism reduces additional computing cycles for key establishment. Typically, each session participant maintains a set of cryptographic information for each SRTP stream, which is referred to as the *cryptographic context.* For each cryptographic context, there are at least one encryption, one salt, and one authentication key for SRTP and SRTCPs respectively. Therefore, the SRTP key derivation algorithm can request only one master key and one salt value, when required, to derive the necessary session keys. Figure 6.6 shows this process. The derivation algorithm can be used repetitively to derive session keys. The frequency of session key generation is based on the value of the *key_derivation_rate,* which is predefined. This can be thought of as a key-refreshing mechanism that can be used to protect against cryptanalysis (which might otherwise be possible if a single master key is used). For example, an attacker can collect large amounts of session data and attempt to perform cryptanalysis. If the same key is used for the entire data, when that key is discovered all data can be recovered. If multiple keys are used, however, successful cryptanalysis will recover only data associated with the respective key (not the entire session). Therefore, multiple session keys can support perfect forward secrecy. Although frequent session key generation may be desirable and applicable for unicast sessions (for example, between small groups of two or four participants), it is not applicable for large multicast communications because each participant would have to maintain several hundred keys (which, in turn, deplete resources and impact processing and performance). One way to manage multiple SRTP and SRTCP keys is to refresh only the SRTP session keys on a specific interval and use only one key for SRTCP (for example, SRTCP key_derivation_rate = 0). Note that rekeying is necessary in cases where participants may join or leave during a group session (for example, conference calls). The determination of when such rekeying needs to occur is typically left up to the implementation, as long as there is a mechanism to alert all the participants to the expiration of the current key and the issuance of a new one. For example, the application might automatically trigger rekeying each time a participant joins the discussion or departs from the discussion. Either way, rekeying can be a costly computation depending on the number of participants and resource capabilities available on each participant's device.

Issues with Early Media

In some cases, media is transmitted to the remote ends before completing the signaling messages exchange and establishing a session. This is called early media, and it is a required condition in converged environments (for example, VoIP/PSTN). For example, when a VoIP subscriber calls a number that resides in a SS7 network (for example, PSTN), it might be necessary for the PSTN gateway to provide the signal progress by sending inband tones or announcements before the call is set up. This scenario introduces challenges as to how the media can be protected. Currently, there are discussions in IETF to use MIKEY with EKT (Encrypted Key Transport) to solve this issue.

SRTCP

Similar to SRTP, the format of the SRTCP packet has the authentication tag and MKI headers, but it also has two additional headers: SRTCP index and "encrypt-flag. Figure 6.7 shows the format of the SRTPC packet. The sensitive information that needs to be protected in an RTCP message includes the originating party of the report and the contents of the report. Therefore, these headers are encrypted.

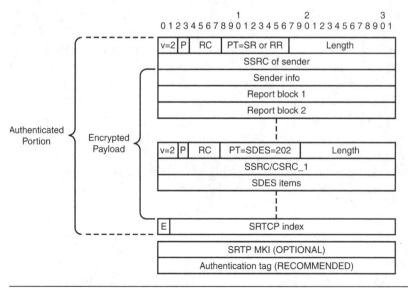

FIGURE 6.7 Format of an SRTCP packet.

The authentication tag, SRTCP index, and encrypt-flag headers are mandatory for SRTCP. For the most part, the processing of SRTCP packets is similar to SRTP packets, including the use of cryptographic algorithms and key lengths.

SRTP provides several properties to protect media streams in multimedia communications. The following list summarizes the strengths and limitations that should be considered when evaluating or implementing SRTP in a network to support multimedia communications.

SRTP strengths

- Provides confidentiality, integrity, and authentication of the message payload (media content).
- Provides protection against replay attacks for both RTP and RTCP.
- Support of AES allows for out-of-order packet reception and processing.
- Minimizes computation and resource consumption for generating cryptographic keys through an external key management mechanism by using a native key derivation algorithm.
- Key derivation algorithm helps protect against certain cryptanalytic attacks and provide perfect forward secrecy.

SRTP limitations

- Lack of RTP header encryption allows for traffic analysis by collecting information from the RTP headers and extensions.
- Cannot maintain end-to-end message integrity and authentication as the media stream is sent from an IP network to an SS7 network (PSTN).
- The key refresh and key management impact processing and resource consumption in large multicast groups. This is not desirable for mobile devices with limited computing resources.

Summary

Currently, SRTP is the standard protocol to provide protection of media streams. It supports authentication, confidentiality, and integrity of media messages to help protect against attacks such as eavesdropping, message replay, call hijacking, and various DoS attacks. One of the long-term challenges and an area for further research remains the key exchange and management in large multicast groups. At the moment, for a variety of reasons, SRTP is not considered a standard practice in VoIP implementations. One reason is the late adoption of SRTP by VoIP vendors in their products and the associated cost to have such functionality available. Another is negligence or lack of expertise to deploy SRTP in VoIP enterprise environments by corporations. Whatever the reason, it will take additional effort to educate users (and, perhaps, disclosure of security incidents [for example, eavesdropping, disruption]) to convince organizations to deploy SRTP as a standard practice.

## CHAPTER 7

KEY MANAGEMENT MECHANISMS

Key management is a fundamental part of protecting Internet multimedia applications such as VoIP. At the same time, key management protocols are difficult to design, especially for multimedia applications that require group participation (for example, videoconferencing, broadcasting or multicast audio, video or file transfer). Until recently, various key-exchange mechanisms such as IKE were proven to support asynchronous communications (that is, file transfer) but were not suitable for group or multicast Internet multimedia applications. Therefore, a distinct effort has been initiated within the IETF to establish such capability. The IETF RFC 4046, "MSEC Group Key Management Architecture," defines an architecture that consists of abstractions and design principles for developing key management protocols. The MSEC architecture defines a set of requirements for developing key management protocols.[1] These requirements discuss the properties and principles that key management protocols should exhibit for scalability, group security policy, associations (encryption key, lifetime, and so on), group membership, rekeying, attack deterrence, and recovery from compromise.

Multimedia communications such as VoIP require key negotiation protocols that can provide robust and extensible capabilities for multicast and unicast communications. For example, protocols such as TLS and IKE do not provide such capabilities. Group key management protocols can be used to protect multicast and unicast communications between users, user groups, and subgroups (through the group security association). In addition, they have to demonstrate resistance to attacks from external and internal sources (that is, impersonations, DoS).

Within the MSEC architecture, a multicast or group security architecture is defined in which key negotiation and key management are components. Negotiation of keying material is one of the most challenging topics

---

1. M. Baugher, et al. Multicast Security (MSEC) Group Key Management Architecture. IETF RFC 4046, April 2005.

for VoIP (and, generally, Internet multimedia applications). Those who want to maintain confidentiality and integrity of their communication need a robust and secure mechanism to reliably exchange cryptographic keys. Primarily, there are two methods of exchanging keying messages:

- Integrated keying, through the session establishment protocol, such as SIP[2]. This approach requires fewer messages to be exchanged, and thus minimizes associated delays introduced by message exchange.
- Native key exchange through a distinct process. This approach requires more messages to be generated between end points, and thus increases the risk of associated delays introduced by message exchange. Furthermore, a device cannot determine in advance whether the remote end point can support a particular key-exchange mechanism. For example, Bob sends an INVITE to Alice, but Bob doesn't know whether Alice's device can support MIKEY[3] because the initial exchange of messages does not contain any corresponding information. At this point, Bob can't determine whether his call will be encrypted or there is a delay in setting up the encryption unless his phone has the capability to alert him.

Cryptographic functions are computationally intensive because of the mathematical computations they must perform to derive the corresponding product (for example, Message Authentication Code or cryptographic keys). Therefore, it is important to define a set of requirements when designing key negotiation protocols, particularly when they are used in conjunction with real-time streaming applications that are time sensitive. When designing key-exchange protocols, you must consider the following:

- **Computational resource consumption**—Key negotiation mechanisms are resource intensive and impact both processing and storage resources (that is, CPU, memory), which also consume power (for example, battery life). In the case of multimedia applications such as VoIP, where processing of media streams is also computational intensive, it is critical to maintain stringent requirements for

---

2. J. Rosenberg, et al. SIP: Session Initiation Protocol. IETF RFC 3261, June 2002.

3. J. Arkko, et. al. MIKEY: Multimedia Internet KEYing. IETF RFC 3830, August 2004.

low resource consumption, especially for mobile devices such as phones and PDAs. Establish a careful balance between the amount of processing required by the cryptographic functions and the resource capabilities of the respective device. A typical question that helps guide the decision is "how much security does this device provide?"

- **Session establishment delay**—In multimedia applications (and naturally, VoIP), key negotiation adds another layer of messages to be exchanged to establish a secure session between two or more parties. This added layer can introduce delays in establishing a session, which may impact the QoS. Therefore, it is necessary to be as conservative as possible and minimize the number of messages required to negotiate keys.

- **Implosion avoidance**—An important consideration when designing a key management protocol is the case of implosion, where a network element can be overloaded by an overwhelming number of legitimate messages. There are two variations of this condition: out-of-sync and feedback implosion. The out-of-sync implosion refers to the simultaneous attempt of legitimate participants to update their security associations or rekey, which will result in overwhelming the key server with update request messages. The feedback implosion refers to the reliable delivery of rekey messages. Typically, reliable multicast protocols are designed to retransmit packets when packet loss occurs. Therefore, many group members may simultaneously transmit feedback messages (that is, NACK or ACK) to the key server, and thus overwhelm the server.

Currently, there are several existing and emerging key management standards, including MIKEY, and MIKEYv2, SRTP Security Descriptions, ZRTP,[4] and GDOI[5] (group key management) for establishing SRTP cryptographic context. This chapter focuses on MIKEY, ZRTP, and SRTP Security Descriptions because they are currently deployed in VoIP environments and supported by VoIP vendors.

---

4. P. Ziemmermann. ZRTP: Extensions to RTP for Diffie-Hellman Key Agreement for SRTP. IETF draft, www.ietf.org/Internet-drafts/draft-zimmermann-avt-zrtp-02.txt.

5. M. Baugher, et al. The Group Domain of Interpretation. IETF RFC 3547.

MIKEY

Internet multimedia applications such as VoIP have demanding performance and QoS requirements. Latency[6] is one[7] property that requires careful consideration to improve or maintain QoS in multimedia communications. Key exchange adds an additional processing burden for edge devices, especially the ones with limited processing power and memory capacity (for example, handhelds). Although memory and processing power have dramatically improved for handheld devices, encryption remains a resource-intensive task that requires consideration when designing protocols. Therefore, MIKEY was developed with the intention to minimize latency when exchanging cryptographic keys between small interactive groups that reside in heterogeneous networks. In addition, the following properties were considered when developing the protocol:

- The protocol should maintain simplicity for ease of implementation, performance, and security.
- Minimize message exchange. The negotiation of key material should be accomplished in one round trip.
- Support secure end-to-end key management.
- Protocol integration. Allow transport of messages within other protocols (that is, SDP).
- Protocol independence. Maintain independence from any security functionality imposed by the underlying transport.
- Low bandwidth consumption and low computational workload.

The MIKEY (Multimedia Internet KEYing) protocol is defined in the IETF RFC 3830 and was developed to support key negotiation for security protocols such as SRTP (Secure Real-time Time Protocol) and IPSec. Although SRTP is currently the only protocol directly supported by MIKEY, IPSec/ESP can also be supported by developing the corresponding profile. The standard describes mechanisms for negotiating keys between two or more parties who want to establish a secure channel of communication. The protocol can be used in the following modes:

---

6. *Delay of packet delivery. ITU-T G.114 recommends a maximum of a 150ms one-way latency.*

7. *Packet loss and jitter are other factors that impact multimedia communications, and there is always a constant effort for improvement.*

7. KEY MANAGEMENT MECHANISMS

- Peer to peer (unicast)
- Simple one to many (multicast)
- Many to many, without a centralized control unit

An additional mode is supported: many to many, with centralized control (applicable to a larger user group that requires the coordination of key exchange). To transport and exchange keying material, three methods are supported, as follows:

- **Pre-shared secret key (PSK)**—The PSK is used to derive subkeys for encryption and integrity. Although it is not scalable for group communications, it is the most efficient way to handle key transport.
- **Public key encryption (PKE)**—The originating user generates a random encryption key, which is then sent to the remote user using the public key to encrypt it. This method requires somewhat more computational resources as compared to PSK, but it supports key negotiation for group communications and provides better scalability in an environment where a central repository for public keys is available (that is, a PKI infrastructure).
- **Diffie-Hellman (DH) key exchange**—Optional to implement. This method is the most resource intensive, but it is the only one of the three listed here that provides Perfect Forward Secrecy (PFS).[8] This method can be used only for peer-to-peer key negotiation, and it requires the existence of a PKI infrastructure.

As you can understand from the preceding list, vendors that implement MIKEY in their products are required to support pre-shared and public key encryption methods to interoperate with other implementations.

MIKEY Protocol Definitions and Constructs

To understand the operations of the MIKEY protocol, it is necessary to understand some of the abstract protocol constructs. The following definitions represent some of the fundamental constructs used in MIKEY.[9]

---

8. *In an authenticated key agreement protocol that uses public key cryptography, Perfect Forward Secrecy (PFS) is the property that disclosure of the long-term secret keying material that is used to derive an agreed ephemeral key does not compromise the secrecy of agreed keys from earlier runs (definition provided by wikipedia.org).*

9. *Some of these definitions are originally captured in the Multicast Security (MSEC) Group Key Management Architecture document RFC 4046.*

- **Data security protocol**—The security protocol used to protect the actual data traffic, such as IPSec and SRTP.
- **Data security association (data SA or SA)**—Information for the security protocol, including a TEK and a set of parameters/policies.
- **TEK-generation key (TGK)**—A bit string agreed upon by two or more parties, associated with the crypto session bundle (defined in this list). From the traffic-generation key, traffic-encrypting keys can then be generated without needing further communication.
- **Traffic-encrypting key (TEK)**—The key used by the security protocol to protect the CS. (This key may be used directly by the security protocol or may be used to derive further keys depending on the security protocol.) The TEKs are derived from the CSB's TGK.
- **Crypto session (CS)**—Uni- or bidirectional data stream(s) protected by a single instance of a security protocol. For example, when SRTP is used, the CS will often contain two streams, an RTP stream and the corresponding RTCP, which are both protected by a single SRTP cryptographic context; that is, they share key data and the bulk of security parameters in the SRTP cryptographic context (default behavior in SRTP). In the case of IPSec, a CS would represent an instantiation of an IPSec SA. A CS can be viewed as a data SA (as defined in GKMARCH) and could therefore be mapped to other security protocols if necessary.
- **Crypto session bundle (CSB)**—Collection of one or more CSs, which can have common traffic-generation keys and security parameters.
- **Crypto session ID.** Unique identifier for the CS within a CSB.
- **Crypto session bundle ID (CSB ID)**—Unique identifier for the CSB.

Establishing a Session

Each key-exchange mechanism (PSK, PKE, and Diffie-Hellman) defined in MIKEY is using the same approach of sending and receiving messages, but the message attributes (that is, headers, payloads, and values) differ from method to method. Ultimately, the objective in each method is to transport the appropriate key material and establish a crypto session. The two important pieces of information contained in the initial message, which is originated by the initiator, is the TGKs (one or more) and the security policies associated with the respective CS. The typical attributes of a message include the following:

- **HDR**—The general MIKEY header, which includes MIKEY CSB-related data (for example, CSB ID) and information mapping to the specific security protocol used.
- *T*—The timestamp, used mainly to prevent replay attacks.
- **ID*x***—The identity of entity *x* (IDi = initiator, IDr = responder).
- **RAND**—Random/pseudo-random byte string, which is always included in the first message from the initiator. RAND is used as a freshness value for the key generation. It is not included in update messages of a CSB.
- **SP**—The security policies for the data security protocol.

When PKE exchange is used between two parties, the initiator sends an I_MESSAGE request, which carries the KEMAC and the desired SP. Figure 7.1 demonstrates this message exchange.

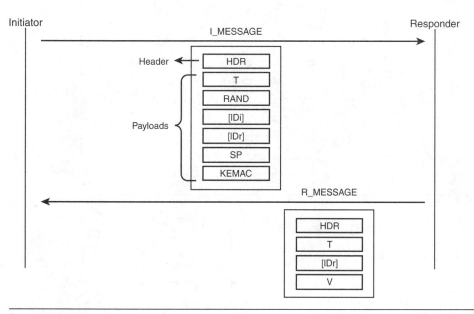

FIGURE 7.1 PSK message exchange in MIKEY.

The main objective of the initiator's message is to transport one or more TGKs and security parameters to the responder in a secure manner. In this case, the KEMAC is computed by encrypting all the TGK and using the predetermined MAC algorithm to provide integrity. The computation is as follows:

```
KEMAC = E(encr_key, {TGK}) || MAC
```

The main objective of the verification message (in the R_MESSAGE) from the responder is to obtain mutual authentication. The verification message, V, is a MAC that is computed over the responder's entire message, the timestamp (the same as the one that was included in the initiator's message), and the two parties' identities, using the authentication key. In the case where PKE is used, the initiator's message contains three additional payloads to support associated certificate information: CHASH, PKE, and SIGNi. The responder's message is the same as in the previous case. Figure 7.2 depicts the message structure when PKE is used.

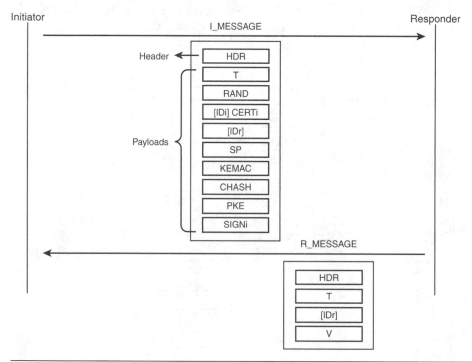

FIGURE 7.2 PKE message in MIKEY.

In this instance, the KEMAC is computed using the following:

```
KEMAC = E(encr_key, IDi || {TGK}) || MAC
```

The KMAC contains a set of encrypted subpayloads and a MAC, as described earlier with regard to the PSK exchange, but the encrypted payload contains the TGK and the identity of the initiator IDi. The IDi does not represent a certificate, but it can be the same ID as the one in the initiator's certificate. Finally, in the Diffie-Hellman exchange, the payloads for KEYMAC, CHASH, and PKE are not used, but a payload DHi that holds the initiator's Diffie-Hellman information is introduced. The main objective of the initiator's message is to communicate securely the security protocol parameters and provide the responder with its DH value (DHi) g^{xi}, where xi *must* be pseudo-randomly and secretly chosen.

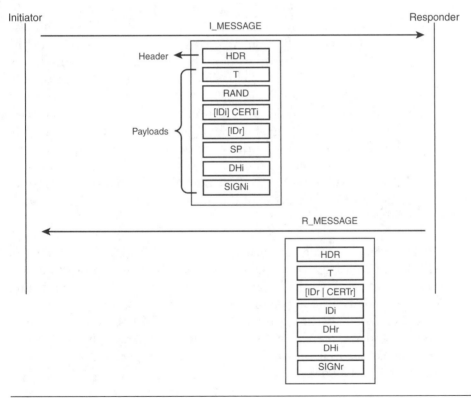

FIGURE 7.3 MIKEY Diffie-Hellman exchange.

In this case, the responder's message is very different compared to the other two response messages. Specifically, the message includes a payload that captures the responder's ID and certificate information, the initiator's ID, and the DH values for the initiator and receiver. Both parties calculate the TGK, g(xi×xr) from the exchanged DH values. The SIGNr is a signature covering the responder's MIKEY message, R_MESSAGE, using the responder's signature key.

Protocol Syntax and Message Creation

Creating a MIKEY message consists of the following steps:

1. Create an initial MIKEY message starting with the Common Header payload.
2. Concatenate necessary payloads of the MIKEY message.
3. As a last step (for messages that must be authenticated, this also includes the verification message), create and concatenate the MAC/signature payload without the MAC/signature field filled in. (If a NEXT PAYLOAD field is included in this payload, it is set to LAST PAYLOAD.)
4. Calculate the MAC/signature over the entire MIKEY message, except the MAC/Signature field, and add the MAC/signature in the field. In the case of the verification message, the Identity_i || Identity_r || Timestamp *must* directly follow the MIKEY message in the Verification MAC calculation. Note that the added identities and timestamp are identical to those transported in the ID and T payloads.

The common header payload must be included at the beginning of each MIKEY message (request and response) because it provides necessary information about the CS and CSB with which it is associated. Figure 7.4 depicts the fields that comprise the header.

MIKEY defines several payloads to support the three key exchange methods and the corresponding architectural scenarios (that is, peer to peer, simple one to many [multicast] many to many, without a centralized control unit), as follows:

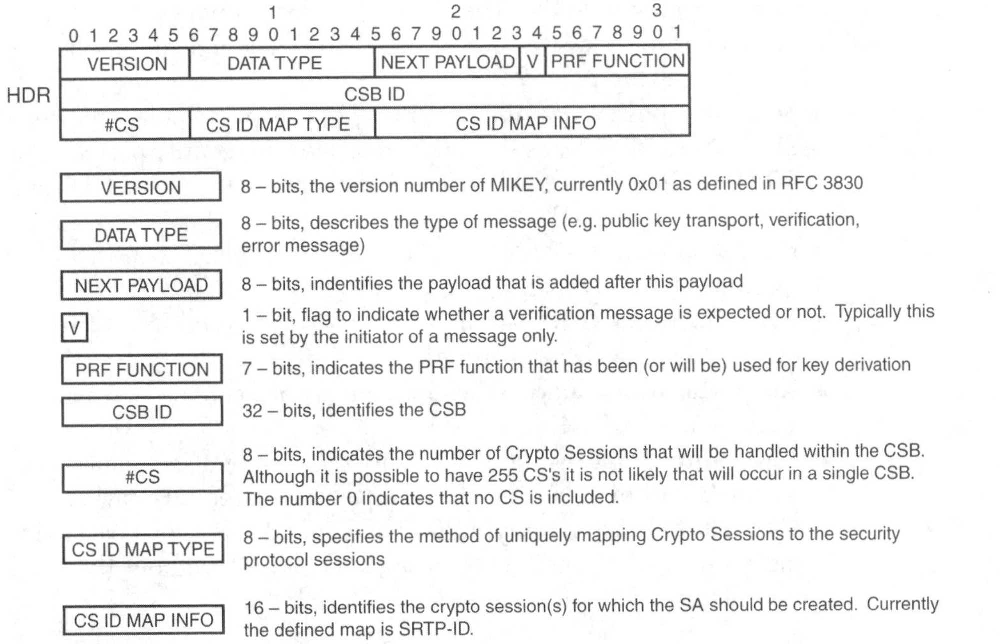

```
                      1                   2                   3
      0 1 2 3 4 5 6 7 8 9 0 1 2 3 4 5 6 7 9 0 1 2 3 4 5 6 7 8 9 0 1
      ┌──────────┬──────────────┬──────────────┬─┬──────────────┐
      │ VERSION  │  DATA TYPE   │ NEXT PAYLOAD │V│ PRF FUNCTION │
HDR   ├──────────┴──────────────┴──────────────┴─┴──────────────┤
      │                       CSB ID                             │
      ├──────────┬──────────────┬────────────────────────────────┤
      │   #CS    │ CS ID MAP TYPE│        CS ID MAP INFO         │
      └──────────┴──────────────┴────────────────────────────────┘
```

| VERSION | 8 – bits, the version number of MIKEY, currently 0x01 as defined in RFC 3830 |

| DATA TYPE | 8 – bits, describes the type of message (e.g. public key transport, verification, error message) |

| NEXT PAYLOAD | 8 – bits, indentifies the payload that is added after this payload |

| V | 1 – bit, flag to indicate whether a verification message is expected or not. Typically this is set by the initiator of a message only. |

| PRF FUNCTION | 7 – bits, indicates the PRF function that has been (or will be) used for key derivation |

| CSB ID | 32 – bits, identifies the CSB |

| #CS | 8 – bits, indicates the number of Crypto Sessions that will be handled within the CSB. Although it is possible to have 255 CS's it is not likely that will occur in a single CSB. The number 0 indicates that no CS is included. |

| CS ID MAP TYPE | 8 – bits, specifies the method of uniquely mapping Crypto Sessions to the security protocol sessions |

| CS ID MAP INFO | 16 – bits, identifies the crypto session(s) for which the SA should be created. Currently the defined map is SRTP-ID. |

FIGURE 7.4 MIKEY header.

- **Key data transport payload (KEMAC)**—Contains encrypted key data subpayloads.
- **Envelope data payload (PKE)**—Contains the encrypted envelope key that is used in the public key transport to protect the data in the key data transport payload.
- **DH data payload (DH)**—Contains the DH value and indicates the DH group used.
- **Signature payload (SIGN)**—Contains the signature and its related data.
- **Timestamp payload (T)**—Carries the timestamp information.
- **ID payload (ID).** The ID payload carries a uniquely defined identifier.
- **Certificate payload (CERT)**—The certificate payload contains an indicator of the certificate provided as well as the certificate data.
- **Cert hash payload (CHASH)**—The Cert hash payload contains the hash of the certificate used.

- **Ver msg payload (V)**—The Ver msg payload contains the calculated verification message in the pre-shared key and the public key transport methods.
- **Security policy payload (SP)**—The security policy payload defines a set of policies that apply to a specific security protocol.
- **SRTP policy.** This field specifies the parameters for SRTP and SRTCP.
- **RAND payload (RAND)**—The RAND payload consists of a (pseudo-)random bit string.
- **Error payload (ERR)**—The error payload is used to specify the error(s) that may have occurred.
- **Key data subpayload**—The key data payload contains key material (for example, TGKs).
- **Key validity data**—The key validity data is not a standalone payload, but part of either the key data payload or the DH payload.
- **General extensions payload**—The general extensions payload is included to allow possible extensions to MIKEY without the need for defining a completely new payload each time.

MIKEY messages can be transported using various signaling protocols including SIP, RTSP, and H.323.

Generating a Crypto Session

MIKEY provides the ability to support multiple crypto sessions for several security protocols or multiple instances of the same security protocol. This notion is represented using a CSB. Figure 7.5 shows a logical representation of the process for establishing a crypto session.

The CSB maintains the traffic-generation key and the security policies associated with each CS. The CSB can facilitate the management of one or more crypto sessions, which in turn represent a distinct communication channel (for example, a phone call, file transfer, video stream). It should be noted that the CSs in a CSB can use the same traffic-generation key mechanism, but each CS inherits a distinct TEK. Each CS is applied to the corresponding data stream through the associated security protocol (that is, SRTP).

The data security association (data SA) is used by the corresponding security protocol (that is, SRTP). The information within the data SA includes the parameters and policies to be used with the corresponding security protocol (that is, encryption algorithms, encryption key size, lifetime of keys, and so on) and a TEK. The TEK can also be used by the respective security protocol to derive additional keys. Figure 7.6 shows a logical representation for the key-derivation process.

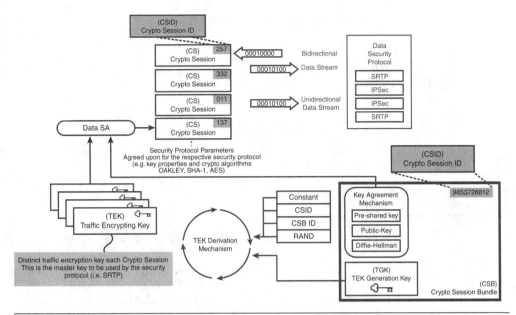

FIGURE 7.5 MIKEY creation of a crypto session.

The TEK is generated using a pseudo-random function (PRF) with the following as input (|| indicates concatenation):

```
inkey : TGK
inkey_len : bit length of TGK
label : constant || cs_id || csb_id || RAND
outkey_len : bit length of the output key
```

The 32-bit *constant* values are taken from the decimal digits of number e (2. 718281828...) in consecutive chunks, where each constant consists of nine decimal digits (for example, the first nine decimal digits 718281828 = 0x2AD01C64). The cs_id is an 8-bit unsigned integer of the corresponding CS. Similarly, the csb_id is a 32-bit unsigned integer of the corresponding CSB. Finally, RAND is a 128-bit pseudo-random sent by the initiator in the initial message exchange.

TEK Derivation in MIKEY

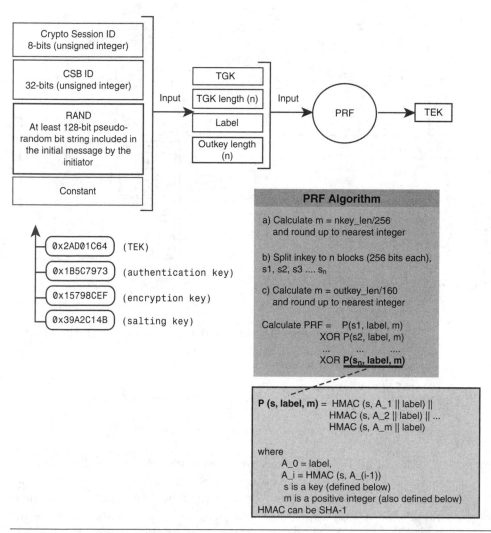

FIGURE 7.6 MIKEY TEK derivation.

Using MIKEY with SIP

MIKEY messages can be exchanged through the signaling protocol that the multimedia application is using. This section describes how MIKEY messages are exchanged using SIP/SDP, but similar approaches are used by signaling protocols such as H.235 and RTSP.

Integrating MIKEY messages within SIP minimizes the number of messages sent between end points to exchange keys. In other words, end points are not required to send separate MIKEY messages and SIP messages to establish a secure session. Therefore, it is desirable to integrate MIKEY messages within the application protocol.

Figure 7.7 shows how MIKEY key exchange is performed using SIP. Bob sends an INVITE to Alice that contains the MIKEY initiator message (I_MESSAGE). If Alice answers the phone, a 200 OK response will be sent back to Bob's phone that contains a MIKEY responder message (R_MESSAGE). Note that the MIKEY R_MESSAGE is not sent in the provisional response 180 Ringing to avoid performing the key exchange prematurely and thus executing cryptographic computations unnecessarily in case the called user does not respond. If the MIKEY R_MESSAGE is included in the 180 Ringing response, an attacker can take advantage of this configuration to perform various DoS attacks.

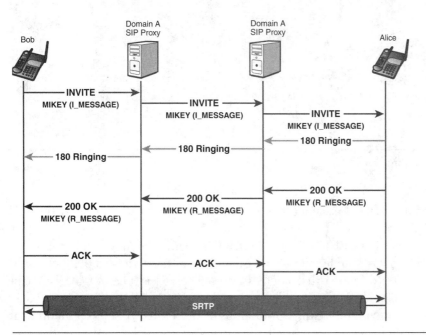

FIGURE 7.7 MIKEY key exchange with SIP.

When Bob's phone receives the 200 OK response, it sends an ACK to Alice's phone and prepares to initiate the media exchange. Each device derives a TEK for the corresponding session based on the key that was negotiated during the session setup. The TEK key is used with SRTP to protect the media. Figure 7.8 illustrates the use of a MIKEY initiation message in a SIP INVITE.

```
Internet Protocol, Src: 192.168.1.35, Dst: 192.168.1.20                    IP

User ??????? Src Port: 5060, Dst Port: 5060                               UDP

INVITE sip:bob@192.168.1.20 SIP/2.0                                       SIP
Route: <sip:192.168.1.20:5060; transport UPD;lr>
From: <sip:alice@192.168.1.35>;tag 2029
To: <sip:bob@192.168.1.20>
Call-ID: 5872@192.168.1.35
Cseq: 301 INVITE
Contact: <sip:alice@192.168.1.35:5060; transport UDP>;expires 1000
Contact-Type: application/sdp
Via: SIP/2.0/UDP 192.168.1.35:5060;branch z9hG4bK1918
Content-Length: 3542


V: 0                                                                      SDP
o: - 3344 3344 IN IP4 192.168.1.35
s: Minisip Session
c: IN IP4 192.168.1.35
t: 0 0
a: key-mgmt:mikey AQQFgAAATbcCAAAAAHK/AAAAAAAAAAAAAAAAAoAx9bH1P3ztk
                  LAAAAJwABAQEBEAIBAQMBFAQBDgUBAAYBAAcBAQgBAQkBAAoBAQs
                  BCgwBAAcQrp33V4S04/yprsxz2nytcQMCBpMwggaPMIIEd6ADAgE
                  CAgkA8+z1SAxBJE4wDQYJKoZIhvcNAQEFBQAwgYsxCzAJB
```

FIGURE 7.8 Using MIKEY with SIP.

The MIKEY parameters are captured in the SDP portion of the SIP INVITE using the *key-mgmt* attribute.

According to RFC 3830, "MIKEY is mainly intended to be used for peer-to-peer, simple one-to-many, and small size (interactive) groups." Therefore, one area that needs to be addressed is whether MIKEY can support key distribution in large groups that require multimedia services (that is, video multicasting for millions of subscribers). This is a theoretical limitation because there haven't been any substantial case studies that use MIKEY for communications in large distributed groups.

Another area that requires attention when implementing MIKEY is selecting the appropriate transport protocol to be used: TCP versus UDP. RFC 3261 mandates that SIP messages that are larger than 1300 bytes must be transmitted using congestion-controlled transport such as TCP. Therefore, in cases where MIKEY requires the exchange of PKI certificates and the use of Diffie-Hellman, TLS must be used. On the other hand, use of TCP impacts the performance of setting up a call that traverses multiple hops because TLS operates over TCP and TCP connections require more messages to set up compared to UDP (for example, three-way TCP handshake versus single UDP packet). If the TLS sessions has already been established, there is no impact.

Regardless of what transport protocol is used to exchange MIKEY messages, it has to provide confidentiality and integrity to protect the keys from being intercepted by an unauthorized party. Therefore, most implementations use TLS, with some experimental adoption of DTLS.

SRTP Security Descriptions

SRTP Security Descriptions[10] is not considered a key management protocol such as MIKEY but rather a mechanism to negotiate cryptographic keys among users in unicast sessions using the SRTP transport (for example, RTP/SAVP or RTP/SAVPF). The Security Descriptions mechanism does not support multicast media streams or multipoint unicast streams.

To communicate the keying material, the *crypto* field is used within SDP (Session Description Protocol). Figure 7.9 shows where the crypto attribute is defined in the SDP portion of a SIP INVITE message.

The format of the *crypto* attribute is as follows:

```
a=crypto:<tag> <crypto-suite> <key-params> [<session-params>]
```

In Figure 7.9, the *crypto suite* is AES_CM_128_HMAC_SHA1_32, *key params* is defined by the text starting with "inline:", and *session params* is implementation dependent.

The *tag* field is a decimal number and is used as part of the offer/answer model to distinguish the crypto attributes chosen by the participants for each media stream in a session. For example, Alice may offer two or more crypto suites to Bob during the initial offer (for example, AES_CM_128_HMAC_SHA1_80, AES_CM_128_HMAC_SHA1_32, and f8_128_HMAC_SHA1_80). Bob can respond to Alice by selecting the option f8_128_HMAC_SHA1_80 as the cryptographic transformation to protect the respective media stream.

---

10. F. Andreasen, M. Baugher, and D. Wing. *Session Description Protocol Security Descriptions for Media Streams. IETF RFC 4568.*

```
INVITE sips:alice@domain-b.com:5601 SIP/2.0
VIA: SIP/2.0/TLS 192.168.1.3:5061;branch=z9hG4bk-d04dcaal
From: bob<sips:bob@domain-a.com:5061>;tag-aed516f97elda529o0
To: <sips:alice@domain-b.com:5061>
Call-ID: ceab1739-db25ale9@192.168.1.3
CSeq: 102 INVITE
Max-Forwards: 70
Contact: bob<sips:bob@domain-a.com:5061>
Expires: 240
User-Agent: 001217E57E31 Linksys/RT31P2-3.1.6(LI)
Content-Length: 335
Allow: ACK, BYE, CANCEL, INFO, INVITE, NOTIFY, OPTIONS, REFER
Content-Type: application/sdp
```

SIP Portion of SIPS Message

```
v=0
o=bob 2890844526 2890842807 IN IP4 192.168.1.3
s=VoIP Security Testing
i=Develop Methodolgy for VoIP Security Testing
e=bob@domain-a.com (Bob The Security Guy)
c=IN IP4 161.44.17.12/127
t=2873397496 2873404696
m-audio 51442 RTP/SAVP 0
a=crypto:1 AES_CM_128_HMAC_SHA1_32
        inline:NzB4d1BINUAvLEw6UzF3WSJ+PSdFcGdUJShpX1Zj|2^20|1:32
```

SDP Portion of SIPS Message

FIGURE 7.9 SIP and SDescriptions.

The *crypto-suite* field is an identifier that describes the encryption and authentication algorithms (for example, AES_CM_128_HMAC_SHA1_80).

The *key-params* field provides one or more sets of keying material for the *crypto-suite* and consists of a method, in this case "inline," which indicates that the actual keying material (master key and salt) is provided in the *key-info* field itself. Additional information includes the associated policy of the master key such as its lifetime and use of MKI (master key identifier). The MKI is used to associate SRTP packets with a master key in a multimedia session. Based on the IETF Security Descriptions standard, each key follows this format:

```
"inline:" <key||salt> ["|" lifetime] ["|" MKI ":" length]
```

The syntax of the key is as follows:

- key‖salt is the concatenated master key and salt encoded in base64 format.
- lifetime indicates the lifetime of the master key.
- MKI:length: indicates the MKI and length of the MKI field in SRTP packets.

The lifetime and MKI parameters may not be present in some implementations because they are defined as *optional* by the standard. Figure 7.10 shows an example of a key without lifetime or MKI values.

Media Attribute (a): crypto: **1 AES_CM_128_HMAC_SHA1_32 inline:UIrbLIfNTNw3bIKHQVLGze6oHsyFdjGj3NheKoYx**

Media Attribute (a): crypto:

```
1 ----------------------------➤Tag
AES_CM_128_HMAC_SHA1_32 -------------➤Crypto-suite
inline: ------------------------➤Method
UIrbLIfNTNw3bIKHQVLGze6oHsyFdjGj3NheKoYx ---➤Master key with salt encoded using base 64
```

FIGURE 7.10 Security Descriptions without lifetime or MKI values.

Figure 7.11 displays the case where the lifetime attribute and MKI are present.

Media Attribute (a): crypto:

```
1 ------------------------------➤ Tag
AES_CM_128_HMAC_SHA1_32 ------------➤ Crypto-suite
inline: -------------------------➤ Method
UIrbLIfNTNw3bIKHQVLGze6oHsyFdjGj3NheKoYx ---➤ Master key with salt encoded using  base 64
|2^20 --------------------------➤ Master key lifetime (optional)
|1:4 --------------------------➤ Master Key Identifier (optional)
```

FIGURE 7.11 Security Descriptions with lifetime and MKI values.

The notation |2^20 (for example, 2 to the power of 20) indicates the lifetime value of the master key measured in packets (for example, the maximum number of SRTP packets that should be encrypted using this particular key).

The notation |1:4 indicates the MKI and its length. This parameter is also optional. The identifier is 1 (one) and its length is 4 bytes long. Another example is this:

```
inline: UlrbLlfNTNw3blKHQVLGze6oHsyFdjGj3NheKoYx |1024:4
```

where the key identifier is 1024 with a length of 4 bytes.

The session parameters [<session-params>] that can be included in an offer/answer interaction are as follows (as defined by the RFC):

- **KDR**—The SRTP key-derivation rate is the rate that a PRF is applied to a master key.
- **UNENCRYPTED_SRTP**—SRTP messages are not encrypted.
- **UNENCRYPTED_SRTCP**—SRTCP messages are not encrypted.
- **UNAUTHENTICATED_SRTP**—SRTP messages are not authenticated.
- **FEC_ORDER**—Order of forward error correction (FEC) relative to SRTP services.
- **FEC_KEY**—Master key for FEC when the FEC stream is sent to a separate address/port.
- **WSH**—Window size hint, which is used to protect against replay attacks.
- **Extensions**—Extension parameters can be defined.

Note that Security Descriptions are defined within SDP, which is typically encapsulated in protocols such as SIP or MGCP. Therefore, it is expected that the underling transport protocol (for example, TLS, IPSec) will provide authentication and confidentiality to protect the keying material from attacks such as eavesdropping, replaying, and message modification.

ZRTP

ZRTP is another key agreement protocol that can be used to support SRTP. The fundamental difference between ZRTP and other existing key-exchange mechanisms is that cryptographic keys are negotiated through the media stream (RTP) over the same UDP port instead of using the signaling path as it is done with MIKEY or SDescriptions. Therefore, the key negotiation is performed directly between peers without requiring the use of intermediaries such as SIP proxies to relay the keying material. If necessary, however, the ZRTP design also provides the option to exchange keying material through signaling messages. Primarily, the protocol uses ephemeral DH (Diffie-Hellman) keys to establish a shared secret between peers, but it does not require a PKI, which makes the protocol an attractive alternative for organizations that do not maintain a PKI. As of this writing, ZRTP is labeled "draft," but it is expected to be ratified as an RFC by the IETF because it has been implemented by vendors.

ZRTP Key Negotiation

Key negotiation in ZRTP is performed using the media path (RTP), and there are two key agreement modes: Diffie-Hellman and pre-shared secret. When Diffie-Hellman mode is used, the key agreement process is performed using five steps to announce support for ZRTP between peers and initiate, manage, and terminate the key exchange, as shown in Figure 7.12.

In pre-shared mode, the end points omit the DH calculation because it is assumed that the shared secret is known from a previous session, but the DHPart1 and DHPart2 messages are still exchanged to determine which shared keys should be used. Instead of DH values (hvi and pvr), the end points use nonces along with the retained secret keys to derive the key material.

In Step 1a, Bob's phone sends a ZRTP Hello message that contains a ZRTP ID (ZID) value, the protocol version, and options to be used with ZRTP. The ZID is a 96-bit random string generated one time during installation of the software shim that implements ZRTP. The options include a hash, cipher, authentication method and tag length, key agreement type, and supported algorithms for SAS (Short Authentication String).

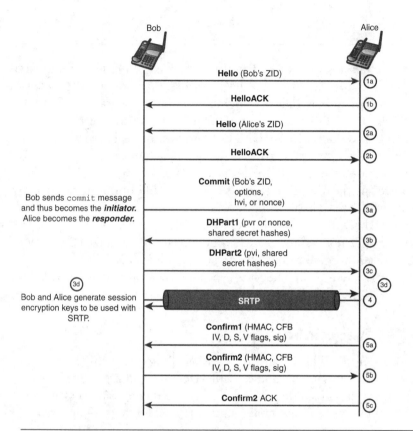

FIGURE 7.12 ZRTP key negotiation using Diffie-Hellman mode.

This initial message (Hello) is used to verify whether the remote end point supports ZRTP and announce the encryption algorithms that can be supported by the callee. The ZID is a unique identifier generated during installation of the ZRTP, and it is used to index cached shared secrets that have been accumulated from previous sessions and identify the corresponding end point's shared secret. This minimizes the need for additional key renegotiation if the key is already known by the end points.

In Step 1b, Alice sends a response to Bob acknowledging his initial ZRTP Hello message. This indicates to Bob's phone that Alice's phone supports ZRTP and announces her ZID if it is not known from a previous session. The HelloACK message can be omitted in cases where an end point wants to enter the negotiation mode immediately, and the commit message is sent instead.

In Step 2a, Alice sends a Hello message similar to Bob's, who in turn responds with a HelloACK (Step 2b).

In Step 3a, the end points can begin the key agreement when the exchange of initial Hello and HelloACK messages is complete. The first party who sends the commit message is considered the *initiator*; the other party becomes the *responder*. If both parties send the commit message simultaneously, the party that generated the highest hvi (hash value) assumes the initiator role. The hvi is computed as hvi = hash(pvi | responder's Hello message), and the pvi (DH public value) is computed as pvi = g^{svi} mod p. The svi (secret value) is a randomly generated string that is used as the exponent of base g (a number based on Diffie-Hellman cyclic group G). In addition to the ZID and hvi value, the commit message contains a set of options that consists of the ZRTP mode, hash value, cipher, at, keya, and SAS type.

In Step 3b, Alice (responder) sends a DHPart1 message to Bob. The message contains a pvr and shared secret hashes (HMACs) that were used in generating the ZRTP secret. There are five HMAC parameters: rs1IDr, rs2IDr, sigsIDr, srtpsIDr, and other_secretIDr.

In Step 3c, Bob sends a DHPart2 message that contains his public DH value and the calculated secret IDs, similar to DHPart1.

In Step 3d, each participant generates the SRTP master key and master salt using the exchanged shared secret. Note that there are two RTP streams in session, one from Bob to Alice and one from Alice to Bob. Therefore, each RTP stream is using different RTP keys and salts. Each end uses the srtpkey(i/r) and srtpsalt(i/r) to encrypt and decrypt the corresponding RTP stream.

In Steps 5a and 5b, the two end points exchange information about the shared secret key's life expectancy (cache expiration interval) using the confirm message. This message is sent only in response to a valid DHPart2 message when the key negotiation has been completed successfully. Part of the confirm message is encrypted using CFB (Cipher Feedback encryption mode) and protected for integrity using HMAC.

In Step 5c the Conf2ACK message is sent upon receipt of a valid Confirm2, and it is used to stop further retransmission of a Confirm2 message.

To terminate encrypting media, the GoClear message is used. The message does not terminate the session, but alters the state of the RTP stream from being encrypted to unencrypted.

Table 7.1 provides a description of the ZRTP header fields.

Table 7-1 ZRTP Key Negotiation Parameter Mapping

Variable	Description	Comments
ZID	Unique identifier of ZRTP end point	96-bit-long random string generated during initial installation.
hvi/r	Hash value initiator/responder	Computed as hvi = hash (pvi | responder's Hello message).
pvi/r	Public value initiator/responder	Computed as pvi = g^{svi} mod p (initiator). Computed as pvr = g^{svr} mod p (responder).
svi/r	Secret value initiator/responder	Random Diffie-Hellman value based on DH-4096 or DH-3072. The svi value is twice as long as the AES key length. For example, if AES key is 128 bits, svi should be 256 bits.
hash	Supported hash type block	S256; SHA-256 is the only one currently supported.
cipher	Supported cipher types	AES1; AES-CM with 128-bit keys, as defined in RFC 3711.
		AES2; AES-CM with 256-bit keys, as defined in RFC 3711.
at	Authentication tag	HS32; HMAC-SHA1 32-bit authentication tag, as defined in RFC 3711.
		HS80; HMAC-SHA1 80-bit authentication tag, as defined in RFC 3711.
keya	Key agreement types	DH3k; DH mode with p=3072-bit prime, as defined in RFC 3526.
		DH4k; DH mode with p=4096-bit prime, as defined in RFC 3526.
		Prsh; Pre-shared non-Diffie-Hellman mode uses shared secrets.
SAS	SAS type	B32; Short Authentication String using Base32 encoding.
		B256; Short Authentication String using Base256 encoding.
		The SAS value is calculated as the hash of the ZRTP messages (responder's Hello, commit, DHPart1, and DHPart2).

Variable	Description	Comments
rs1IDi/r	Retained secret ID	Computed as rs1IDi = HMAC(rs1, "Initiator").
		Computed as rs1IDr = HMAC(rs1, "Responder").
rs2IDi/r	Retained secret ID	Computed as rs2IDi = HMAC(rs2, "Initiator").
		Computed as rs2IDr = HMAC(rs2, "Responder").
sigsIDi/r	Signaling secret	The HMAC of the initiator's/responder's signaling shared secret. These values are exchanged using the signaling protocol (for example, SIP) and passed to ZRTP.
		Computed as sigsIDi = HMAC(sigs, "Initiator").
		Computed as sigsIDr = HMAC(sigs, "Responder")
srtpsIDi/r	SRTP secret ID	The HMAC of the initiator's/responder's SRTP secret.
		Computed as srtpsIDi = HMAC(srtps, "Initiator").
		Computed as srtpsIDr = HMAC(srtps, "Responder").
other_secretIDi/r	Other secret	HMAC of an additional shared secret in case multiple shared secrets are available.
		Computed as other_secretIDi = HMAC(other_secret, "Initiator").
		Computed as other_secretIDr = HMAC(other_secret, "Responder").
srtpkeyi/r	SRTP key	The ZRTP initiator and responder generate this value using the following:
		srtpkeyi = HMAC(s0,"Initiator ZRTP key")
		srtpkeyr = HMAC(s0,"Responder SRTP master key")
srtpsalti/r	SRTP salt	The ZRTP initiator and responder generate this value using the following:
		rtpsalti = HMAC(s0,"Initiator HMAC key")
		rtpsaltr HMAC(s0,"Responder HMAC key")

(continues)

Table 7-1 ZRTP Key Negotiation Parameter Mapping *(continued)*

Variable	Description	Comments
hmackeyi/r	HMAC key	This value is used only with ZRTP but not SRTP. The ZRTP initiator and responder generate this value using the following: hmackeyi = HMAC(s0, "Initiator HMAC key") hmackeyr = HMAC(s0, "Responder HMAC key") This HMAC key is used to ensure that GoClear messages are unique and cannot be replayed by an attacker to force a connection to go in to unencrypted mode.

Using Zfone

The initial implementation of ZRTP is Zfone, which interfaces with existing soft phones such as X-Lite, Gizmo, and SJphone, but vendors have started to support the protocol; therefore, it is expected that it will gain additional acceptance. Figure 7.13 depicts Zfone with X-Lite.

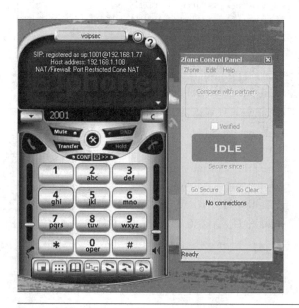

FIGURE 7.13 ZRTP interface.

7. KEY MANAGEMENT MECHANISMS

During key negotiation, Zfone displays a message to the user indicating its current state, as shown in Figure 7.14.

FIGURE 7.14 ZRTP key negotiation state indicator.

When the two parties establish the key exchange, their session is encrypted, as shown in Figure 7.15.

The ZRTP key exchange helps alleviate many of the complexities found in other key-exchange protocols that require the use of signaling messages, but it has its limitations. ZRTP works well in a peer-to-peer network in which RTP is used, but it cannot support calls that traverse between VoIP networks and PSTN. Therefore, another mechanism needs to be established to support such interconnection.

FIGURE 7.15 ZRTP in secure mode.

ZRTP and Man in the Middle

Because DH is susceptible to *man-in-the-middle* attacks, the ZRTP design provides a Short Authentication String (SAS). The SAS is used by the participants to determine whether their key exchange has been compromised. The legitimate parties announce the SAS string to each other when the initial handshake is completed, and they also set the V flag (SAS verified). This is available only in implementations in which the user can set the SAS verified flag, such as a soft phone. If the option to set the SAS flag is not available to the user, it is possible to perform a man-in-the-middle attack.[11]

ZRTP DoS

One common method to attack key-exchange protocols is by performing a DoS through resource consumption and exhaustion. In ZRTP, an attacker

11. P. Gupta, and V. Shmatikov. *Security Analysis of Voice-over-IP Protocols. The University of Texas at Austin. Cryptology ePrint Archive,* 2006.

may send spurious Hello messages to end points, thus forcing them to allocate resources and eventually causing them to degrade or terminate operation.[12] This attack requires that the exchange of signaling messages has preceded the ZRTP negotiation. The signaling messages may be an easier target for attack instead of waiting until the end points initiate RTP media exchange and exploit ZRTP.

ZRTP DTMF Disclosure

Although ZRTP is designed to protect the RTP stream, the current implementation of Zfone fails to protect DTMF (Dual Tone Multi Frequency) tones. RFC 2833 defines the payload format to transmit DTMF tones in RTP.[13] Many automated answering systems use DTMF tones to allow menu navigation and provide customer support and services. For example, when users dial their bank or health-care provider, they are prompted to enter their account number or Social Security number or other personal-identifiable information. It is possible for an attacker to capture a conversation between end points and retrieve credit card numbers, birthdates, PINS, Social Security numbers, or other confidential information. Figure 7.16 depicts a failed attempt to decode an RTP stream that is protected using ZRTP.

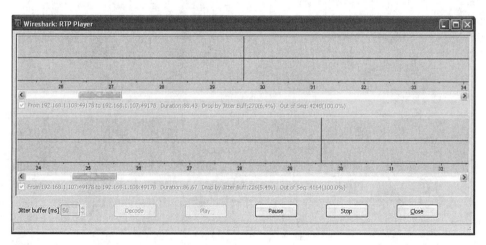

Figure 7.16 ZRTP and eavesdropping.

12. P. Gupta, and V. Shmatikov. *Security Analysis of Voice-over-IP Protocols. The University of Texas at Austin. Cryptology ePrint Archive 2006.*

13. H. Sculzrinne, and S. Petrck. RFC 2833, *"RTP Payload for DTMF Digits, Telephony Tones and Telephony Signals."*

Figure 7.16 depicts a sniffer capture of the same RTP stream protected by ZRTP. In this figure, the user has pressed various numbers on his keypad that translated into DTMF tones. One of the DTMF tones is the number 2, which is clearly depicted in Figure 7.17.

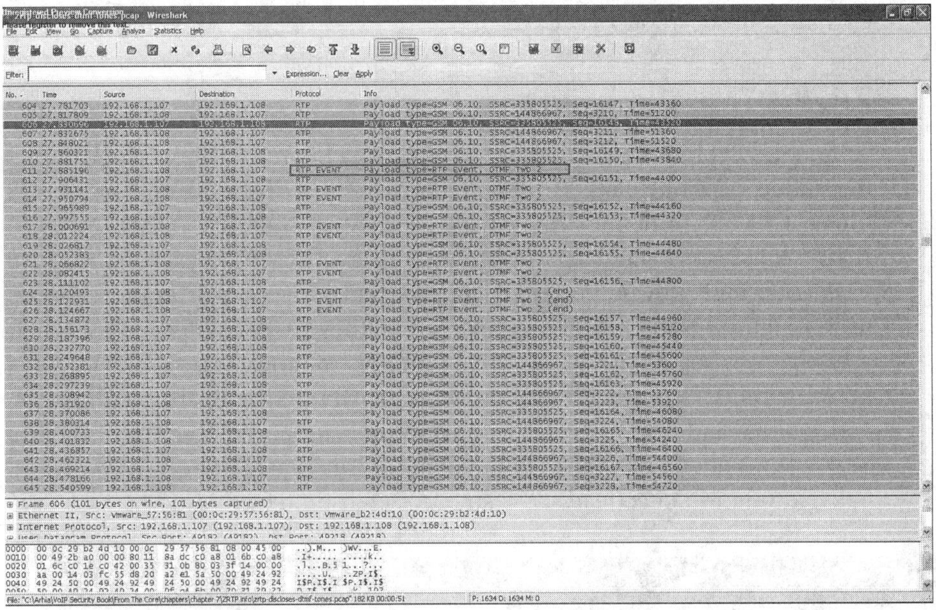

FIGURE 7.17 DTMF disclosure in ZRTP.

Figure 7.18 depicts the captured message.

This vulnerability can have great impact in VoIP implementations in which sensitive information is exchanged through DTMF tones. One approach to address this weakness is to introduce a capability in the design of ZRTP to extend its protection of DTMF tones (for example, encrypting the RTP payload format of named events).

```
IP    ⌠ Source: 192.168.1.108 (192.168.1.108)
      ⌡ Destination: 192.168.1.107 (192.168.1.107)
      ┌ User Datagram Protocol, Src Port: 49218 (49218), Dst Port: 49182 (49182)
      │   Source port: 49218 (49218)
      │   Destination port: 49182 (49182)
UDP   ┤   Length: 24
      │   Checksum: 0x19fe [correct]
      │     [Good Checksum: True]
      └     [Bad Checksum: False]
      ┌ Real-Time Transport Protocol
      │   [Stream setup by SDP (frame 43)]
      │     [Setup frame: 43]
      │     [Setup Method: SDP]
      │   10.. .... = Version: RFC 1889 Version (2)
      │   ..0. .... = Padding: False
      │   ...0 .... = Extension: False
      │   .... 0000 = Contributing source indentifiers count: 0
      │   1... .... = Marker: True
RTP   ┤   Payload type: telephone-event (101)
      │   Sequence number: 3213
      │   Timestamp: 51840
      │   Synchronization Source indentifier: 144866967
      │ RFC 2833 RTP Event
      │   Event ID: DTMF Two 2 (2)
      │   0... .... = End of Event: False
      │   .0.. .... = Reserved: False
      │   ..00 1010 = Volume: 10
      └   Event Duration: 0
```

FIGURE 7.18 ZRTP and DTMF disclosure: example packet.

Summary

Key management is a *must* to protect Internet multimedia applications such as VoIP, video on demand, conferencing, and others. This chapter covered two methods, MIKEY and SRTP Security Descriptions, currently implemented by vendors to support security requirements to provide authentication, confidentiality, and integrity of media streams. In addition, this chapter discussed ZRTP, which is currently an IETF "draft" but is likely to become a viable solution for peer-to-peer confidentiality. The MIKEY protocol provides the scalability and flexibility to support unicast and multicast communications, but it can be more complex to implement compared to SRTP Security Descriptions. Nevertheless, both approaches provide the ability to exchange cryptographic material and support the SRTP protocol to adequately protect the media streams between participants. ZRTP provides a level of transparency compared to MIKEY or

SDescriptions because it is signaling protocol independent and it requires changes on the peer software but not the core VoIP components such as a SIP proxy or an H.323 gatekeeper. One limitation that all key-exchange protocols suffer is that they cannot extend their properties to calls that traverse between VoIP networks and PSTN. Forking and media clipping are additional issues that require further research and need to be addressed by any key-exchange mechanism or protocol.[14] Currently, the IETF is working on several options, including EKT and redesigning MIKEY (MIKEYv2), to provide additional mechanism for key management.

14. D. Wing, et al., *Media Security Requirements. IETF draft, www.ietf.org/Internet-drafts/ draft-wing-media-security-requirements-00.txt, October 2006.*

## CHAPTER 8

VoIP AND NETWORK SECURITY CONTROLS

This chapter discusses network security controls that can be used to protect a VoIP deployment. Note that network security controls are only one dimension in the effort to secure VoIP networks. Chapter 9, "A Security Framework for Enterprise VoIP Networks," outlines additional areas that should be considered as part of an organization's process to secure VoIP communications. Because of the intricacies of VoIP protocols, specific mechanisms have been developed to protect against attacks that take advantage of the associated weaknesses. Therefore, it is necessary to discuss network security controls in relation to VoIP in a distinct chapter to help you understand the relationship of these controls and VoIP communications. Defending against threats and attacks requires a well-defined process that aims to establish a layered approach to maintain an adequate security posture. The process should be designed to incorporate controls that can address the following:

- Identify applicable threats
- Identify avenues of attack and minimize the opportunity for an attack
- Minimize the impact of an attack if it occurs
- Manage and mitigate a successful attack in a timely fashion

Therefore, security in VoIP or any network that provides Internet multimedia applications requires similar approach. Furthermore, security policies, standards, and procedures should be developed and enforced as part of the process to maintain a uniform approach to managing information security.

Networks security controls in VoIP encompass the use of security policies and components used to control access to resources and prevent attacks. This chapter focuses on architectural considerations; mechanisms that can be used to support authentication, authorization, and accounting (for example, Diameter); and components that can be used to provide controls and protection against attacks (for example, SBCs).

Architectural Considerations

A fundamental element for a secure VoIP deployment is a well-defined architecture. The VoIP architecture should incorporate requirements for reliability, availability, confidentiality, authorization, and integrity.

To support these objectives, we need to identify, prioritize, and categorize the types of data and information that are exchanged through the VoIP network (for example, secret, confidential, public). In addition, we need to identify security requirements that the infrastructure should support to meet the previously mentioned objectives (confidentiality, authorization, and integrity). The development of security requirements will help build a robust and scalable architecture that incorporates security and availability in addition to QoS. Generally, the security considerations of the VoIP architecture should include proper network segmentation, out-of-band network management, and private addressing.

Network Segmentation

Network segmentation is one of the architectural considerations that need to be incorporated in the deployment of VoIP communications. In enterprise and carrier-grade environments, network segmentation provides the ability to streamline and control the traffic that flows between components. Figure 8.1 depicts a configuration of a segmented enterprise VoIP network.

In this sample architecture, all the critical components are logically isolated. Traffic filtering can be enforced by the supporting network elements such as routers and switches or the use of VoIP firewalls or session border controllers (SBCs).

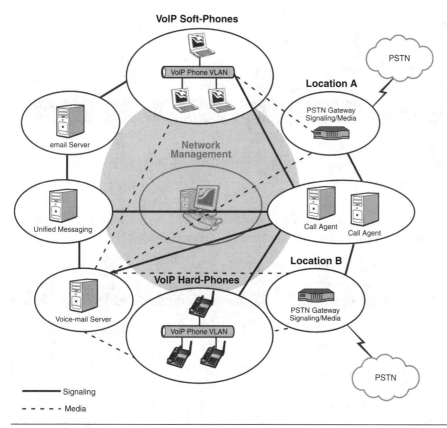

FIGURE 8.1 Enterprise network architecture segmentation.

For example, the call agents, PSTN gateways, voicemail servers, unified messaging server, email server, VoIP hard phones, and VoIP soft phones are all located in their distinct VLAN (virtual LAN). In addition, signaling and media traffic between VLANs is restricted. If traffic filtering is enforced by routers or switches, the use of access control lists (ACLs) is the typical choice. In this example, most of the signaling traffic will flow between the VLAN that houses the call agents and all the other VLANs. Therefore, the ACLs on the call agent VLAN will be lengthier compared to the other VLANs.

Because signaling traffic can be SIP, H.323, MGCP, or another signaling protocol (for example, Skinny), additional filtering can be enforced to restrict the type of signaling that can flow between VLANs. Table 8.1 shows an example of an ACL that allows SIP signaling between the VoIP phones and the call agent VLANs.

Table 8-1 Example ACL Filtering for Signaling Traffic

Source	Destination	Transport	Port
Call agent VLAN	VoIP phone VLAN	UDP	5060
VoIP phone VLAN	Call agent VLAN	UDP	5060

Table 8.2 shows another example of an ACL that allows MGCP signaling between the call agent and the voice gateway VLANs.

Table 8-2 Example ACL Filtering for Signaling Traffic

Source	Destination	Transport	Port
Call agent VLAN	Voice gateway VLAN	UDP	2427
Voice gateway VLAN	Call agent VLAN	UDP	2727

In addition, the call agent may have the ability to enforce call admission controls (including authentication and authorization) based on the user's credentials, profile (for example, executive management, warehouse, sales), and policy (for example, discard international calls or calls to specific internal or external numbers).

The media traffic is allowed between certain VLANs, such as the PSTN gateway VLAN, the VoIP phone VLAN, and voicemail server VLAN. Note that media ports are negotiated dynamically between end points. Therefore, using ACLs to restrict RTP traffic requires defining a range of UDP ports to be allowed between end points. Typically, ports between 16,384 and 32,767 are used for audio; ports between 49,152 and 65,535 are used for video. A vendor may be using a different range, but it should be possible to identify the low and high values of the range to implement the corresponding ACL.

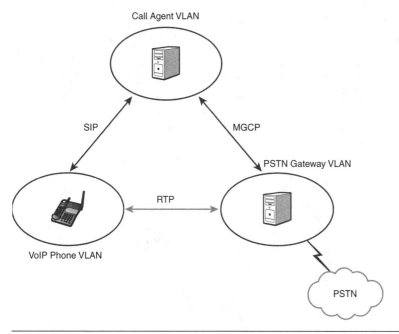

FIGURE 8.2 Example of ACL filtering between VoIP components.

Figure 8.2 depicts an example of ACL filtering between VoIP components in distinct VLANs. This configuration restricts VoIP signaling and media traffic to flow only between the corresponding VLANs. In addition, it provides a layer of defense for signaling and media from attacks that originate from networks other than the designated VLANs. For example, an attack that originates from another point in the network against the signaling port of the voice gateway will fail.

In the case where signaling traffic is exchanged between VLANs, the ACL can be further tailored to control traffic between network elements based on individual IP addresses rather than the entire subnet. In other words, the ACL can enforce the exchange of signaling traffic that originates from the call agent IP address and the voice gateway IP address on the corresponding ports. Such granularity obviously depends on the size of the network and associated components that need to be managed. For large enterprise environments, this configuration might not be optimal.

Network Management Configuration

Management of the VoIP infrastructure is also a dimension that needs to be considered in VoIP architecture. The network management VLAN has visibility to all the VLANs in the network to monitor the health of all the VoIP components. Typically, the core VoIP components are configured with two network interfaces. One interface is assigned to the management VLAN, and the other to the production VLAN where the signaling and media streams are handled, as shown in Figure 8.3.

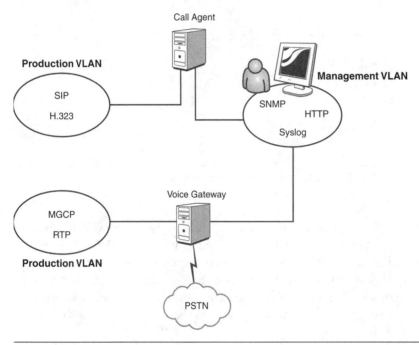

FIGURE 8.3 Network management.

This architectural configuration provides out-of-band network management and system administration that eliminates the associated risk of an attack against the management or administrative ports (for example, SNMP, HTTP, Telnet). This is a typical configuration for telecommunication carriers, service providers, and large enterprise networks.

In cases where the organizational resources or requirements do not permit for dual network interface configuration, the management traffic has to be restricted with ACLs. And as with signaling and media protocols, all network management protocols are explicitly permitted between the VLANs and the network management VLAN. This approach allows enforcing granular filtering between VLANs and the traffic that traverses between the VLANs to enforce stronger network security.

Private Addressing

Private addressing is used as another mechanism to protect against external attacks. The exponential growth of the Internet in the early 1990s signaled the rapid depletion of globally unique IP addresses. The IETF published RFC 1918, "Address Allocation for Private Internets," in an effort to encourage organizations to use nonroutable IP addresses for systems that were not intended to be directly connected to the Internet. By configuring the internal hosts of an organization with one set of IP addresses and using only a small set of IP addresses to route Internet traffic, the depletion of Internet-routable IP addresses was decelerated. An internal host will send all its traffic through a component that is responsible for routing traffic to the Internet and also perform Network Address Translation (NAT), as depicted in Figure 8.4. NAT devices can perform address-to-address translation or address and port translation.

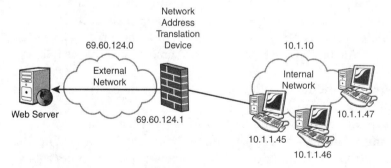

FIGURE 8.4 Private addressing.

The NAT device maintains a table that associates the IP address and ports of internal hosts with the IP address and ports of external hosts (source and destination). This option provides an added benefit to the security of the organization's internal network. Any external malicious traffic targeting internal systems is dropped unless the NAT has established an association in its state table. Therefore, it is encouraged to use private addressing in VoIP deployments to provide another layer of protection. At the same time, NAT has introduced issues with VoIP signaling and security. These issues are discussed later in this chapter.

Authentication, Authorization, and Auditing: Diameter

As discussed earlier, access to the network is a fundamental security control that needs to be incorporated in the architecture of the VoIP network. Some of the protocols support authentication mechanisms that are not sufficient for certain environments (for example, SIP digest). This section discusses the Diameter protocol, which is defined in RFC 3588, "Diameter Base Protocol." The protocol is an evolution from RADIUS (Remote Authentication Dial In User Service), defined in RFC 2058, and it provides the basis for developing Diameter applications. Diameter provides authentication and authorization to network resources, and it can be used to capture accounting information for billing network resource usage. Diameter is designed as a peer-to-peer protocol and uses the client/server architecture to exchange messages between Diameter nodes (similar to SIP).

A Diameter node can be a client, a server, or an agent. The base protocol defines seven entities that support the Diameter sessions, as follows:[1]

- **Diameter client**—Resides at the edge of a network, and it performs access control.
- **Diameter server**—Handles AAA for a particular realm.
- **Diameter node**—A network element process that implements the Diameter protocol and acts either as a client, a server, or an agent.

---

1. *RFC 3588 defines a* session *as "a logical concept at the application layer, and is shared between an access device and a server, and is identified via the Session-Id AVP."*

- **Proxy agent**—A network element that forwards Diameter messages on behalf of clients and makes policy decisions for resource usage. In addition, it provides admission control and provisioning.
- **Relay agent**—A network element that forwards requests and responses based on routing-related information and realm-routing table entries. Relay agents are allowed to modify only routing-related data of Diameter messages.
- **Redirect agent**—Refers clients to servers to allow them to communicate directly.
- **Translation agent**—A network element that acts as a Diameter client, server, relay agent, redirect agent, or translation agent.

Diameter is a binary protocol and consists of attribute value pairs (AVPs). There can be a number of AVPs in a Diameter message, and they typically carry AAA data, as shown in Figure 8.5.

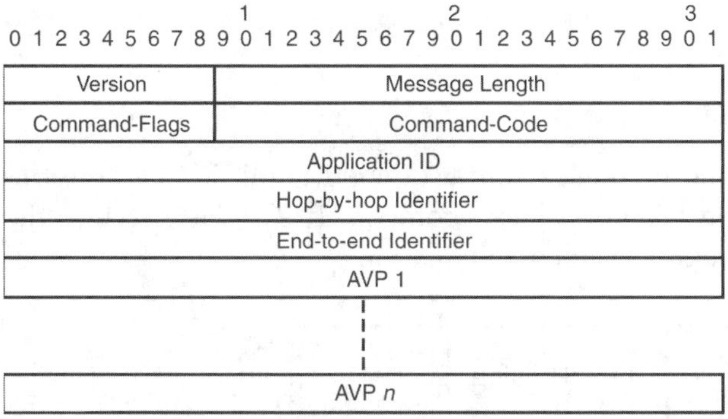

FIGURE 8.5 Diameter message format.

- **Version**—Indicates the current Diameter version. The current version is 1.
- **Message Length**—Indicates the length of the entire Diameter message, including the header fields.
- **Command Flags**—Indicates the type of message, as follows:
  R(equest). If the first bit is set (position 0), the message is a request; otherwise, it's an answer.
  P(roxiable). If it is set (position 1), the message *may* be proxied, relayed, or redirected. Otherwise, the message *must* be locally processed.

E(rror). If it is set (position 2), the message contains a protocol error.

T(Potentially retransmitted message). This flag is used during a link failover to eliminate the transmission of duplicate messages. This bit is never set when sending a request for the first time. If it is used, the bit at position 3 is set.

r(eserved). Reserved for future use and set to zero. The remaining positions are set to zero.

- **Command-Code**—Used to indicate the associated command in the message (see Table 8.3).
- **Application-ID**—Identifies the associated application that the message pertains to. In the case of a SIP application, the value is 6.
- **Hop-by-Hop Identifier**—A 32-bit integer identifier used to match requests and replies.
- **End-to-End Identifier**—A 32-bit integer identifier used to detect duplicate messages.

SIP and Diameter

Figure 8.6 depicts some of the currently defined application extensions developed based on the Diameter base protocol.[2] RFC 4740 specifies the Diameter Session Initiation Protocol application.

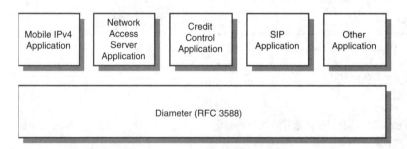

FIGURE 8.6 Diameter base protocol and applications.

---

2. *RFC 4004 defines the Diameter Mobile IPv4, and RFC 4005 defines the Diameter Network Access Server application.*

The specification discusses how a SIP implementation can use AAA to support authentication, authorization, and auditing. Although it focuses on the SIP digest authentication, the architecture can be extended to adopt other authentication mechanisms. An example of how Diameter authentication is performed in a SIP environment is shown in Figure 8.7. In this scenario, the SIP proxy in domain A authenticates a SIP INVITE request through the Diameter server.

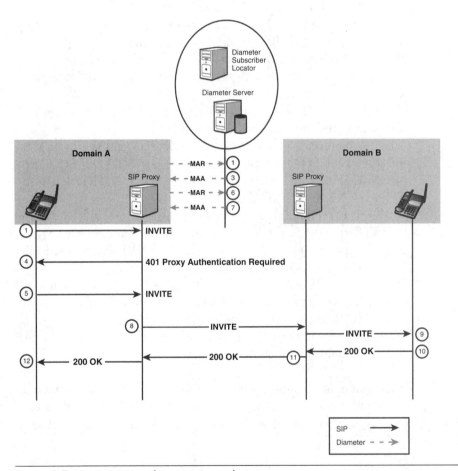

FIGURE 8.7 SIP INVITE authentication with AAA.

The message flow is as follows:

1. The SIP UA (phone) sends an INVITE to its proxy server.
2. The SIP proxy sends a MAR (see Table 8.3) message to the Diameter server.
3. The Diameter server sends an MAA message back to the SIP proxy that contains a nonce and any additional information to challenge the SIP UA (for example, digest authentication).
4. The server sends a 407 Proxy Authentication Required message that contains the challenge and nonce information.
5. The SIP UA sends a new INVITE request to the SIP proxy containing the user's credentials. The credential may have been previously cached or preconfigured in the user's phone profile.
6. The SIP proxy (Diameter client) sends a new MAR message with the user's credentials for validation.
7. The Diameter server validates the credentials and sends an MAA message back to the SIP proxy indicating DIAMETER_SUCCESS or DIAMETER_ERROR (for example, DIAMETER_ERROR_USER_UNKNOWN 5032).
8. If the user credentials are validated, the SIP proxy forwards the INVITE request to the intended domain (domain B).
9. The SIP proxy in domain B forwards the INVITE request to the destination SIP UA (called party).
10. The remote SIP UA sends a 200 OK to its SIP proxy in domain B indicating willingness to participate in the session (call).
11. The 200 OK is propagated to the SIP proxy in domain A.
12. The SIP proxy in domain, in turn, forwards the 200 OK to the SIP UA in domain A (caller).

Another example of how Diameter authentication is performed in a SIP environment is shown in Figure 8.8. This scenario may be of a roaming wireless user who is a subscriber of domain B, but he is roaming in domain A.

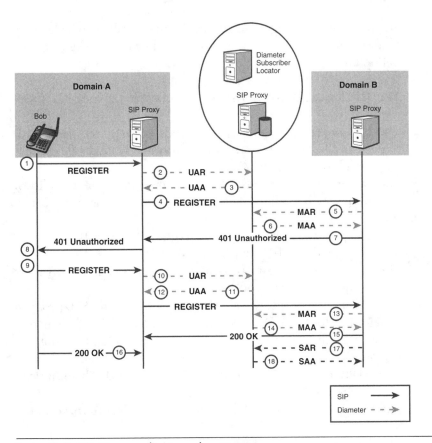

FIGURE 8.8 SIP-Diameter basic authentication.

The Diameter Subscriber Locator (SL) is used to discover the Diameter server that contains the corresponding user's account information. The subscriber locator maintains a database of mappings between the SIP address of record (AOR) and the diameter server URI. The AOR is a permanent SIP address associated with a subscriber, and it is not bound to an IP address or a device. The SIP URI is composed of a domain name or IP address and port, and it is used by the location server while the registration is active. The Diameter URI points to the corresponding server that keeps profile information associated with a SIP AOR (subscriber).

The example shown in Figure 8.6 describes the process in which a user is granted access to use the service in a foreign domain. The steps of the authentication are as follows:

1. The SIP device sends a REGISTER request to the local SIP proxy (domain A).
2. The SIP proxy (Diameter client) sends a UAR (see Table 8.3) request to the Diameter server to determine whether the user is authorized to use the service.
3. The Diameter server sends a UUA response that contains a list of capabilities such as the remote server (domain B) and the corresponding URI.
4. The SIP proxy in domain A forwards the REGISTER request to the corresponding SIP proxy in domain B.
5. The SIP proxy in domain B (diameter client) sends a MAR message to the diameter server.
6. The diameter server sends an MAA response to the SIP proxy in domain B. The MAA message contains a nonce and a challenge to be used by the SIP proxy (domain B) in the 401 Unauthorized response.
7. The SIP proxy in domain B sends a SIP 401 Unauthorized response to the SIP proxy in domain A.
8. The SIP proxy in domain A forwards the 401 Unauthorized to the SIP phone.
9. The SIP phone generates a new REGISTER request that contains the response to the challenge from the Diameter server, and it sends it to the local SIP proxy.
10. The local SIP proxy (diameter client) sends a UAR message to the diameter server to locate the SIP server that corresponds to the user (SIP proxy in domain B) and authenticates the user using the updated information.
11. The Diameter server responds with a UAA that contains the domain B SIP proxy URI.
12. The SIP proxy (domain A) forwards the new REGISTER request (from Step 9) to the SIP proxy in domain B.
13. The SIP proxy in domain B forwards the user's credentials to the Diameter server for verification in a MAR message.

14. The Diameter server verifies the user's credentials and returns an MMA message. If the verification is successful, the message contains a Result-Code set to DIAMETER_SUCCESS value; otherwise, a DIAMETER_ERROR is returned (DIAMETER_ERROR_USER_UNKNOWN 5032).
15. If successful, the SIP server in domain B returns a 200 OK to the SIP proxy in domain A.
16. The 200 OK is forwarded to the SIP phone to complete the dialogue.
17. The SIP proxy in domain B sends a SAR message to perform some housekeeping in case it has been configured to update domain A's SIP URI on the Diameter server downloads and caches the user's profile information.
18. The Diameter server responds with an SAA message to acknowledge the request to update the SIP proxy URI information or the user's profile information.

Diameter Commands

Table 8.3 summarizes the SIP application Diameter commands.

Table 8-3 SIP Application Diameter Commands and Codes

Command Name	Abbreviation	Code
User-Authorization-Request	UAR	283
User-Authorization-Answer	UAA	283
Server-Assignment-Request	SAR	284
Server-Assignment-Answer	SAA	284
Location-Info-Request	LIR	285
Location-Info-Answer	LIA	285
Multimedia-Auth-Request	MAR	286
Multimedia-Auth-Answer	MAA	286
Registration-Termination-Request	RTR	287
Registration-Termination-Answer	RTA	287
Push-Profile-Request	PPR	288
Push-Profile-Answer	PPA	288

User-Authorization-Request Command

This message is used by the Diameter client on a SIP proxy to request authorization from a Diameter server on behalf of a SIP user agent (phone) to route a SIP REGISTER request. Currently, the SIP Diameter application supports only the SIP digest authentication (or more specifically, HHTP digest, as defined in RFC 2617). It is expected that other mechanisms will be supported in the future.

User-Authorization-Answer Command

The User-Authorization-Answer (UAA) message is sent by the Diameter server in response a previously received Diameter User-Authorization-Request (UAR) command. In this response, the Diameter server indicates whether the registration authorization request was successful (SUCCESS) or failed (for example, DIAMETER_AUTHORIZATION_REJECTED) and provides a list of SIP capabilities.

Server-Assignment-Request Command

The Server-Assignment-Request (SAR) message is used by the Diameter client to indicate the completion of the authentication process to the Diameter server. In addition, the message contains the URI of the user's corresponding SIP proxy, and it instructs the Diameter server whether the URI should be stored or cleared from the Diameter server. Furthermore, the Diameter client can indicate to download the user profile for further processing. The user profile contains user preferences that define service requirements for the corresponding user that need to be executed by the SIP proxy.

Server-Assignment-Answer Command

The Server-Assignment-Answer (SAA) is sent in response to a previously received Diameter Server-Assignment-Request message. The response includes a success or error in executing the SAR command, and it may also include the user profile (or part of it) if it was requested.

Location-Info-Request Command

The Location-Info-Request (LIR) is sent by the SIP proxy to the Diameter server to request routing information such as the URI of a remote SIP proxy that serves a corresponding user (for example, visitor).

Location-Info-Answer Command

The Location-Info-Answer (LIA) is sent by the Diameter server in response to a previously received Diameter Location-Info-Request (LIR) command. If the request fails, the response contains an error message indicating the failure (for example, DIAMETER_ERROR_USER_ UNKNOWN). Otherwise, the requested information is sent in an AVP format.

Multimedia-Auth-Request Command

The Multimedia-Auth-Request (MAR) command is sent by the SIP proxy to the Diameter server to authenticate and authorize a user's request to use a SIP service (for example, REGISTER, INVITE). This message is also used to register the SIP proxy's URI to the Diameter server for future use.

Multimedia-Auth-Answer Command

The Multimedia-Auth-Answer (MAA) is sent by the Diameter server in response to a previously received Diameter Multimedia-Auth-Request (MAR) command. If the request fails, the response contains an error message indicating the failure (for example, DIAMETER_ERROR_ IDENTITIES_DONT_MATCH).

Registration-Termination-Request Command

The Registration-Termination-Request (RTR) command allows an operator to administratively deregister one or more users from a centralized Diameter server. The message is sent from the Diameter server to the Diameter client (on a SIP proxy) indicating that one or more SIP AORs have to be deregistered.

Registration-Termination-Answer Command

The Registration-Termination-Answer (RTA) is sent by a Diameter client to a Diameter server in response to a previously received Diameter Registration-Termination-Request (RTR) command.

Push-Profile-Request Command

The Push-Profile-Request (PPR) command is sent by a Diameter server to a Diameter client (running on a SIP proxy) to update the user profile of an existing user. In addition, the Diameter server can request to update accounting information on the SIP proxy. This is useful for provisioning purposes where user profile modifications are necessary to support service changes.

Push-Profile-Answer Command

The Push-Profile-Answer (PPA) is sent by the Diameter client to a Diameter server in response to a previously received Diameter Push-Profile-Request (PPR) command. If the command is successful, the SIP proxy (Diameter client) can download the user profile and store it for future processing. Otherwise, an error message is returned (for example, DIAMETER_ERROR_NOT_SUPPORTED_USER_DATA).

The Diameter protocol is exposed to various attacks, one being eavesdropping (discussed in Chapter 3, "Threats and Attacks"). To protect against eavesdropping, the transport protocol between the Diameter client and server must be protected using TLS or IPSec. Furthermore, the Diameter SIP application should be configured to perform all final authentications by the Diameter server instead of delegating it to other remote Diameter nodes.

VoIP Firewalls and NAT

VoIP firewalls help protect against various attacks by enforcing policies on inbound and outbound traffic and supporting Network and Port Address Translation (NAPT). NAT provides internal network topology hiding and suppresses external attacks against internal hosts.

Providing NAT also introduces an impediment to properly manage Internet multimedia sessions. One of the deployment issues with VoIP and firewalls is proper session management. When a VoIP phone that is located behind a NAT firewall initiates a call to another phone, the signaling messages include information that reflect properties of the originating phone. This information includes the phone's local IP address and port that the message was sent from and the ports on which signaling and media messages should be received. If the remote phone is located outside the NAT firewall, the information contained in the signaling messages will be invalid because they reflect the addressing of the internal network.

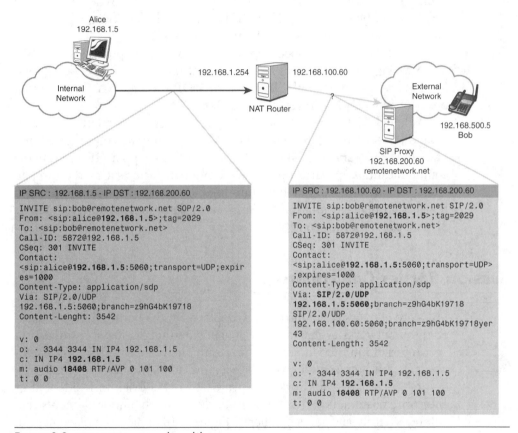

FIGURE 8.9 SIP NAT traversal problem.

Figure 8.9 provides an example in which a signaling message from host 192.168.1.5 is sent to Bob's phone at bob@remotenetwork.com with address 192.168.200.5. Note two important items here. First, the IP address of the message has changed from 192.168.1.5 to 192.168.100.60.

Second, the IP address advertised in the SIP message where the signaling and media messages should be sent is 192.168.1.5, which is incorrect. When Bob answers the phone, it will start transmitting media to IP address 192.168.1.5 rather than 192.168.100.60, and all packets will be discarded. The NAT firewall has to be able to inspect the SIP messages and make the necessary modifications to the SIP/SDAP headers to reflect the appropriate IP addresses and ports that should be used (in this case, the NAT firewall's external IP address and port from which the request was sent). In addition, the NAT firewall should be ready to accept RTP traffic from Bob's phone by inspecting the SDP headers and identifying which ports have been negotiated between the two end points.

The IETF has developed approaches to overcome problems with SIP and NAT'ing. These solutions are defined within the ICE methodology and include the STUN (Simple Traversal of UDP through NAT, RFC 3489) protocol and TURN (Traversal Using Relay NAT).

Although VoIP firewalls provide some protection, as mentioned earlier, and they can recognize and handle VoIP communications, they cannot offer the necessary scalability that is required to support IP multimedia communications in carrier-grade environments where it is required to manage millions of simultaneous multimedia sessions. Therefore, the functionality to manage multimedia sessions is dedicated to devices such as SBCs (session border controllers).

Session Border Controllers

SBCs are network elements that are deployed at the border between packet-based networks to manage the signaling and media messages that support Internet multimedia services (for example, voice or video). For example, they can be placed between service providers in a peering configuration or in an access network that provides VoIP service to residential or enterprise customers. SBCs are considered network border elements that enforce security and service policies. Figure 8.10 depicts the placement of the SBC in an IP network.

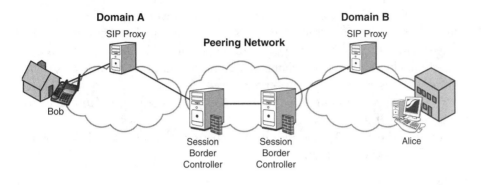

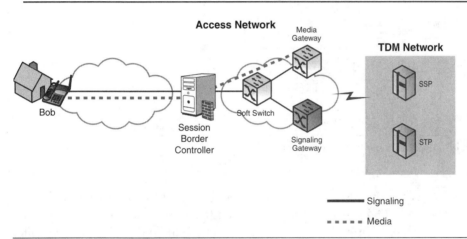

FIGURE 8.10 SBC network placement.

When Bob makes a call to Alice (from domain A to domain B), the signaling messages generated from Bob's phone that are sent to the local SIP proxy (or H.323 gatekeeper in case H.323 is used) traverse domain A's SBC and then domain B's SBC, which in turn will contact Alice's SIP proxy. Finally, Alice's SIP proxy will signal her phone to alert her that Bob would like to initiate a session. When Alice picks up the phone, a SIP response is generated and traverses the intermediate SIP proxies and SBCs (Alice's SIP proxy, SBC domain B to SBC domain A, and finally Bob's SIP proxy) until it reaches Bob's phone. When the signaling to set up the session is complete, the two end points start transmitting voice using the RTP protocol. Note that although the signaling messages traverse the SBCs and the intermediate SIP proxies, the media packets traverse only the SBCs but not the proxies. This allows the SBCs to control signaling and media messages and provides the ability to enforce policies to protect against associated attacks (for example, malicious messages and bandwidth-consuming attacks to disrupt or degrade service).

The remote components (for example, phones or proxies) interact with the SBC as if it were the other remote end and not an intermediary, and therefore the SBC is labeled a back-to-back user agent (B2BUA). Figure 8.11 depicts this configuration.

FIGURE 8.11 A logical representation of an SBC (B2BUA).

When the SBC receives an incoming request to set up a call (for example, INVITE), it acts as if it were the end point (for example, Alice's phone) and sends a provisional response (for example, 100 Trying) to the caller (for example, Bob's phone) to indicate that the dialogue is in progress. At the same time, the SBC initiates a new request to contact the callee (for example, Alice). When the SBC receives a response from the callee, it forwards it to the caller. Figure 8.12 depicts the call flow in which an SBC is terminating and reinitiating signaling messages.

The SBC also terminates the incoming RTP stream and initiates a new RTP stream to the remote end. This ability allows managing the media format (for example, CODEC) that is used in a session to modify the RTP stream as needed. This is called *transcoding*, in which a network element encodes an RTP stream from one format to another (for example, from Pulse Code Modulation u-law PCMU to G.726). The same functionality is also available for signaling (for example, SIP-to-H.323 translation).

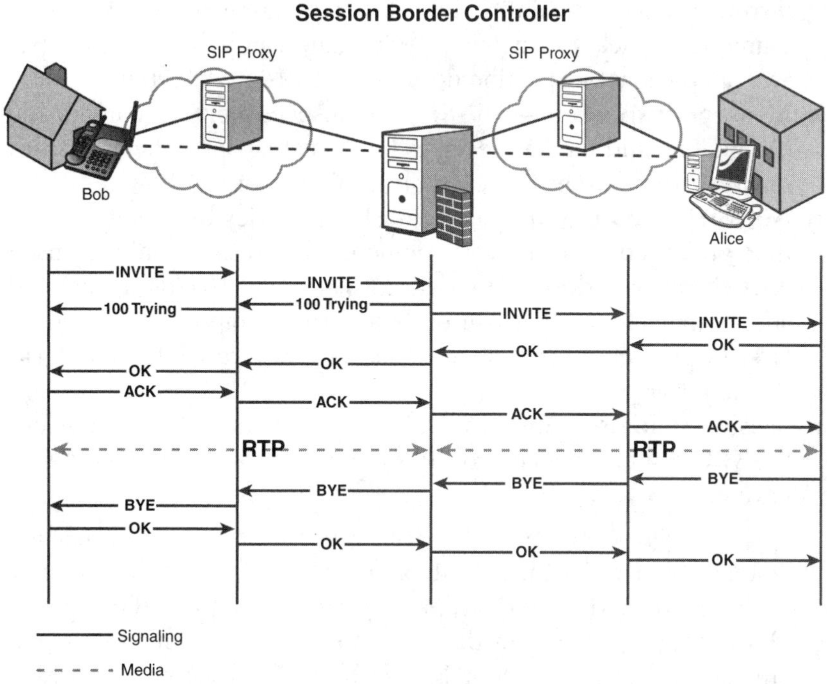

Session Border Controller

FIGURE 8.12 SBC call flow example.

The ability of the SBC to manage multimedia sessions provides the means to enforce various controls to support security objectives.[3] The controls that can be used by an SBC to protect against attacks include the following:

- **Traffic rate limiting**—This functionality provides the ability to control the number of simultaneous sessions (calls) from a given source, which can be a collection of devices or a distinct device caller. In addition, this control helps prevent from occupying PSTN links of backend components. This helps mitigate against DoS attacks, including DDoS (distributed DoS), that aim to impact or

---

3. *J. Hautakopi, et al.* Requirements from SIP (Session Initiation Protocol) Session Border Control Deployments, *IETF draft-camarillo-sipping-sbc-funcs-04.txt.*

disrupt service availability. Rate limiting can also be enforced by inline deep packet inspection devices and can be detected by passive deep packet inspection devices or intrusion detection sensors.

■ **Message inspection**—The SBC can inspect the syntax and format of signaling and media messages to protect against attacks that use malformed messages (for example, DoS, buffer overflow).

■ **Network topology hiding**—An SBC provides the ability to hide the configuration of network elements that reside behind it using NAT (Network Address Translation). The ability to hide the network addressing scheme that is used by internal components provides a layer of protection from attacks that require direct interaction with the target.

■ **Session management**—In addition to providing QoS for sessions, the SBC can enforce controls to support security, including the following:

–*Access control.* Because the SBC can manage the signaling and media streams dynamically, it can control traffic flow based on IP, SIP URI, and other properties (for example, RTP ports). Furthermore, it can provide authentication of signaling messages at the network and application layers to enforce call/session admission.

–*NAT traversal.* Provides network topology hiding and message modifications to overcome issues with private IP addresses (RFC 1918) in signaling messages (for example, SIP/SDP).

–*Modification and termination of sessions.* The SBC can modify the state and parameters of a multimedia session, including parameters in the signaling and media stream (for example, SIP/H.323, SDP, RTP), to enforce a policy. For example, a policy may dictate that sessions that originate from specific networks are not admitted or they should be redirected to another SBC that serves a corresponding geographic region. Or another policy would be to discard and log any calls that are made between 12 a.m. and 8 a.m.

–*UDP stream management.* Dynamic allocation and management of UDP ports to protect from unsolicited UDP traffic and attacks (for example, DoS, SPIT, UDP injection). In addition, the SBC may perform transcoding of media packets to meet certain audio/visual requirements. This allows the SBC to inspect the RTP traffic and detect and discard any malicious or erroneous packets. The SBC can detect whether end points have properly completed the exchange of signaling messages before sending RTP traffic and reflect more accurate information for billing (see the related discussion about fraud in Chapter 3). Also, in a scenario in which a calling card is used, the SBC can terminate a call if the user runs out of available minutes.

In addition, SBCs tend to be ideal components to enforce lawful intercept because they are in the communication path of participants and control both the signaling and media stream. At the same time, this opportunity increases the security requirements for SBCs when it comes to management and administration, especially if the SBC is deployed to manage traffic originating from the Internet, which increases the threat level and number of attacks that can be performed. Imagine the consequences to the network operator and law enforcement agency if an SBC is compromised while executing a surveillance warrant.

These controls are defined in the SBC's security policy, which organizes and enforces operational, organizational, and service requirements. For example, a policy may dictate that sessions that originate from specific networks are not admitted or they should be redirected to another SBC that serves a corresponding geographic region. These functions may be found in the IMS architecture distributed across various components, such as P-CSCF (Proxy-call/Session Control Function), I-CSCF (Interrogating-Call/Session Control Function), or a SEG (Security Gateway).

Limitations of SBCs

Every good story comes to an end. Although SBCs provide several features to protect from various attacks, they also get in the way of supporting certain security functions and objectives. The limitations associated with security include the following:

- **Confidentiality and end-to-end privacy is hampered**—SBCs intercept signaling and media traffic to make decisions based on the enforced policy. If the SBC receives an encrypted signaling or media packet, it will have to decrypt the incoming packet to process it, and therefore it must maintain a set of cryptographic keys associated with the corresponding session. So, the SBC will have to decrypt, process, and re-encrypt the packets if necessary to maintain confidentiality on the other end. This procedure limits end-to-end confidentiality because the SBC acts as man in the middle, and encryption parameters do not remain consistent (for example, digital signatures).

- **Authentication**—Verifying user and device identity is important in Internet multimedia applications, including VoIP. Features such as caller ID are used by businesses to identify customers. If caller ID information can be spoofed in a call, it can be used to perform a number of attacks. For example, a well-known international cellular carrier performs voice mailbox authentication using caller ID. An attacker can use this weakness to spoof the caller ID and manage, modify, retrieve, or delete messages on subscriber mailboxes. There are currently VoIP service providers which offer service to residential and enterprise customers that may not enforce proper message authentication controls. For example, a service provider may deploy security components such as an SBC the products do provide the ability to validate a subscriber's identity and thus allowing attacks such as Caller-ID spoofing.

- **Proprietary extension support**—As vendors strive to maintain competitiveness, they will introduce features and extensions to the protocols used for VoIP (for example, SIP, SDP, RTP). In some cases, vendor extensions might not be supported by the SBC, and thus might limit the ability to extend services or enforce security policies (for example, a proprietary authentication mechanism, message inspection).

- **Reliability of session state**—One of the fundamental functions of the SBC is maintaining session state. If the SBC operation is disrupted (for example, hardware/software malfunction or attack), all session state information is lost, and it will cease processing packets from sessions that were established prior to the outage. For example, if the SBC removes Via entries from a request and then restarts, losing state, the SBC will not be able to route responses to that request. It is advisable to maintain a redundant SBC configuration to overcome service unavailability introduced by the use of a single SBC in case of a failure.

Intrusion Detection and VoIP

Although intrusion detection techniques and products have matured during the last decade, the evolution of Internet multimedia applications, such as VoIP, has introduced a new opportunity for research in intrusion detection. There are two categories of intrusion detection systems (IDSs): signature based and anomaly based. Signature-based IDSs identify malicious activity by inspecting individual packets and matching a pattern to a known signature. Anomaly-based IDSs identify attacks by analyzing aggregate streams of network traffic and performing pattern matching based on predefined traffic heuristics (for example, if activity occurs within normal or abnormal parameters). Both approaches have strengths and weaknesses, but they are effective when used appropriately. One fundamental limitation of current IDS techniques is the orthogonal approach for inspecting and correlating network traffic to identify malicious activity. For example, a typical IDS system is configured to look for specific properties in a protocol (for example, UDP, TCP, HTTP) that match certain rules. In addition, the inspection can be extended to a specific application and analyze the contents of an application message (for example, Web application queries, SQL queries).

VoIP communications use a combination of protocols to relay signaling messages, and they can use dynamically allocated ports. In addition, different routes can be used for signaling or media traffic. These properties introduce challenges to the existing IDS systems. Although they can detect some of the VoIP-related attacks using current techniques, they cannot yet detect attacks such as call or session hijacking, call-flow manipulation, or media manipulation. For example, the Snort IDS uses signature-based techniques to detect malicious activity associated with SIP signaling (see Listing 8.1). These rules include detection for attacks such as SIP signaling flooding, port scanning against SIP ports, SYN floods, and others.

The IDS needs to be able to detect the following:

- DoS; through application resource exhaustion (for example, attacks against the signaling or key management protocols)
- Masquerading of signaling and media messages
- Detection of malformed messages

- Call-flow manipulation attacks (for example, message reordering, insertion, deletion)
- Access control and authorization attacks (for example, authentication replay attacks, application functionality violation attacks, bid-down attacks)
- Fraud

Therefore, in addition to using some of the existing IDS techniques, new methods need to be developed to identify attacks associated with Internet multimedia applications.

Event correlation is one technique that can be used in VoIP to aggregate events from multiple agents that reside on VoIP network elements, including phones, SIP proxies, gateways, and SBCs. Event correlation techniques rely on the characteristics of the network and transport layer, which is insufficient. Instead, correlation techniques need to be developed to incorporate characteristics from the protocols used to support multimedia applications. One research effort that attempts to address this issue is SpaceDive, in which a hierarchical approach to event correlation is used.[4]

Another approach is based on protocol state machines.[5] This approach inspects the state transitions associated with the protocol state machines rather than the properties associated with the protocols and network traffic. The protocol state machine is developed from the protocol specification in which state and transition are clearly defined. Because VoIP communications are depended on protocol state transitions, any deviation from normal communication patterns can be flagged and analyzed for malicious activity.

Although these techniques are promising and help establish the direction, additional attention should be given to expedite research and product development to meet the forthcoming demand.

4. *V. Apte, et al. SpaceDive: A Distributed Intrusion Detection System for Voice over IP environments. CERIAS Tech Report 2006-17.*

5. *H. Sengar, D. et. al. VoIP Intrusion Detection Through Protocol State Machines. 2006 International Conference on Dependable Systems and Networks.*

Listing 8.1 Example of Snort Rules for Detecting VoIP Attacks

```
# Ruleset for the detection of attacks to SIP based VoIP
networks
# Created within the Snocer project www.snocer.org
# Jiri Markl, jiri.markl@nextsoft.cz, Nextsoft s.r.o.

#Here customize variables to fit your network
#Port where SIP proxy is listening
var SIP_PROXY_PORTS 5060

#SIP proxy IP address
var SIP_PROXY_IP any
# Example: var SIP_PROXY_IP 192.168.1.110

#Used DNS server address
var DNS_SERVERS any
# Example: var DNS_SERVERS 192.168.1.20 192.168.1.30

#Known SIP proxy addresses
#var KNOWN_PROXY _ENTER_HERE_


################## PORTSCAN preprocessors
##########################################
#Example of configuration of Portscan Detector:
#alert when more then 5 ports is scaned within 7 seconds
preprocessor portscan: $SIP_PROXY_IP 5 7

#don't alert if portscan arrive from this network and host
#Replace _IGNORE_PORTSCAN_ by hosts or networks from which you
want to allow portscans
#and uncomment the following line
#preprocessor portscan-ignorehosts: _IGNORE_PORTSCAN_


################## COMMON TCP/IP
ATTACKS##############################################
#TCP SYN flood detection rule (from single source IP address):
```

(continues)

Listing 8.1 Example of Snort Rules for Detecting VoIP Attacks *(continued)*

```
alert tcp any any -> $SIP_PROXY_IP any \
(msg: "TCP SYN packet flooding from single source"; \
threshold: type both, track by_src, count 200, seconds 20; \
flow:stateless; flags:S,12; sid:5000001; rev:1;)

#TCP SYN flood detection rule (all TCP SYN packets with
different source IP address):
alert tcp any any -> $SIP_PROXY_IP any \
(msg: " TCP SYN packet flooding (simple or distributed)"; \
threshold: type both, track by_dst, count 10000, seconds 60; \
flow:stateless; flags:S,12; sid:5000002; rev:1;)

#SMURF attack
alert icmp any any -> $SIP_PROXY_IP any \
(msg: "Smurf attack directed against SIP proxy"; \
itype: 0; \
threshold: type both, track by_dst, count 1000, seconds 60; \
sid:5000003; rev:1;)


################### FLOODING BY SIP MESSAGES
##########################################
#Rule for alerting of INVITE flood attack:
alert ip any any -> $SIP_PROXY_IP $SIP_PROXY_PORTS \
(msg:"INVITE message flooding"; content:"INVITE"; depth:6; \
threshold: type both , track by_src, count 100, seconds 60; \
sid:5000004; rev:1;)

#Suppresion of alerting for known proxy
#suppress gen_id 1, sig_id 5000004, track by_src, ip
KNOWN_PROXY

#Rule for alerting of REGISTER flood attack:
alert ip any any -> $SIP_PROXY_IP $SIP_PROXY_PORTS \
(msg:"REGISTER message flooding"; content:"REGISTER"; depth:8; \
threshold: type both , track by_src, count 100, seconds 60; \
sid:5000005; rev:1;)
```

```
#Suppresion of alerting for known proxy
#suppress gen_id 1, sig_id 5000005, track by_src, ip
KNOWN_PROXY


################### FLOODING BY COMMON TCP/UDP PACKETS
##################################
#Rule for alerting common TCP/UDP flood attack:
alert ip any any -> $SIP_PROXY_IP $SIP_PROXY_PORTS \
(msg:"TCP/IP message flooding directed to SIP proxy"; \
threshold: type both , track by_src, count 300, seconds 60; \
sid:5000007; rev:1;)


################### USING UNRESOLVABLE DNS NAMES
######################################
#Rule for alerting attack using unresolvable DNS names:
alert udp $DNS_SERVERS 53 -> $SIP_PROXY_IP any \
(msg:"DNS No such name treshold - Abnormaly high count of No
such name responses"; \
content:"|83|"; offset:3; depth:1; \
threshold: type both , track by_dst, count 100, seconds 60; \
sid:5000008; rev:1;)


################### UNAUTHORIZED RESPONSES
############################################
#Threshold rule for unauthorized responses:
alert ip any any -> $SIP_PROXY_IP $SIP_PROXY_PORTS \
(msg:"INVITE message flooding"; \
content:"SIP/2.0 401 Unauthorized"; depth:24; \
threshold: type both, track by_src, count 100, seconds 60; \
sid:5000009; rev:1;)


################### SQL INJECTION ATTACKS
############################################
#Detection of always true expressions injection:
alert ip any any -> $SIP_PROXY_IP $SIP_PROXY_PORTS \
(msg:"SQL Injection - Injection of always true expression"; \
pcre:"/\w*\'or/ix"; \
sid: 5000010; rev:1;)
```

(continues)

Listing 8.1 Example of Snort Rules for Detecting VoIP Attacks *(continued)*

```
#Detection of SQL statements:
#DROP statement injection:
alert ip any any -> $SIP_PROXY_IP $SIP_PROXY_PORTS \
(msg:"SQL Injection - Injection of DROP statement"; \
pcre:"/\'drop/ix"; \
sid: 5000011; rev:1;)

#DELETE statement injection:
alert ip any any -> $SIP_PROXY_IP $SIP_PROXY_PORTS \
(msg:"SQL Injection - Injection of DROP statement"; \
pcre:"/\'delete/ix"; \
sid: 5000012; rev:1;)

#SELECT statement injection:
alert ip any any -> $SIP_PROXY_IP $SIP_PROXY_PORTS \
(msg:"SQL Injection - Injection of DROP statement"; \
pcre:"/\'select/ix"; \
sid: 5000013; rev:1;)

#INSERT statement injection:
alert ip any any -> $SIP_PROXY_IP $SIP_PROXY_PORTS \
(msg:"SQL Injection - Injection of DROP statement"; \
pcre:"/\'insert/ix"; \
sid: 5000014; rev:1;)

#UPDATE statement injection:
alert ip any any -> $SIP_PROXY_IP $SIP_PROXY_PORTS \
(msg:"SQL Injection - Injection of DROP statement"; \
pcre:"/\'update/ix"; \
sid: 5000015; rev:1;)

#UNION statement injection:
alert ip any any -> $SIP_PROXY_IP $SIP_PROXY_PORTS \
(msg:"SQL Injection - Injection of DROP statement"; \
pcre:"/\'union/ix"; \
sid: 5000016; rev:1;)
```

Summary

This chapter discussed architectural options that should be considered during the design of a VoIP network to support overall robustness and security. In addition, specific mechanisms and components were discussed that can be used to protect against attacks such as DoS and unauthorized access. Although these mechanisms and components are not the only options to support security requirements and controls, they are typically the most commonly used. It is expected that other protocols and components may emerge as new attacks and threats emerge. The controls and mechanisms outlined in this chapter can be considered the fundamental components for deploying a robust VoIP network.

## CHAPTER 9

A SECURITY FRAMEWORK FOR ENTERPRISE VoIP NETWORKS

This chapter focuses on defining a security framework for enterprise VoIP networks to facilitate their design, deployment, and maintenance throughout the life of the implementation. The framework comprises the following:

- Security policy
- External parties
- Asset management
- Physical and environmental security
- Operations management
- Access control
- System acquisition, development, and maintenance
- Incident management
- Business continuity
- Compliance

These areas are similar to the ISO 17799/27001 standard. The standard offers an industry-acceptable approach to managing information security in an enterprise environment. In addition, some controls reflected in this framework are similar to the controls discussed in NIST SP800-58, *Security Considerations for Voice over IP Systems*. The security framework defined in this chapter is based on the author's experience with assessing and architecting security in VoIP networks and controls found in ISO 17799/27001 and NIST SP800-58 standards.

Note that the ISO 17799/27001 standard is considered a superset of controls defined in standards and regulatory requirements such as the NIST 800 series, the Sarbanes-Oxley Act (SoX), the Gramm-Leach-Bliley Act (GLBA), and others. In other words, if an enterprise chooses to align

its operations with ISO 17799/27001, it will naturally fulfill requirements
defined by the aforementioned standards or regulations. Therefore, the
controls defined in this chapter can be used as a guide during an ISO
17799/27001 certification of a VoIP network.

For each category defined here, a number of VoIP controls are discussed to help organizations implementing VoIP to follow a clear and consistent roadmap for deploying and managing a secure VoIP network.
Although the framework focuses on enterprise networks, several controls
can be used in telecommunication carrier environments.

VoIP Security Policy

When organizations decide to deploy VoIP, they also have to recognize the
strengths and limitations that the technology will introduce in their operations. Recognizing these strengths and limitations will help develop a gov-
erning VoIP security policy. The policy in turn will help derive standards
and technical controls that will support regulatory requirements and the
overall security posture of the network.

The security policy associated with VoIP communications (or any
packet-based multimedia applications) should address the following areas:

- Acceptable use of organizational VoIP equipment (for example,
  hard phones, soft phones, WLAN phones, voicemail, conferencing
  servers). The acceptable use includes calling plan restrictions (for
  example, calls to 900 numbers or international calls). These restrictions are also translated to configuration parameters on the respective VoIP components (for example, IP-PBX or SIP proxy).
  Acceptable use of VoIP equipment pertains also to contractors, vendors, and other third parties who interact with the organization.
- Protection of VoIP services, including the following:
  Service access (for example, password-protected conferencing sessions, voice mailbox access controls).

  Signaling and media encryption for interactions in which sensitive
  information is handled (for example, calls or videoconferencing in
  which customer/patient health information or financial information
  is communicated).

- Media retention based on the minimum duration that media should be kept based on regulatory or other industry, state, or federal requirements. The type of media includes, but is not limited to, CDRs (customer detail records), voicemail, call or videoconferencing recordings, instant messages, presentation slides, or whiteboard interactions.
- Signaling or media interception to satisfy law enforcement requirements (for example, CALEA). Although the requirement for lawful intercept pertains to carrier networks, it is helpful to provide such capability in an enterprise network to support the investigation of unforeseen incidents or circumstances.
- A vulnerability management process should be in place to categorize and prioritize the impact of vulnerabilities that may affect the organization's VoIP infrastructure and service.

Although these areas are the most common ones, additional areas may be defined by the organization as needed.

External Parties

In many cases, organizations need to provide access to the VoIP infrastructure or interface with another VoIP infrastructure to support operations with business partners or vendors. The interaction with third parties introduces another dimension in managing the associated threats related to accidental cause or malicious intent. Therefore, an organization needs to identify risks related to external parties, such as liability when VoIP equipment or services are misused, abused, or vandalized.

In the case of VoIP, the associated requirements include the following:

- Addressing security when dealing with customers and partners, including confidentiality and protection of VoIP communications and assets. The associated requirements should address, at least, the following:
  - Call admission controls to protect against unsolicited calls. This requirement is typically implemented by enforcing authentication of signaling messages to initiate calls.

–Signaling and media confidentiality for communications between
the various user groups (for example, executive management, marketing, sales, production, engineering). Certain user groups may
require media confidentiality; others may not. Encryption will be
dictated based on the role and type of information typically
exchanged between the respective users.

–Management of VoIP traffic exchanged between core components
(for example, IP-PBX, SIP proxy), including inspecting messages
for malformed headers.

■ Identifying security requirements for customer access to VoIP components such as hard phones, interfacing with IP-PBX, and so on.
The security requirements may include the following:

–Restricting access to configuration settings of VoIP phones or conferencing devices. Much of the VoIP equipment provides configuration information such as IP addresses of the phone, call managers, DNS servers, and so on, which can be used to construct an
attack. Therefore, access to such information should be protected.

–Dial plan restrictions. For example, restrict international calls and
allow only internal company and 911 calls from specified phones
that reside in conference rooms, lobbies, or other designated areas
in which customers may be present.

■ Addressing security of VoIP components and communications in
third-party agreements. Requirements in this area may include the
following:

–The type of information or data that is permissible to be exchanged
using the VoIP infrastructure

–Disclosure requirements of captured media or data associated with
VoIP communications

–The type of access that should be permitted between third parties
and the organization

–The requirements for managing VoIP components by third parties
such as managed service providers

Asset Management

One critical way to maintain proper security in enterprise and carrier networks is asset management. It provides the means to account for assets, asset allocation, and resource management, In addition, it helps measure compliance of controls across the network during VoIP security evaluations or audits. Asset management must be established for VoIP networks to manage the following:

- **Inventory of assets**—Assets should be clearly identified and inventoried on a scheduled basis (for example, semi-annually or annually) and accounted to maintain a consistent view of the deployed or reserved infrastructure components.
- **Ownership of assets**—VoIP components, including edge and core devices, should be assigned to organizational personnel, and their assignment should be documented clearly.
- **Acceptable use of assets**—The organization should develop and document rules for acceptable use of VoIP components, including hard phones, soft phones, conferencing equipment, and so on. The rules should address proper use of user-to-device interactions, use of the VoIP service (for example, restrict calls unrelated to organizational operations), and the improper use of VoIP equipment to commit fraud or other crimes.

Physical and Environmental Security

The overall security of the VoIP infrastructure is also dependent on the physical and environmental controls that are available. If an attacker gains access to core VoIP components, the attacker can perform a number of attacks, including eavesdropping, call manipulation, or fraud commission. This section discusses various controls to prevent unauthorized physical access and damage to and interference with the VoIP service and infrastructure components. The areas that need to be considered include the following:

- **Physical security perimeter**—VoIP core network elements and supporting components (for example, DNS, email, NTP, servers, network routers and switches, and so on) should be protected by a perimeter that provides physical isolation from external access (for example, physical barriers such as walls, badge-controlled entries) and provide appropriate entry and access controls for authorized personnel. Physical security perimeter controls extend to offices, rooms, and any facilities in which VoIP core and supporting components are located.

- **Protecting the VoIP infrastructure against external and environmental threats**—There should be defined physical and environmental controls to protect the VoIP components against threats such as damage from fire, flood, earthquake, vandalism, explosion, civil unrest, and other forms of natural or manmade disaster. These controls may already be in place to protect other parts of the organizational computing infrastructure, and therefore it might be easier to extend this protection to the VoIP infrastructure.

Note that in incumbent telecommunication carrier environments, a considerable number of controls aim to protect and prevent unauthorized access to the physical facilities (for example, wiring, network elements) that support the telecommunication services. These controls include alarms. Therefore, similar controls should be considered in VoIP implementations.

Equipment Security

Another dimension to protecting the VoIP infrastructure is equipment security. Although asset management and physical security provide a level of protection and control, individual equipment security extends the radius of protection (and thus increases overall security in cases in which other defenses are compromised). Equipment security concentrates on defining controls to protect VoIP components from threats such as direct unauthorized access, vandalism, theft, or damage, which will in turn impact the organization's operations. Primary controls in this area include the following:

- **Supporting power utilities**—It is essential that VoIP equipment be supported by backup power (for example, UPS and power generators) to protect against power disruption caused by natural or man-made catastrophes. This control will support the continuous operation of the VoIP network and communications across the organization, including placing emergency calls for aid (for example, 911).

- **Cabling security**—As in any other network, security of the cabling that interconnects the various VoIP components is an important aspect of protecting against attacks (for example, service disruption, eavesdropping). Therefore, cabling that supports VoIP communications should be protected by proper concealment in walls or other protective mediums that do not provide an easy avenue for attack.

- **Equipment maintenance**—Components that support the VoIP service or comprise the VoIP network should be stowed in facilities with the appropriate climate controls (for example, at temperatures between 69 degrees and 73 degrees Fahrenheit and 45 percent and 50 percent relative humidity). In addition, the components should maintain deterrents (for example, locks) to prevent unauthorized access to external media devices, networks, USBs, console ports, removable hard drives, and so on.

- **Security of equipment off-premises**—Many organizations deploy VoIP to minimize telecommunication costs between headquarters and remote sites. Therefore, VoIP equipment deployed in remote sites should be inspected on a scheduled basis to ensure that they maintain adequate security controls and do not deviate from the organization's standards. Organizations should also consider the threats and risks associated with remote locations before deploying VoIP equipment, especially if these locations are in international locations (where the threats may be dissimilar to threats found at headquarters).

- **Secure disposal or reuse of equipment**—Although this control may be considered premature because VoIP is a new technology, the organization should maintain a set of procedures that describe secure disposal of VoIP equipment (for example, voicemail servers, call managers, VoIP hard phones and so on).[1]

---

1. *An example of such procedures can be found at http://csrc.nist.gov/fasp/FASPDocs/
inoutput-control/NIHDataSanBSP.htm.*

- **Removal of property**—In cases where VoIP equipment needs to be taken offsite (for example, for service or repair), an authorization procedure should be enforced. The procedure should clearly reflect the transition of ownership and configuration of the VoIP equipment. This will help maintain proper asset management and tracking.

Operations Management

Operations management is fundamental to helping maintain an adequate security posture of a VoIP network. In addition to administering the components at the operating system level, it is required to maintain procedures for managing and provisioning securely the services supported by the VoIP network. The controls that should be considered for managing the VoIP network include the following:

- **Documented operating procedures**—The procedures for administering, managing, and provisioning the VoIP network and associated services should be clearly documented. The documentation should capture the methods and mechanisms that should be followed by administrators and personnel involved in provisioning and managing the VoIP services and components (for example, use of secure sessions using SSH/TLS to manage components, logging of activities, and which user groups are responsible for administration and management).
- **Change management**—Changes in the VoIP environment should follow the organization's process for change management procedures. Changes should be reviewed by a group of subject matter experts and stakeholders, tested in a lab environment, and documented before being committed. In addition, a rollback strategy should always be identified to avoid possible service disruption by changes that may impact VoIP service.
- **Segregation of duties**—Depending on the size of the organization, the tasks for administering, managing, and provisioning the VoIP network should be clearly defined and performed by distinct individuals.

- **Separation of development, test, and operational facilities—** It is recommended that a clear separation exists between production VoIP components, development, and testing. Although most organizations don't perform VoIP application development at the moment, it is expected that as the technology evolves there will be instances in which VoIP applications will be developed by in-house developers to accommodate specific needs. For example, companies such as Wal-Mart or Pepsi that focus on streamlining supply-chain operations leverage in-house development teams to enhance current systems or develop new ones. As new methods for processing and operational procedures are developed to accommodate organizational objectives, it is expected that development of real-time applications will also increase. Protocols such as SIP and RTP offer the flexibility to support the development of rich real-time applications such as voice and video collaboration (for example, whiteboard, screen sharing).

- **Third-party service-delivery management—**In cases where the organization outsources the management of the VoIP infrastructure or requires service support by vendors, the service level agreement should ensure that the security controls, service definitions, and delivery levels included in the third-party service-delivery agreement are implemented, operated, and maintained by the third party. The service performance should be monitored regularly (for example, by reviewing reports generated by the third party and conducting technical evaluations) to ensure compliance and identify possible inconsistencies. Furthermore, the organization should have the freedom to verify the state of the security controls maintained by the third party by performing scheduled and unscheduled security evaluations.

- **System planning and acceptance—**As the organization evolves, it is necessary to provide the flexibility for the VoIP network to scale to the needs of the organization. Capacity planning helps determine scaling requirements to minimize system or service failure due to resource exhaustion. Therefore, the VoIP network's components should be monitored to identify hardware, software, and bandwidth limitations (for example, memory and disk capacity for call managers, media gateways, voice channels, software licensing, router memory, bandwidth allocation, and so on). Capacity requirements and acceptance criteria should be in place to ascertain whether software or hardware upgrades are suitable before deployment. Therefore, a testing facility should be maintained to support the evaluation and acceptance process.

- **Protection against malicious code**—Malicious code can become evident in VoIP components and impact service in an unexpected way. For example, VoIP phones may require downloading their operating system image during the boot process. An attacker may corrupt or replace the bootable image with another image that contains malicious code to carry out an attack (for example, DoS, eavesdropping, fraud, and so on). To protect from attacks associated with malicious code injection, a combination of security controls should be in place. Some of these controls include maintaining a cryptographic signature of the bootable image, enforcing signature verification by the device loading the image, and enforcing network and system access controls to restrict unauthorized users from gaining access to the image server (for example, network ACLs, user ID/password, read/write restrictions).

- **Backup**—To support business and service continuity, it is necessary to back up components that support the VoIP service. These components include core VoIP components (for example, voicemail servers, proxy servers, call managers) but also peripheral components such as DNS and email servers. One important aspect of backing up VoIP components is the organization's data-retention policy, which may be dictated by regulatory requirements (depending on the state or country in which the organization resides). Backups may include voicemail messages, email messages, and system files. Therefore, there should be security requirements to address confidentiality and integrity of the stored data along with theft deterrence and physical damage protection mechanisms.

- **VoIP network security management**—Operations management in VoIP networks also includes network security management to monitor, enforce, and maintain network security controls uniformly. Network security management in VoIP networks includes monitoring events at three levels: network, operating system, and service. This means the organization should maintain a capability that allows retrieving and analyzing events from network interfaces (for example, SNMP traps/alarms), operating system logs (for example, kernel events, audit logs for user events and exceptions, administrator logs), and service events (for example, service logs, dropped calls, failed call admissions). An important aspect of monitoring is clock synchronization. Internal system clocks should be synchronized using an accurate time source. Clock synchronization is important when troubleshooting problems but also when performing network or system forensics. In addition, the procedures for managing the security of the VoIP components should be documented to provide a uniform approach.

Access Control

Access control in VoIP implementations is required in many levels of the network. There are typically three dimensions of access controls:

- Device access to the VoIP network
- User access to the VoIP services
- Administration access of the VoIP components

Figure 9.1 depicts the logical representation of access control layers in a VoIP network. User access is typically established through the use of a device. In some cases, the user may be required to authenticate to the device to receive service and also modify profile preferences on the respective device. In cases where user authentication on the device is not required, the device acts as a medium to relay the user authentication information to the network.

Administration and management access can be dictated in a similar way as user/device authentication. The administrator authenticates to the management station and consequently authenticates to the VoIP component to be managed (for example, SIP proxy server, H.323 gatekeeper). Various mechanisms can be used to authenticate users and devices in a VoIP network. Some mechanisms are provided by the VoIP protocols and some by the operating system or firmware running on the VoIP component.

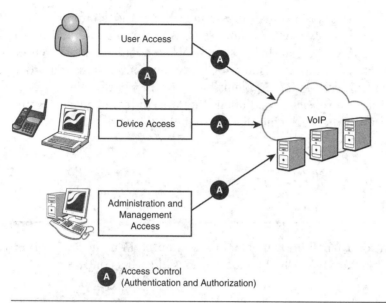

FIGURE 9.1 Logical access control layers in VoIP.

Table 9-1 Examples of Access Control Mechanisms in VoIP

Authentication/Authorization Mechanism	Device	User
IEEE 802.1x. Port-based authentication for devices.	✓	✓
Diameter client/server-based protocol that can be used to authenticate users or devices in the VoIP network. Also used in the IMS architecture (IP Multimedia Subsystem). See RFC 3588 and IETF draft *Diameter Session Initiation Protocol (SIP) Application 1*	✓	✓
SIP digest authentication. Supported in SIP for message authentication (INVITE and REGISTER).	✓	
H.235.1 Baseline Security Profile recommendation provides support for message authentication and integrity of H.245, H.225.0, RAS, and call signaling messages. The challenge authentication is implemented using a HMAC-SHA1-96 to produce a 20-byte hashed password.	✓	
Network service / operating system login (for example, SSH, SSL).		✓

1. http://www.ietf.org/internet-drafts/draft-ietf-aaa-diameter-sip-app-12.txt

The following controls should be considered as part of the access control policy:

- The access control mechanisms should be dictated and defined clearly in the organizational access control policy in alignment with the operational requirements of the organization.
- There should be a distinct capability (for example, designated personnel such as a security officer) and a process for the following:

    User credential issuance and revocation for VoIP devices, including phones, core components administration, and management stations

    Issuance of unique user IDs

    User credential management, including password strength enforcement and password expiration/reset and account auditing on a schedule basis

- User awareness on security topics such as credential confidentiality and password strength, clear desk/screen, and device locking.
- Network access control should be enforced to restrict access to VoIP services, devices, and management interfaces (for example, enforcement of ACLs on the Ethernet switch to segregate VLANs or firewall policies to restrict the flow of traffic between internal or external networks). In addition, message authentication should be enforced for signaling and media messages.
- Intercommunication between core components should be performed by establishing a trust relationship (for example, allowing signaling messages to flow between a call manager and a media gateway by enforcing network or local ACLs).
- VoIP network elements should be configured to allow connections on management ports from designated hosts (for example, enforce network/local ACLs).
- Network segregation should be enforced between the core VoIP components, phones, and other network elements that support VoIP services (for example, DNS servers, mail servers). For example, subnets that contain the core VoIP components should not be accessible from the corporate network. Access between the VoIP phone subnet and the core VoIP network should be restricted to signaling and media protocols. In addition, the subnets that contain all VoIP phones should not be accessible by other networks (for example, corporate or guest).

- Guest and third-party networks should be restricted from accessing the VoIP core components and phone subnets. If guests or subcontractors require access to VoIP services, a stateful VoIP firewall should be considered for deployment, and appropriate access controls (for example, user credentials, signaling protocol restrictions) should be enforced.

- Operating system controls should be enforced for user interaction, administration, and management, including secure logon (for example, SSH, SSL, Diameter) and session timeout.

- Third-party utilities or applications should not be deployed on core VoIP components unless they are inspected and certified through a security certification and validation process.

- VoIP service and application access should be restricted to authorized users who have been assigned proper credentials. Reuse of credentials by users other than the designated owners should not be permitted.

- Mobile devices that have VoIP capabilities (for example, PDAs and laptops with soft phones, wireless VoIP phones) should be assigned to a distinct subnet/VLAN and segregated through a firewall. Workstations with VoIP soft phones that are connected to the corporate data network should have the capability to encrypt signaling and media traffic.

- Port-based access controls should be enforced to restrict unauthorized access. Such controls include the deployment of IEEE 802.1x and deactivation of unused Ethernet ports on the switch.

- User and device registration should be enforced before allowing origination or reception of calls or related multimedia sessions. Device and user registrations should be authenticated with a corresponding VoIP network element such as a gatekeeper or SIP registrar.

- Controls for signaling and media messages should be enforced to protect against unauthorized communications or generation/ propagation of malicious messages (for example, authentication, confidentiality, and integrity of signaling and media messages). See Chapter 5, "Signaling Protection Mechanisms," and Chapter 6, "Media Protection Mechanisms," for additional information about protecting signaling and media messages.

- Authentication, authorization, and cryptographic controls should be enforced to restrict access to CDRs only to authorized personnel.

- Authentication, authorization, and cryptographic controls should be enforced to restrict access to voicemails only to authorized personnel.
- Key management mechanisms should be defined and standardized to support authentication, confidentiality, and integrity of VoIP communications.

Information Systems Acquisition, Development, and Maintenance

As organizations decide to adopt VoIP, they should establish a process in which they define security requirements for acquisition, development, and maintenance. It is expected that as organizations mature, their understanding and use of the deployed VoIP infrastructure will provide the means to develop innovative applications to support operations. Therefore, proper controls should be in place to support development and maintenance of multimedia applications that will utilize the VoIP protocols and infrastructure. The following are some of the controls to be considered:

- Security requirements and standards should be defined as part of the acquisition process of VoIP components and applications. The requirements should capture the fundamental security objectives of confidentiality, integrity, and availability. For example, VoIP components should support signaling confidentiality, integrity, and authentication (for example, H.235 security profiles, SIPS, SRTP, and so on). Additional security requirements include administrative and management controls (for example, SSH/HTTPS, role-based authorization).
- API security controls should be defined and made available to facilitate secure interexchange of data, signaling, or media messages between multimedia applications and supporting components (for example, email servers, unified messaging). These controls should provide the ability to support strong authentication, integrity, and confidentiality.

- VoIP component functionality and data validation. A process should be defined in which VoIP products (software and hardware) are evaluated prior to being deployed in production. This process should outline security requirements and test methodology for evaluating VoIP products according to the organizational security policy and standards.
- VoIP component deployment. A process should be in place that defines security requirements, procedures and controls for deploying VoIP components (for example, installation and configuration of software and hardware).
- VoIP component retirement. A process should be in place that defines security requirements and procedures for retiring VoIP components (software and hardware).
- Change control procedures should be defined to support modification and updates to the VoIP network and to provide the ability to recover from erroneous implementation, which ultimately can impact VoIP service availability. Typically, a test environment, a replica of the production environment, should be used before evaluating the intended change to identify potential impact.

Security Incident Management

To properly manage future events that may occur in the VoIP network, a well-defined incident management plan should be established. (for example, to deal with fraud or unauthorized access). Incident management has been written about widely, and so I recommend you find a book dedicated to the subject. This section identifies some recommended controls related to VoIP that can be useful in incorporating in an organization's incident response and management plan. These controls include the following:

- Customer detail records (CDRs) are useful in forensic investigations, and therefore should be maintained and securely archived for a defined period. Typically, the time retention requirement is dictated by regulatory requirements.
- There should be organizational requirements for voicemail archiving, similar to CDRs.

- Cryptographic mechanisms should be implemented to protect the integrity and confidentiality of CDRs, voicemail, and related media-capture components (for example, conferencing servers, unified messaging servers).

Business Continuity Management

VoIP provides a cost-effective and flexible alternative to maintain communications during a disaster. Therefore, organizations should consider incorporating VoIP communications as an alternative communications channel in case of a disaster. Some of the considerations should include the following:

- Alternative communication mechanisms should be defined as part of the business continuity plan.
- Interoperability of VoIP equipment configuration and protocols with VoIP alternative service providers (for example, soft phones, gatekeepers, SIP proxies).
- There should be a service level agreement with VoIP service providers in case of a disaster.
- A VoIP recovery site should be established to support continuation of operations.
- A core set of VoIP components should be available for operation and assist in the recovery process.
- The communications recovery plan should be tested on a scheduled basis.

Compliance

VoIP communications compliance with standards and regulatory requirements is a topic under development. Some standards and regulations have been defined, but compliance is questionable. The following are some of the well-known standards and regulatory requirements associated with VoIP that should be considered:

- **Standards**

  Security Considerations for Voice over IP Systems, NIST publication (Special Publication 800-58)

  IP Telephony & Voice over Internet Protocol, Security Technical Implementation Guide, DISA (Defense Information Systems Agency)

- **Regulatory requirements**

  FCC requirements for VoIP service providers to support E911 service

  FCC requirements to enable Law Enforcement to access certain broadband and VoIP providers (Communication Assistance to Law Enforcement Act) (see www.fcc.gov/omd/pra/docs/3060-0809/3060-0809-10.doc)

  FDIC, Voice over Internet Protocol Guidance on the Security Risks of VoIP (see www.fdic.gov/news/news/financial/2005/fil6905.pdf)

There are also general IT regulatory requirements such as Sarbanes-Oxley and HIPAA (the Health Insurance Portability and Accountability Act) that can mandate controls for VoIP indirectly.

Summary

This chapter outlined the core areas that need to be considered when deploying enterprise VoIP networks. For each area, a number of recommendations were made that align with industry standards such as ISO17799 and NIST's publication SP800-58, *Security Considerations for Voice over IP System*. These recommendations should be used in conjunction with the protection mechanisms discussed in Chapters 5, 6, and 7 to maintain an adequate security posture against threats and attacks. Furthermore, the ISO 17799/27001 standard is considered to include controls that pertain to regulatory requirements such as the Sarbanes-Oxley Act (SoX) and the Gramm-Leach-Bliley Act (GLBA). Therefore, the outlined framework fulfills requirements outlined in regulatory requirements and can also be used as a guide during an ISO 17799/27001 certification of a VoIP network.

## CHAPTER 10

PROVIDER ARCHITECTURES AND SECURITY

This chapter describes the logical components and network topology of various architectures currently used in service provider VoIP deployments. Carrier-grade VoIP architectures aim to provide a scalable, secure, robust, and interoperable network for residential and enterprise customers using standard mechanisms and protocols. Although this philosophy is claimed by many companies that provide VoIP services, some take a more mature approach to meet these objectives. The two issues that surface frequently are QoS and security, which also tend to be somewhat interrelated. If a network element (for example, SIP proxy) suffers from a vulnerability which can be used to cause a DoS (or a related Byzantine behavior), it can cripple the provider's QoS and its objective of maintaining 99.999 percent uptime. The next few paragraphs discuss the configuration of a typical carrier-grade environment. The objective is to provide you a basic understanding of the convergence between PSTN and IP communications and highlight security strengths and weaknesses that we have encountered in the similar architectures.

Components

Every carrier-grade VoIP architecture may be distinct in terms of services, components/network elements, requirements, and the configuration that it supports. However, some components remain the same in most architectures. These components are considered to be fundamental and exist in every VoIP implementation. In some cases, their physical implementation may be collocated on the same host, but there is a logical distinction in the functionality they provide. Note that the IMS (IP Multimedia Subsystem) architecture defines a number of functions that are implemented by various components, but it maintains a similar set of components when it comes to interconnecting with the PSTN. The fundamental components that support the interconnection between IP and PSTN in a typical carrier-grade VoIP network include the following:

- **Signaling gateway**—Translates signaling messages between the PSTN (SS7) signaling network and IP (ISUP/SIP). The signaling gateway coordinates with the soft switch the setup, modification, and teardown of calls. The function of this component is essential to the converged network (VoIP <> PSTN).
- **Media gateway**—Performs bidirectional conversion of media streams from TDM circuits to IP packet streams (RTP). In addition, it communicates with the signaling gateway and the soft switch to allocate resources (for example, voice channels) and set up, maintain, or tear down calls (bearer path). In some implementations, CDRs (call/customer detail records) are generated by the media gateway. The function of this component is essential to the converged network (VoIP <> PSTN).
- **Soft switch**—The soft switch (also called call agent) maintains a set of instructions that specify the way that phone calls should be handled. This includes, but is not limited to, provisioning, call control and routing, signaling, and support for other applications. In the IMS architecture, the soft switch can be thought of as the MGCF (media gateway control function).
- **SBC (session border controller)**—The SBC is an application-aware firewall that provides the ability to manage real-time multimedia applications such as VoIP. Some of the distinctive functions supported by SBCs include network topology hiding using NAT; signaling; and voice call traffic management, including inspection and

suppression of malicious signaling or media messages. These functions allow protecting against malicious traffic (for example, DoS) and at the same time support operational and functional requirements of protocols used in multimedia applications (for example, maintain and manage the state of sessions). In the IMS architecture, the SBC functionality is distributed among the various components. For example, the inspection of malicious SIP messages may be performed by the P-CSCF (proxy call/session control function) component.

- **STP**—The signal transfer point is responsible for performing routing decisions in the PSTN. When a signaling message is received, the STP performs the necessary lookup operations to determine where to route the message.
- **SSP**—The service switching point is processing signaling messages to set up, manage, and release voice circuits required to complete a call. Signaling messages are transported to SSP through STPs.
- **SCP**—The service control point is a centralized database that is used in SS7 to support services such as toll-free calling (800/888).

The loss of operation of any of the aforementioned components will adversely impact the VoIP service. Therefore, these components are fully redundant in a carrier network. Figure 10.1 shows a redundant configuration in a converged network.

Traditionally, circuit-switch networks are architected with redundant components to maintain high service availability. This requirement is also reflected in packet-based networks such as IP. Figure 10.1 shows redundant connections between the signaling and media gateways on the IP network and the STP and SSP network elements, respectively, in the SS7 network. Additional components such as DNS, NFS, and NTP servers can also be used as part of the architecture to support VoIP services.

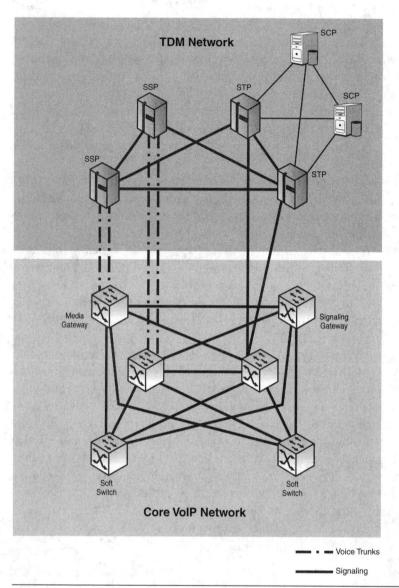

FIGURE 10.1 Redundancy in a converged network.

Network Topologies

The flexibility offered by the protocols that provide multimedia services over IP allows many companies to provide VoIP service. Although this drives competitive pricing, because there are more providers and therefore more choices by customers, not all of them maintain the same standards in terms of quality and security. The typical VoIP service provider architectures available today include the following:

- **Converged telco**—An incumbent telecommunications provider that maintains and provides telecommunication services through a PSTN and a VoIP infrastructures (for example, ATT, Global Crossings, SBC)
- **ISP-based voice service provider (ISP-VSP)**—An Internet service provider that provides VoIP service to existing customers (for example, Cablevision)
- **Internet-based voice service provider (I-VSP)**—A VoIP service provider that provides telecommunication services using VoIP but does not maintain a PSTN infrastructure or provide Internet access to customers

Each architecture has its benefits and limitations, as discussed in the following paragraphs.

Converged Telco

A converged telco maintains a TDM infrastructure that interconnects with the VoIP infrastructure. In some cases, the TDM and IP networks may be interconnected with a cellular network. The interconnection of these networks (IP and cellular) is the focus of the IMS architecture, a 3GPP initiative that aims to provide new services and personalized experience to subscribers. Figure 10.2 shows the configuration between a TDM and IP network.

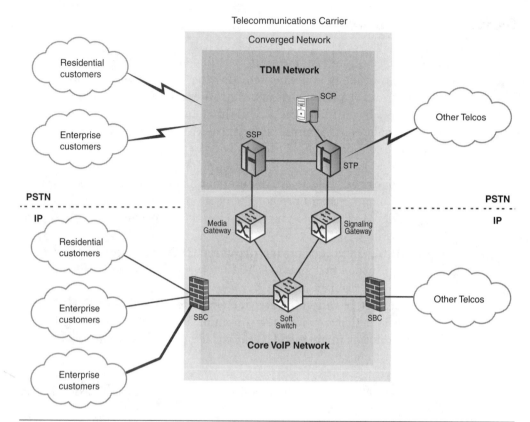

FIGURE 10.2 Converged telco architecture.

In this environment, the telecommunications carrier provides traditional PSTN services and VoIP services to enterprise and residential customers through points of presence throughout a geographic region (hub-and-spoke configuration). Enterprise customers can interconnect to the VoIP network through the Internet or an IP VPN network (using MPLS). Connecting residential or enterprise customers to the VoIP network over the Internet requires a residential VoIP gateway or an enterprise-grade component that acts as a gateway (for example, MGCP- or

SIP-based router, IP-PBX, SIP proxy, H.323 gatekeeper). The physical connection may be over a DSL modem or another medium (for example, T1-OC3 in the case of an enterprise customer) that can support high bandwidth. Although connecting over the Internet might be a more cost-effective alternative than connecting through a provider's VPN, there is an associated risk because of attacks that originate from the Internet.

Interconnecting through an IP VPN provides QoS and a higher level of security as compared to Internet-based connectivity because the VPN network is managed by the telecommunications carrier. Companies, such as Vonage, that offer VoIP services lack the ability to provide adequate QoS because they cannot manage the underlying transport between the subscriber and the subscriber's ISP. For example, the quality of the calls for a New Jersey Vonage customer who subscribes to a local ISP (for example, Cablevision) for their Internet service is not as adequate as a subscriber that obtains Internet and VoIP service from the ISP.

In addition to routing calls between TDM and IP, this architecture offers the ability to exchange VoIP traffic with other telcos using static IP routing (for example, VoIP to VoIP). Currently, there are efforts in the IETF (the SPEERMINT working group) to establish guidelines for dynamic peering among VoIP providers.

The primary components that facilitate the convergence in this architecture are the signaling and media gateways because they perform message translation between IP and SS7/C7 (signaling and media codecs). In addition, the soft switch manages signaling for calls that traverse the VoIP network and coordinates the allocation of resources on the signaling and media gateway. It is obvious that attacks against these three fundamental components, such as DoS, will impact service. Therefore, service providers deploy various security controls, such as SBCs, to protect these components from attacks. The SBC provides protection against attacks that originate from external networks, and they can be used to enforce policies to manage traffic originating from enterprise, residential customers, or peering with other VoIP service providers.

Figure 10.3 shows examples of attack origins in this architecture.

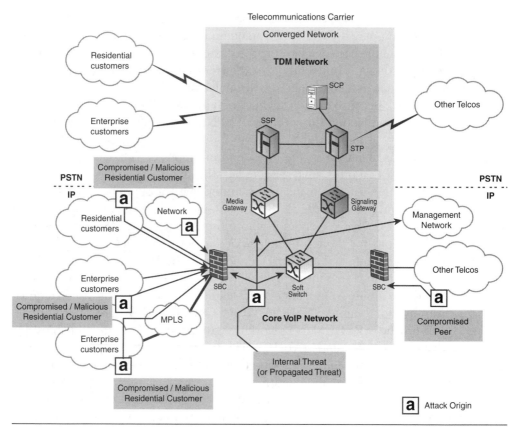

FIGURE 10.3 Attack origins in a converged telco architecture.

The origin of the attack may be from an external interconnection or an internal vantage point that has been previously compromised or used maliciously by an internal operative (for example, an employee or a vendor). One of the critical areas is the management network, which, if targeted, can have a devastating impact on the operations of the VoIP service provider. Therefore, management networks should be isolated from other networks, and traffic between the management network and the production network should be monitored accordingly. A typical oversight that introduces security risks is the lack of adequate security controls with other VoIP providers (peers). In a recent VoIP fraud case that was investigated by the FBI, attackers used basic attack methods to compromise VoIP provider and enterprise networks and route calls across continents, resulting in the loss of millions of dollars within months. One of the techniques used by the perpetrators was a brute-force attack of peer calling access codes that were used by the VoIP service providers to identify and bill traffic originating from peer telcos. In some cases, a three-digit code was used as an identifier. This demonstrates that some VoIP service providers don't enforce the proper controls to protect against attacks (for example, network element hardening, traffic filtering, and proper authentication).

ISP-Based Voice Service Provider

ISPs are well positioned to offer VoIP services to their subscribers at competitive prices. For example, cable providers that offer cable service and Internet access may also offer VoIP service as a bundle (cable/Internet/voice). In fact, some cable companies have started offering VoIP service to enterprise customers as well as residential. Figure 10.4 depicts a typical architecture of an ISP that provides VoIP service.

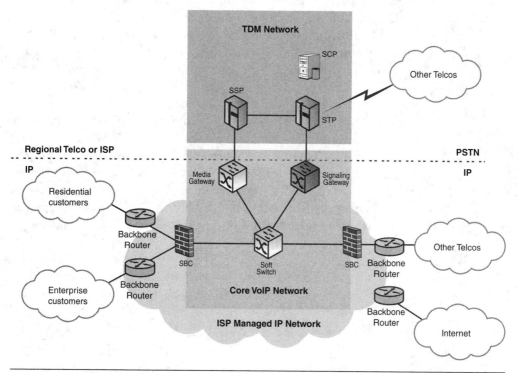

FIGURE 10.4 ISP-VSP architecture.

In this architecture, the IP network interconnects with the TDM using the same network elements as the converged telco (signaling and media gateway). The ISP can protect the core VoIP infrastructure from certain attacks by deploying a combination of security controls, such as SBCs for traffic management, and enforcing device and user registration along with authentication and integrity of signaling messages. In cases where the ISP does not maintain a TDM infrastructure, it can route calls destined for the PSTN through a regional telco. Large ISPs tend to maintain PoPs (points of presence) throughout a geographic region, and therefore they can route calls within their IP backbone from one site to another at minimal or no cost (for example, San Francisco and New York). At the same time, they can expand their customer base by offering competitive VoIP service to enterprise customers. Attacks against the various components of the architecture can originate from external networks (for example, peer or Internet) and internal networks.

A good example of an ISP-VSP is cable television providers. Figure 10.5 shows the PacketCable architecture that cable providers are using to offer VoIP service to subscribers.

The PacketCable architecture (PacketCable[1] is based on the DOCSIS [Data-Over-Cable Service Interface Specifications] PacketLabs Publication 1.1) defines an IP-based service-delivery architecture for services such as VoIP, videoconferencing, interactive gaming, and so on, and it is based on Release 6 of the IMS, developed by the 3rd Generation Partnership Project (3GPP). You might note that the two components defined as the demarcation points between IP and PSTN are the signaling and media gateways. These two components are the heart of a converged network, and proper protection mechanisms should be enforced to minimize the impact from attacks. Additional components exist to support signaling and media functions within the IP network of the provider, such as call agents (similar to soft switches), gate controllers, DNS, and others.

---

1. *See PacketCable, Security technical Report, [PKT-TR-SEC-V01-060406] and PacketCable Architecture Framework Technical Report [PKT-TR-ARCH- ARCHFRM-V01-060406].*

Packet Cable Architecture

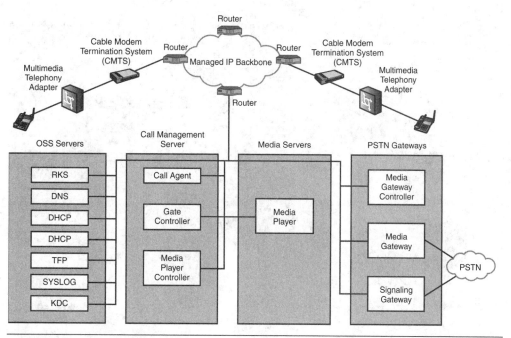

FIGURE 10.5 PacketCable architecture.

Internet-Based Voice Service Provider

The topology of an Internet-based VSP maintains similar core components as the previous architectures. The fundamental differences are the ability for the VSP to provide QoS and adequate security to its subscribers because they are accessing the VoIP network through their respective ISPs. An example of such provider is Vonage. Figure 10.6 shows this relationship.

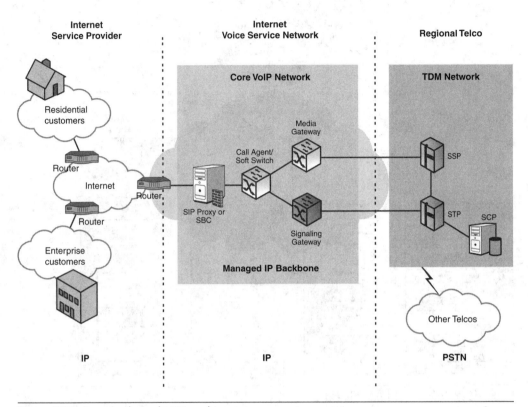

FIGURE 10.6 Internet-based VSP architecture.

In this architecture, subscribers connect to the Internet through their corresponding ISPs and place and receive calls by using the VoIP provider's network. Calls destined for the PSTN are routed to the local exchange carrier (LEC) through the signaling and media gateways.

The customer's edge device (for example, VoIP router) registers with the VoIP service provider upon startup and maintains the registration (binding) as long as there is Internet connectivity. If the subscriber's Internet access gets disrupted (for example, because of a DoS attack against their cable/DSL modem or an ISP outage), their phone service also gets disrupted. This architecture provides less QoS, reliability, and security as compared to the other two architectures (converged telco and ISP-VSP).

Security in Provider Implementations

Carrier-grade VoIP architectures maintain a distinct set of operational and architectural requirements because the primary objective is to stay profitable by maintaining and continuously expanding customer subscriptions by offering competitive features and services. These requirements include QoS, availability, innovative features and services, and security. Security tends to be an expected and embedded requirement in VoIP implementations, but it is often misunderstood and, worse, improperly implemented by some. To protect against current and emerging threats (for example, DoS, fraud, unauthorized access), a layered protection framework should be used when architecting and deploying networks to support VoIP (and generally any Internet multimedia services and applications).

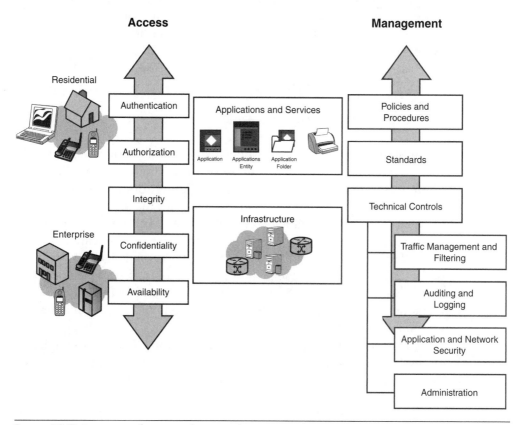

FIGURE 10.7 Protection framework example.

Figure 10.7 shows an example of a framework that is partially used in current deployments. One of the main areas emphasized in the framework is subscriber access. To protect against and minimize the impact of various attacks, proper access controls should be enforced to provide authentication, authorization, integrity, and confidentiality of the signaling and media streams exchanged between the subscriber's device (for example, phone, PBX). In addition, strong access controls help minimize the opportunity to perform DoS attacks and service fraud by unauthorized parties (and thus increase availability and provide fraud prevention). At the same time, there is the scenario in which a legitimate subscriber may attempt to defraud services, launch an attack to affect service availability, or perform a number of other attacks. This threat (the authorized insider) is managed by enforcing strong security management controls, including defining policies, procedures, and standards and enforcing technical controls to provide adequate network and application security, auditing, and logging.

Currently, VoIP service providers enforce security controls in the following areas:

- Subscriber device authentication
- User authentication
- DoS attack protection

Subscriber device authentication focuses on authenticating the subscriber's device that is used by the user, but not the user himself. This is different from authenticating the user to the network or the user to the device and the device to the network. This means that other users can use the same device to originate or receive calls even when it is not clear which user originated a call. The methods used for device authentication depend on the hardware controls available on the device and signaling protocol implemented by the provider. The hardware controls may include MAC address authentication, certificate authentication, a combination of both, or another set of device characteristics (for example, a digest of a device's serial number). When the subscriber's device boots, it uses its predefined configuration file to retrieve the necessary parameters (for example, IP address) to contact the service provider's configuration/registration server. This process ensures that the device is using the latest firmware and up-to-date configuration. When the device receives its configuration, it initiates a registration process to associate the device with the VoIP network. This association allows the device to receive calls and originate calls depending on the signaling protocol used and how it is implemented (for example, SIP, H.323, or MGCP). If SIP is used as the signaling protocol, the SIP digest authentication is used as the authentication mechanism. The shared secret is typically preconfigured in the configuration of the device. Depending on the service provider's implementation, the network might perform challenge authentication of the device during registration or during the initiation of a call or both. This means that every REGISTER/INVITE request is authenticated. The device may be configured to refresh registration requests regularly (for example, every minute or 20 seconds) to maintain a current association with the remote network. The registration requests include the current IP address of the device and signaling port that should be used to send signaling messages. By inspecting that the device has registered within the typical time frame, the service provider can determine whether a device is connected and can accept calls or divert incoming call to voicemail or generate an error message to the caller. Of course, the same conclusion (whether it is active or inactive) can be derived by attempting to contact the remote device without relying on the registration record, but doing so can cause the service provider to originate unnecessary traffic on the network. In addition, if the subscriber's device resides in a network where IP addresses are reassigned, the service provider might accidentally send VoIP traffic to the wrong device. Therefore, most service providers rely on the IP address and port that was included in the registration messages. A similar approach is taken when H.323 is using an RRQ (registration request) message in which transport and alias addresses of the respective device are included.

User authentication in a VoIP provider's network attempts to associate a subscriber with its corresponding account. The process is similar to the device authentication, but in this case the user supplies a predefined password that is used to authenticate signaling messages. This method allows the subscriber to subscribe from virtually any place and any device as long as there is an Internet connection and the device supports the service provider's signaling and media protocols. For example, a user traveling in Europe can use a soft phone installed on her laptop to subscribe to her VoIP provider in the United States to originate or receive calls over the Internet.

DoS attacks represent one of the most significant areas of concern for VoIP providers because they impact directly on QoS. DoS attacks can be launched against the subscriber equipment or the VoIP components to disrupt service. In addition, annoyance attacks can influence user subscription (and may, therefore, negatively impact revenue growth). Therefore, VoIP providers are trying to protect against DoS and annoyance attacks by deploying SBCs and enforcing traffic filtering on their network. Depending on the architecture used by the service provider, some may be more effective than others in protecting against DoS attacks.

Although the current approach taken by carriers provides protection against some attacks, many improvements can be made to elevate the overall security posture. Figure 10.8 shows an example of a zoned approach to enforcing security throughout the infrastructure. The primary objectives of this approach are service availability and resiliency to attack.

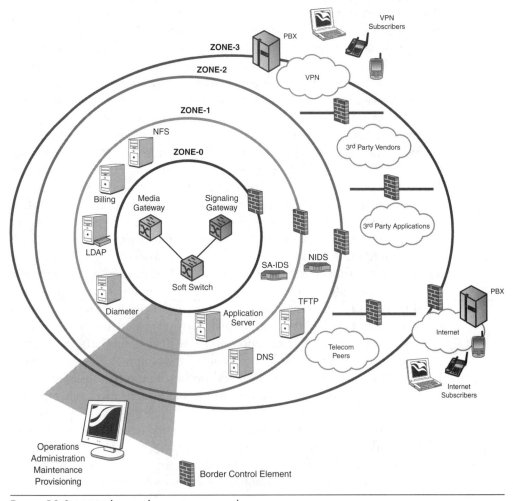

FIGURE 10.8 NGN layered security example.

In this example, a border control element (BCE) is the demarcation component between the zones that separate the various components of the infrastructure. The functionality offered by the BCEs is dependent on the type of protection required when transitioning between zones. For example, the BCE that controls zone 3 may enforce controls (for example, rate limiting, message inspection) at the network layer (IP) to filter traffic from untrusted networks. Application layer controls may be enforced by BCEs in zone 0 and zone 1 to protect against signaling and media stream attacks. The following list describes the relationships between the BCEs and the zones:

- **BCE zone 3**—Enforces traffic management and filtering at the network layer and protects against attacks that originate from the Internet. Between zone 2 and zone 3, there is a logical segregation among the trusted networks that interact with the components that reside in the inner zones. These trusted networks are composed of subscribers, partners, vendors, or peers, and the segregation provides an added layer of protection from attacks that may impact any of the participants within this trusted layer.

- **BCE zone 2**—Enforces traffic management and filtering at the transport and application layers and protects against attacks that originate from the trusted networks that may have been compromised or from trusted users with malicious intentions. The components that reside in zone 2 typically provide device configuration services. Therefore, attacks that aim to compromise the initialization of VoIP devices to obtain service can be suppressed by enforcing network and operating system controls and isolating the associated components (for example, DNS, TFTP, BOOTP, DHCP).

- **BCE zone 1**—Protects the components such as application servers, NFS (used to store billing information), authentication servers (for example, Diameter), directory servers (for example, LDAP), or billing servers from attacks that may originate from zone 2 or zone 0. Although host-based intrusion detection (HIDS) and network-based intrusion detection sensors (NIDS) can be deployed through the infrastructure, our example depicts a NIDS between zone 1 and zone 2 as a minimum measure to monitor for malicious traffic that originates from external networks. The BCE in zone 1 may be used to terminate SSL or SRTP streams to enforce signaling and media message inspection and meet lawful surveillance requirements.

■ **BCE zone 0**—Protects the core components that support multimedia services (for example, voice, conferencing, and so on). The components within this zone must continue to support the exchange of signaling and media messages even if billing or other components have been affected. Therefore, they must be isolated from the rest of the infrastructure, and stringent traffic controls must be enforced by the BCE that protects zone 0 (for example, signaling and media inspection). An application intrusion detection (AP-IDS) capability should be established between zone 0 and zone 1 to detect and alert about attacks associated with the signaling and media messages. This capability may also be enforced by the BCE depending on the traffic load and performance limitations of the respective architecture.

Chapter 8, "VoIP and Network Security Controls," discusses the various controls that protect carrier-grade VoIP architectures. When developing security requirements or evaluating the security controls of such implementations, consider the following:

■ Subscriber security controls (for example, authorization, authentication, and confidentiality for signaling and media streams)
■ Network security controls (for example, IDS, firewalls/SBC, reliability, and resiliency)
■ Service application security controls (for example, provisioning, fraud control)
■ Application security controls (for example, third-party applications, access to functionality)
■ Peering security controls (for example, policy enforcement and traffic control)
■ Regulatory (for example, CALEA)
■ Billing security controls
■ Provisioning security controls
■ Network management security controls

Another fundamental area that should be addressed is the definition and development of security requirements of critical areas associated with VoIP networks, including the following:

- Design and architecture
- Deployment
- Operations
- Management and administration
- Product certifications
- Service level agreements with other carriers/service providers

Traditionally, organizations do not incorporate well thought-out security controls during the design and deployment phases of the VoIP network. Therefore, when threats and vulnerabilities surface post deployment, security controls are considered "added" cost. Defining security requirements during the design phase (in addition to deployment and operational phases) decreases the perceived cost of security when threats and attacks surface in later stages and security is needed. Currently, the IMS and the PacketCable architectures have security controls defined that can be used to protect against various attacks associated with VoIP (and generally Internet multimedia services and applications).

Summary

This chapter discussed the network topology, components, and security considerations associated with VoIP service provider environments. This foundational information will help you gain additional insight into a typical VoIP service provider environment and assess the associated strengths and weaknesses. VoIP service providers have to maintain a distinct set of operational and architectural security requirements to protect against current and emerging attacks. Therefore, a layered approach was presented that enables you to confine and control network traffic at a granular level. Note that this approach incorporates concepts from ITU's X.805 and IMS, and it is just one approach, which may or may not be applicable to all VoIP service providers. Nevertheless, it can provide a starting point to further develop a framework specific to a service provider's VoIP environment.

## CHAPTER 11

ENTERPRISE ARCHITECTURES AND SECURITY

Security in enterprise VoIP architectures adopts many of the protection mechanisms discussed in earlier chapters, but there are also several distinctions compared to carrier architectures, and therefore different security requirements need to be defined in those areas. This chapter focuses on identifying the primary areas of enterprise VoIP architectures in which security can be applied to maintain an adequate security posture. Initially, the chapter discusses the components most likely used in enterprise architectures, and then the architectures with respect to the areas that require security to be closely examined. The contents of this chapter are helpful to security engineers, consultants, managers, and personnel involved in deploying, maintaining, and evaluating the security of enterprise VoIP implementations.

Components

Organizations may integrate VoIP in their environment using different approaches, but the aim is to build a converged network to support any multimedia application (for example, data, voice, video, conferencing). This evolution is not intended just to replace the current telecommunications, but rather to develop a capability to adopt new technologies to improve operations and transform how services are delivered throughout the organization. The type of components used in enterprise networks depends on the particular vendor's implementation, but they typically support most open protocols (such as SIP, H.323, MGCP, and RTP). Some vendors may use proprietary signaling protocols such as Skinny by Cisco, UNIStim (Unified Networks IP Stimulus) by Nortel, or IAX by Asterisk.

Generally, the types of components used in enterprise VoIP implementations include the following:

- **Call manager/agent**—This component is one of the most important in a VoIP implementation because it controls communications between end users and the rest of the VoIP infrastructure. In addition, it provides a variety of functions depending on the implementation. For example, in Cisco implementations, the call manager may act as a subscriber or publisher and support signaling protocols such as Skinny, H.323, MGCP, and SIP. Most of the Cisco implementations use the Skinny protocol by default. In implementations where SIP is used, the call manager acts as a SIP proxy or SIP registrar. If H.323 is used, it acts as a gatekeeper. Because the call manager is the focal point in a VoIP network, it is typically implemented with failover.

- **IP-PBX**—This component facilitates the interconnection between the enterprise IP network and the PSTN. It combines the functionality of a signaling and media gateway and helps medium- and small-size enterprise organizations migrate from an existing TDM-based PBX system.

- **Signaling gateway**—This component is used in larger deployments of enterprise VoIP and translates signaling messages between the PSTN (SS7) signaling network and IP (for example, SIP/H.323). The signaling gateway coordinates with the call agent (or call manager) the setup, modification, and teardown of calls.

- **Media gateway**—This component performs bidirectional conversion of media streams from TDM circuits to IP packet streams (RTP). In addition, it communicates with the signaling gateway and the soft switch or call agent to allocate resources (for example, voice channels) and set up, maintain, or tear down calls (bearer path).

- **Voice mail server**—This component is primarily used to store multimedia messages (voice and video) for later retrieval. The voice mail server interacts with other components such as signaling and media gateways using standard protocols such as SIP, H.323, MGCP, and RTP; therefore, it is exposed to associated attacks such as signaling or media message manipulation, denial of service, eavesdropping, and so on. In addition, the administrative and management interfaces can be targeted to gain unauthorized access. Because this component archives multimedia messages (voice and video) that might contain sensitive information (for example, customer-identifiable information, financial data, and so on) various regulatory requirements apply, including HIPAA, GBLA, and SoX.

- **Unified messaging server**—This component has the ability of a voice mail server to archive messages and converts text messages to voice messages and vice versa. The unified messaging server interacts with the email server to retrieve messages through the use of interactive voice prompts. For example, the user calls the VoIP network's voice mail system by dialing a specific number (for example, 1234), and the corresponding component (for example, IP-PBX, SIP proxy, call manager) routes the call to the unified messaging server, which provides all the intelligence needed to retrieve the user's messages. This provides the user with the flexibility to retrieve messages in different formats (for example, retrieve a voice mail message as an email or access an email message from a payphone). At the moment, in most implementations the unified messaging server archives voice mail messages and notifies users via email of new messages. No conversion occurs. Depending on the environment, the unified messaging server can be deployed on a single physical box and includes all the functions needed to support unified messaging; alternatively, its functionality can be distributed across components.

- **IVR (interactive voice response) system**—The interactive voice response system is used in many environments (for example, banking, health) and enables users to navigate through an organization's voice mail system, customer support center, service, or application (for example, search a company directory, check a bank account balance, activate a credit card, vote for a favorite singer). Because this component provides routing selection at the application or service level, it can be targeted by malicious users to perform various attacks, including annoyance (for example, routing loops through maliciously configured prompts), masquerading (for example, rerouting the CFO's extension), or passive message eavesdropping (for example, routing an extension to an attacker's voice mailbox). An example attack is voice mail phishing, which can be exploited by gaining unauthorized access to the organization's IVR and reconfiguring the extension of a user to be automatically forwarded to the attacker's voice mailbox. The attacker can copy the legitimate user's greeting message on his voice mailbox to impersonate the legitimate user to callers.

The functionality of these components can be combined in one physical node or distributed across the network. For example, the media and signaling gateways may be combined in a single physical device depending on the size of the network and the architecture that is implemented.

Network Topologies

Three variations of enterprise PBX architectures are typically deployed: TDM-PBX, hybrid IP-PBX, and IP-centric (or distributed). The type of IP-PBX architecture being used depends on the size of the organization and the applications required to be supported.

In the hybrid IP-PBX architecture, the IP network is interconnected with the PSTN using a single component, as shown in Figure 11.1.

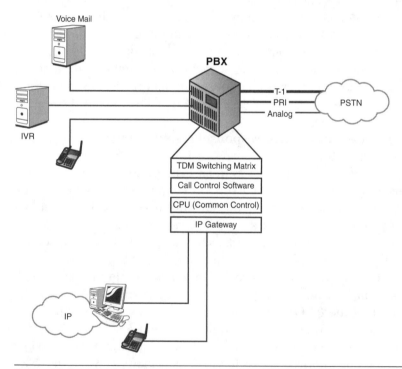

FIGURE 11.1 Hybrid IP-PBX architecture.

The hybrid IP-PBX leverages the enterprise's data infrastructure for both IP phone and PC connectivity, and it coordinates signaling and media exchange between all the components, including VoIP phones, POTS phones, voice mail, and so on. The benefits of the hybrid IP-PBX architecture include the following:

- Entails low-risk/cost transition plan because it supports existing and new technologies.
- Simplifies connectivity in environments with many distributed locations
- Scales very well for architectures that must support large numbers of callers in queues (for example, a technical support center)

At the same time, this architecture introduces some limitations, including the following:

- Requires investment in a proprietary technology that is no longer a priority for the vendor's R&D efforts.
- In a distributed site architecture, it might be necessary to add additional proprietary components (for example, media gateways), which further increases the investment in a single-vendor solution.
- Increases management complexity of TDM and IP components (compared to an IP-centric architecture).

Although the hybrid IP-PBX architecture has its limitations, it remains the primary choice for enterprise networks to evolve from TDM to VoIP. Figure 11.2 displays the projected PBX shipments for enterprise networks.

This demonstrates that although there might be an initial investment cost to IP-PBX, most organizations realize the benefits and have established a migration path. This migration path requires investing in hybrid PBXs to accommodate easier transition from TDM-PBX to a pure IP-PBX architecture. One of the most well-known IP-PBXs is the open-source PBX Asterisk. Figure 11.3 shows an example of a PBX configuration using Asterisk.

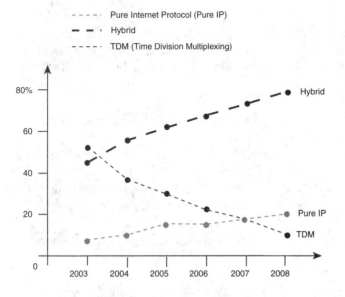

Source: Infornetics Research Enterprise Telephony Market Share 3Q05 (Novermber 2005)

FIGURE 11.2 PBX projected shipments.

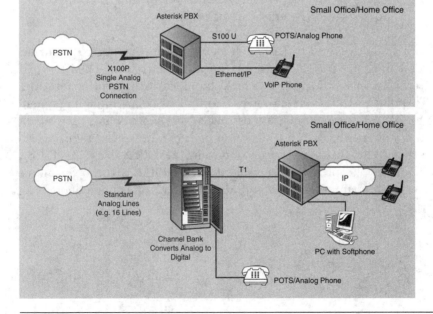

FIGURE 11.3 Asterisk IP-PBX.

This architecture can support everything from small/home offices up to medium-size enterprise networks (for example, 250 users).

In the IP-centric (or pure IP) architecture, the functionality is distributed among various components, as shown in Figure 11.4.

Large Enterprise VoIP Architecture

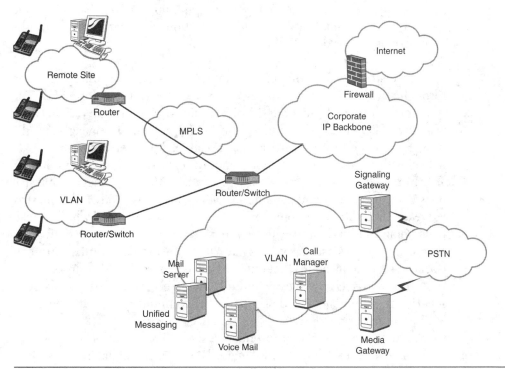

FIGURE 11.4 Large enterprise VoIP architecture.

In a large enterprise environment, the applications and services offered are supported by components distributed across the network. These components include the signaling and media gateways, the call agent/manager, voice mail, and the edge devices (VoIP phones).

Because the VoIP components are distributed across networks (trusted, semi-trusted, and untrusted), they are exposed to external and internal threats. The areas that need to be examined include the following:

■ Interconnections with local and remote networks, including internal data networks, partners, VPNs, remote sites, and service providers

- Network segmentation between networks and components that support the VoIP service (for example, between VoIP core components, VoIP phones, data networks, and so on)
- Traffic policy enforcement points, to control traffic and interaction between users, components, and networks
- Protection mechanisms to maintain the security of infrastructure components, the access to services and applications (signaling and media streams), and the administration and management of the infrastructure

In a distributed architecture, remote sites are typically interconnected through an MPLS network managed by a network service provider. The remote site exchanges data and VoIP traffic with the core VoIP network over the MPLS network. Because the MPLS network is managed by the provider, its security posture is questionable. Many erroneously equate MPLS with Frame Relay when it comes to security. Although both MPLS and Frame Relay enforce policies to route traffic over specific links, it doesn't ensure that the information traveling across is protected from prying eyes. In addition, the enterprise customer cannot verify whether traffic is being routed domestically or internationally and how the network is shared with other customers. The inability to ensure how traffic is protected raises several questions that enterprise customers should address before subscribing to such services. Therefore, it is recommended that a set of security requirements be developed and communicated with potential MPLS network providers.

Another important area to enhance the VoIP network's security posture is network segmentation. By logically compartmentalizing the various VoIP components into virtual LANs (VLANs), it is easier to manage policy enforcement and network traffic controls. Chapter 8, "VoIP and Network Security Controls," discusses network segmentation in more detail.

Traffic policy enforcement refers to maintaining control of the application, administrative, management, and control traffic exchanged between the VoIP components and internal and foreign networks. The policy may be enforced on various layers of the traffic, depending on the organization's operational and security objectives. Examples of traffic policy enforcement include traffic shaping and network topology hiding using NAT or filtering of IP, TCP/UDP layers, or filtering based on caller or callee credentials (for example, SIP URI) or day and time of the traffic (for example, discard all incoming calls between 7 p.m. and 6 a.m. on Sundays).

Protection mechanisms must address all layers of the VoIP infrastructure, including the following:

- Operations, management, and administration protection mechanisms (for example, role-based access controls, authentication, HTTPS, SSH, SNMPv3)
- Network protection mechanisms (for example, SBCs, IDS/IPS)
- Network element protection mechanisms (for example, local system security, authentication, and authorization)
- Signaling and media protection mechanisms (for example, IPSec, TLS, DTLS, SRTP)
- Service and application functionality protection mechanisms (for example, role-based access controls, authentication)

This layered approach supports the defense-in-depth concept to maximize the VoIP network's security posture.

Security Considerations

As discussed in Chapter 3, "Threats and Attacks," enterprise VoIP networks are at risk of various attacks, and most enterprise implementations lack the proper controls to protect against current and emerging threats. Some organizations are more security conscious than others and take proper precautions to ensure that their VoIP implementations provide the appropriate security controls to minimize the impact from attacks.

The IEEE 802.1x standard provides a protocol that helps organizations enforce device authentication in an enterprise network. The mechanism is effective in preventing unauthorized access to the network by unauthorized hosts, and thus limits the attack vectors that can be exercised against the VoIP network and supporting components. Although 802.1x is an effective mechanism, it is costly to implement; therefore, many organizations have yet to deploy this capability. Instead, they approach node access control by enforcing mechanisms such as MAC address authentication, which requires more management effort to maintain MAC address associations with nodes and corresponding permissions.

User authentication is something else that many enterprise VoIP implementations avoid, and thus allow user access to VoIP services and applications without restrictions. Depending on the VoIP implementation, it is feasible to enforce user authentication for VoIP applications, including signaling and media message authentication. Earlier chapters discuss in detail signaling and media protection mechanisms and capabilities, including authentication.

Signaling and media confidentiality is another important area that organizations tend to shy away from because of the cost, vendor support, or complexity involved in implementing the associated controls. To overcome such obstacles, it is recommended that a security requirements document be defined as an extension of the VoIP network architecture document, to discuss how signaling and media messages are to be protected. Chapter 5, "Signaling Protection Mechanisms"; Chapter 6, "Media Protection Mechanisms"; and Chapter 7, "Key Management Mechanisms," discuss signaling and media confidentiality in detail.

Logging and auditing is an important and sensitive area associated with VoIP and security. Logging abnormal or security-related events allows enterprises to perform proper forensics analysis in case of an incident. Each VoIP core network element and associated component—including signaling/media gateway, call manager/agent, voice mail server, email server, and so on—should maintain a log of events, including who, when, how, and what (for example, who accessed a network element, when it was accessed, how it was accessed, and what was accessed) . Furthermore, systems that support billing and provisioning require additional attention to logging and auditing

Summary

This chapter focused on the security of enterprise VoIP networks and discussed the architecture and core components that comprise a typical VoIP enterprise network. Although other components must be considered when securing a VoIP enterprise network—such as routers, switches, and DNS and NTP servers—they are purposefully omitted because they are discussed in great detail in other publications (and therefore unnecessary to repeat here). Nevertheless, these devices that support the VoIP core components should be equally secured by using current best security practices and by extending the security requirements to protect the core VoIP components. In addition, to strengthen the configuration of the core VoIP components and secure the signaling and media streams, significant attention should be given to protecting the management and APIs (application programming interfaces) used to manage, administer, and interact with the VoIP components.

INDEX

A

AAA (authentication, authorization, and auditing). *See* Diameter Base Protocol

ACA (Australian Communications Authority), 6

access
  enterprise VoIP architecture, 307-311
  unauthorized access, 58, 76-80
    exploiting software vulnerabilities, 83
    SIP authentication dictionary attack, 80-82

Address Resolution Protocol, 88

addressing, private, 269-270

ADSL (Asymmetric Digital Subscriber Line), 31

Advance Intelligent Network (AIN), 4

agents, 271

AIN (Advance Intelligent Network), 4

ALE (Annual Loss Expectancy), 20

ALG (Application-Level Gateway), 43

analyzing vulnerabilities, 160-162

annoyance, 75-76

Annual Loss Expectancy (ALE), 20

Application-Level Gateway (ALG), 43

architecture, 32, 264
  carrier VoIP networks. *See* carrier VoIP networks
  enterprise VoIP networks. *See* enterprise VoIP networks
  IMS, 41
  network management configuration, 268-269
  network segmentation, 264-267
  peer-to-peer IP telephony, 32-34
  private addressing, 269-270
  service provider architectures, 39
  softswitch architecture, 39-40

asset management, 301

asterisk IP-PBX architectures, 339

Asymmetric Digital Subscriber Line (ADSL), 31

at variable (ZRTP key negotiation), 254

attacks. *See also* threats
  defined, 54
  DoS. *See* DoS attacks
  telephony services
    call forwarding, 62
    caller ID, 62
    confidentiality, 63
    emergency services, 64
    follow-me service, 62
    lawful intercept, 63
    location and presence services, 63
    voicemail, 61
    vulnerabilities, 129-130

auditing (Diameter Base Protocol)
  Diameter clients, 270
  Diameter servers, 270
  Location-Info-Answer (LIA) command, 279
  Location-Info-Request (LIR) command, 279
  message format, 271-272
  Multimedia-Auth-Request (MAR) command, 279
  proxy agents, 271
  Push-Profile-Answer (PPA) command, 280
  Push-Profile-Request (PPR) command, 280
  redirect agents, 271
  Registration-Termination-Answer (RTA) command, 280

Safari®
BOOKS ONLINE
ENABLED

THIS BOOK IS SAFARI ENABLED

INCLUDES FREE 45-DAY ACCESS TO THE ONLINE EDITION

The Safari® Enabled icon on the cover of your favorite technology book means the book is available through Safari Bookshelf. When you buy this book, you get free access to the online edition for 45 days.

Safari Bookshelf is an electronic reference library that lets you easily search thousands of technical books, find code samples, download chapters, and access technical information whenever and wherever you need it.

TO GAIN 45-DAY SAFARI ENABLED ACCESS TO THIS BOOK:

● Go to **http://www.awprofessional.com/safarienabled**

● Complete the brief registration form

● Enter the coupon code found in the front of this book on the "Copyright" page

Addison
Wesley

If you have difficulty registering on Safari Bookshelf or accessing the online edition, please e-mail customer-service@safaribooksonline.com.